. . . .

PRAISE FOR
Elements of Magic

Gede Parma and Jane Meredith have excelled themselves in putting together one of the most comprehensive compilations of practices found in the Reclaiming tradition. This will not only be useful for anyone who is following the Reclaiming path, but also those who are solitary or want to build on their coven practices.

—*Janet Farrar and Gavin Bone, teachers
and authors of* The Inner Mysteries
and Lifting the Veil

Elements of Magic is a soulful and grounded offering that honors the past while inviting the future.

—*Ivo Dominguez Jr., author and elder
in the Assembly of the Sacred Wheel*

In this approachable, engaging guide, Jane Meredith and Gede Parma seamlessly weave together an introduction to Reclaiming and a course in the foundations of natural magic. With brilliant contributions by more than a dozen witches, activists, priestesses, and storytellers, there is something here for you. . . . You'll experience the Craft as practiced by one of its most long-standing and entrenched traditions.

—*Thorn Mooney, Gardnerian priestess
and author of* Traditional Wicca

Reclaiming has so much to offer with its insights into community work, activist magic, and bringing healing to this planet. . . . This book is like a dandelion seed-head, spreading wild wisdom and ecstatic practice.

—*Tony Rella,*
author of Circling the Star

This array of essays, exercises, and rituals at once honors the practices from which our knowledge of the elements comes and explores the depth and richness that the Reclaiming movement has developed over the years. *Elements of Magic* will be a valuable resource for those who seek a spiritual connection to our world, whatever their tradition.

—*Diana L. Paxson,*
author of Trance-Portation

ELEMENTS
of
MAGIC

Photo © David Brazil

Jane Meredith

An author and ritualist who lives in Australia and presents workshops worldwide, Jane's passions include mythology, magic, and ritual. Her other books are:

- *Aphrodite's Magic: Celebrate and Heal Your Sexuality*
- *Aspecting the Goddess: Drawing Down the Divine Feminine*
- *Journey to the Dark Goddess: How to Return to Your Soul*
- *Rituals of Celebration: Honoring the Seasons of Life Through the Wheel of the Year*
- *Circle of Eight: Creating Magic for Your Place on Earth*
- *Magic of the Iron Pentacle*

For more information, visit Jane online at www.janemeredith.com.

Photo © Luke Brohman

Gede Parma

A Balinese-Australian witch, priestess, and award-winning author, Gede is an initiate of the Wildwood, Reclaiming, and Anderson Feri traditions. A hereditary healer and seer, his other books include:

- *Spirited: Taking Paganism Beyond the Circle*
- *By Land, Sky & Sea: Three Realms of Shamanic Witchcraft*
- *Ecstatic Witchcraft: Magick, Philosophy & Trance in the Shamanic Craft*
- *Magic of the Iron Pentacle*

For more information, visit Gede online at www.gedeparma.com.

Edited by JANE MEREDITH
& GEDE PARMA

ELEMENTS
of
MAGIC

Reclaiming
Earth • Air • Fire • Water • Spirit

Foreword by STARHAWK

Llewellyn Publications
Woodbury, Minnesota

First Edition
Sixth Printing, 2024

Cover design by Shira Atakpu

Llewellyn Publications is a registered trademark of Llewellyn Worldwide Ltd.

Library of Congress Cataloging-in-Publication Data
Names: Meredith, Jane, editor. | Parma, Gede, editor. | Starhawk,
author of foreword.
Title: Elements of magic : reclaiming earth, air, fire, water, and spirit /
edited by Jane Meredith & Gede Parma ; foreword by Starhawk.
Description: First edition. | Woodbury, Minnesota : Llewellyn Publications,
2018. | Includes bibliographical references.
Identifiers: LCCN 2018035861 (print) | LCCN 2018046012 (ebook) | ISBN
9780738759005 () | ISBN 9780738757148 (alk. paper)
Subjects: LCSH: Magic. | Witchcraft. | Four elements
(Philosophy)—Miscellanea.
Classification: LCC BF1621 (ebook) | LCC BF1621 .E44 2018 (print) | DDC
133.4/3--dc23
LC record available at https://lccn.loc.gov/2018035861

Llewellyn Publications
A Division of Llewellyn Worldwide Ltd.
2143 Wooddale Drive
Woodbury, MN 55125-2989

www.llewellyn.com

Printed in the United States of America

...

We acknowledge and honor the traditional peoples of the lands on which we live, write, make magic, and weave community. We hope that the work of Reclaiming and our communities might help to bring healing to the earth and her peoples. We acknowledge and respect all indigenous elders—past, present, and emerging.

We honor and acknowledge the immeasurable and immense body of technique, process, lore, and ritual craft woven together into the entity that is the class known as Reclaiming's Elements of Magic. We are grateful for all the classes that have existed through the years and to all who have developed and taught this content, from Diane Baker and Starhawk in 1980 in the Bay Area to Canadian feminists to Witch-Camps all over the world.

We acknowledge those who have gathered to facilitate and participate in Elements of Magic in living rooms, attics, halls, paddocks, forests, and churches—including queer men's classes, women's classes, children's paths in the redwoods, and teens drawn to empowerment and witchery. Elements of Magic has traveled from the United States out as far as Perth, Australia; Somerset, England; and Germany, Iceland, and Guatemala.

And we know that this work will develop, deepen, and live as it continues to be taught worldwide and with each person who takes a step into this work and who dares to open this book.

Jane Meredith & Gede Parma
AUSTRALIA, 2017

Welcome to this adventure called the Elements of Magic. Ground yourself; know your body and being to be part of this beautiful earth we live on. You might like to name the sacred land you live on. Draw in a deep breath and find your center. Perhaps you are calm and settled, perhaps excited, nervous, or filled with curiosity. Know that many others share this journey with you across time and space. Our hands and voices, our stillness and silence, reach out to you from the center, from the circumference—and we cast the circle. We step between the worlds to discover our origins, awaken to our divinity, and become the magic-weavers our ancestors and descendants know we can be.

Earth is here—we feel it under our feet, place a hand on it, or reach for it through layers of floor. Air is here—we breathe deep, maybe we sing or sigh or speak. Fire is here—we look to the sky for the sun or stars or moon; we feel the warmth of our skin. Water is here—we feel the moisture in the air, turn toward a river or ocean, feel the blood pumping in our veins. Spirit is here—we look into each other's eyes, we remember our lineage, we open to the divine. Earth—air—fire—water—and that mysterious everything and nothing, spirit. We cherish, we adore, we welcome all the elements of life!

In this book is a depth and breadth of knowledge, experience, insight, humor, power, and presence. These pages are written for you. We invite you in. We welcome your voice, your thoughts, your experience, your magic. You are welcome here. This is your sacred space; this is our sacred space. Let it begin.

CONTENTS

Air   63

Fire   115

Water   165

Spirit   213

Creating a Ritual   263

FOREWORD

* * *

On the Fourth of July, 1980, I sat in my back yard with Diane Baker while my then-husband Eddie barbecued hamburgers. For three or four years, Diane and I had been part of a women's coven we called Raving, and the previous autumn, together with an extended community of witches, artists, and activists, we had created a powerful public ritual for Samhain/Halloween. We called it the Spiral Dance ritual, and it also celebrated the publication of my book *The Spiral Dance*. We thought we knew something about ritual and also about sharing power and working together, as our coven ran collectively.

But now Diane was in love and planning to follow her boyfriend to Washington, DC. She asked if we could teach a class together so she could get some experience teaching ritual and magic and be prepared to offer classes in her new home. While fireworks erupted in the distant sky, we brainstormed our curriculum. We'd teach together to model shared power, and over time we'd turn over more and more power to the students. The class would run for six weeks. Each week we'd focus on a different element. The next week the students would invoke that element. By the sixth week, they'd be prepared to create their own ritual.

The class was successful, and the students wanted to continue. Quickly, we came up with another curriculum, this one based on the Iron Pentacle of Victor Anderson's Feri tradition. The students still wanted to continue, so we created a third course, the Rites of Passage, based on the structure of the Hero's Journey. By then we had recruited the others in our coven—Lauren Gale, Susan Stern, and Kevyn Lutton—into teaching and roped in some of our students from the first course, including Rose May Dance, Carol McAnnally, and Pandora Minerva O'Mallory. The classes, rituals, and gatherings proliferated, but they kept our original model: shared teaching and a gradual turnover of power to the students themselves.

Today, Reclaiming has spread all over the world, from North America to Europe and Australia. A typical Reclaiming ritual still follows the model of shared leadership. Many people take roles: one person might welcome the participants and introduce the ritual. Another might ground, another cast the circle, and others invoke elements, ancestors, and deities. Someone else might lead a trance or a spiral dance or offer a benediction. The form allows many people to shine, to offer a bit of wisdom or inspiration or create a moment of beauty through song or dance or poetry. No one person is the fount of wisdom—the inspiration of Goddess and spirit demonstrably comes through in great diversity.

This book is true to that spirit of shared power. Guided, shaped, we might say hosted by Jane Meredith and Gede Parma, who have planted some of the seeds of Reclaiming in Australia, it contains a multiplicity of voices. Some of them are old and dear friends. Others are newly stepping into leadership in the broad Reclaiming community. Some I have never met in person, yet through their words I can appreciate their experience and wisdom.

For me personally, it's a great gift to receive this treasure trove of voices adding to our tradition, and I see it as a measure of Reclaiming's health and vitality. There was a time when I was at the center of almost everything in Reclaiming. I taught at all the WitchCamps, was on a multitude of cells and committees, and wrote some of the core texts. Then, one summer day when I was walking on a trail at Spiral-

Heart WitchCamp, I heard a clear message: an inner voice that said, "Get out of the center!"

I wasn't sure I wanted to, for I knew that withdrawing would require a lot of letting go of influence and control. I would have to trust that others would carry on the work—and if they didn't, it might die away. But I saw clearly that if I stayed so central to everything, I was like a narrow bottleneck that ultimately would strangle the tradition. Slowly, I began pulling back, and others stepped up. They took the teachings, the exercises, and the rituals in new directions. Sometimes I was alarmed or disappointed, but more often I have been excited, inspired, and nourished by the amazing creativity and inherent wisdom of our extended community. Stepping back freed me to move in new directions, such as deepening my practice and teaching of permaculture. And it freed others to step forward and bring forth their own vision. Now, as I enter into cronehood, I can feel confident that Reclaiming will survive even when I'm no longer alive.

Over the years, we've had many conflicts in Reclaiming. We've made mistakes. We've grappled with many of the overriding social issues that surround us. How do we honor sexuality in all its forms and move beyond a binary vision of gender and still retain what has been so powerful for many women in the imagery and mythology of the Goddess? How do we forge a mythology that is truly welcoming, across barriers of race and class, and embraces a diversity of pantheons without falling into cultural appropriation? How do we do more than sing about honoring the earth but actually live in ways that are regenerative and resilient?

One of Reclaiming's greatest strengths is that we don't, at our best, demand singular answers to these deep questions. Instead, we forge a spiritual community that is willing to wrestle with them together and support one another through the personal changes that result. In that work, we are grounded in our experiential practice of ritual and magic, the applied, ancient psychology that teaches us awareness and offers tools for change.

This book is a beautiful introduction to that practice. The many voices lay out the values, the reasoning, and the how-to of numerous exercises and rituals. Together they create a powerful training guide for those who are drawn to ceremony and magic.

Today we face immense challenges with the breakdown of so many environmental and social systems. We see the weather systems of the planet spinning into chaos while inequality grows and injustice abounds. Many people of good heart struggle with alienation and despair and long for a spiritual community that can support them in taking action for change.

So this is a potent moment for a guide to a magical practice that does not ask for blind faith in dogma, but rather the courage to engage on both inner and outer levels in the great struggles of our time.

I am grateful to all who have contributed to this book and to Jane Meredith and Gede Parma for conceiving of it and bringing it together with their own beautiful writing and teachings. Reclaiming's mission statement has long spoken of the need to create a new culture. May this book be a seed to help grow that vision.

Starhawk
JANUARY 1, 2018
CAZADERO

RECLAIMING'S PRINCIPLES OF UNITY

My law is love unto all beings...
—from *The Charge of the Goddess*
by Doreen Valiente

. . .

The values of the Reclaiming tradition stem from our understanding that the earth is alive and all of life is sacred and interconnected. We see the Goddess as immanent in the earth's cycles of birth, growth, death, decay and regeneration. Our practice arises from a deep, spiritual commitment to the earth, to healing and to the linking of magic with political action.

Each of us embodies the divine. Our ultimate spiritual authority is within, and we need no other person to interpret the sacred to us. We foster the questioning attitude, and honor intellectual, spiritual and creative freedom.

We are an evolving, dynamic tradition and proudly call ourselves Witches. Our diverse practices and experiences of the divine weave a tapestry of many different threads. We include those who honor Mysterious Ones, Goddesses, and Gods of myriad expressions, genders, and states of being, remembering that mystery goes beyond form. Our community rituals are participatory and ecstatic, celebrating the cycles of the seasons and our lives, and raising energy for personal, collective and earth healing.

We know that everyone can do the life-changing, world-renewing work of magic, the art of changing consciousness at will. We strive to teach and practice in ways that foster personal and collective empowerment, to model shared power and to open leadership roles to all. We make decisions by consensus, and balance individual autonomy with social responsibility.

Our tradition honors the wild, and calls for service to the earth and the community. We value peace and practice non-violence, in keeping with the Rede, "Harm none, and do what you will." We work for all forms of justice: environmental, social, political, racial, gender and economic. Our feminism includes a radical analysis of power, seeing all systems of oppression as interrelated, rooted in structures of domination and control.

We welcome all genders, all gender histories, all races, all ages and sexual orientations and all those differences of life situation, background, and ability that increase our diversity. We strive to make our public rituals and events accessible and safe. We try to balance the need to be justly compensated for our labor with our commitment to make our work available to people of all economic levels.

All living beings are worthy of respect. All are supported by the sacred elements of air, fire, water and earth. We work to create and sustain communities and cultures that embody our values, that can help to heal the wounds of the earth and her peoples, and that can sustain us and nurture future generations.

Reclaiming Principles of Unity
CONSENSED BY THE RECLAIMING COLLECTIVE IN 1997
AND UPDATED AT THE BIRCH COUNCIL MEETING OF
DANDELION GATHERING 5, PORTLAND, OREGON, 2012

INTRODUCTION

. . .

Elements of Magic will introduce you to a world of magical practices, skills, and knowledge.

If you have yearned to be a witch, a priestess, a spirit worker, or a magician, or if you long to learn what magic is and how it works, or if you want magic to be real, this book is for you.

Perhaps you hear the call of the winds, of thoughts below the surface, the whispers of possibility. Maybe you see patterns in the world and in your life and the lives of those around you, or you can read auras or the meaning in a bird's flight. Can you sense the change of seasons and know the turning point in a life and the beckoning tug of the unknown? Do you feel the phase of the moon and know where to seek it on the horizon? Do you listen to dreams, dance steps of becoming and unbecoming, paint pictures of places that have never been, or write words or music that take you into another realm?

Magic calls out to us—the magic of fairy tales, of childhood, of dreams. Magic to make a spell, call up a vision, read the future, and choose the path that leads to our heart's desire. Magic to speak to gods and goddesses, fly on the wind, read the stars, summon healing or clear sight or a friend when we need one. Magic to make a good luck charm or overcome the odds. In the stories there is magic raised with wands in the battle against evil; there's magic with wax candles, chalk-drawn circles, and incantations in stone basements; magic of unicorns and shapeshifting and spells of power. And of all the magics—older than old, as old as humans and older, as old as the planet, older, as old as the universe—is the magic of the elements, the forces that shape this planet.

Fire. Stars, comets, volcanoes, molten rock birthing the world. Fire that tears apart darkness, that warms and cooks, that burns the landscape black, that releases new life past the destruction. Fire to burn away the old; fire for creativity, passion, and inspiration.

Air. Air held close to the earth by the atmosphere, making life possible. Breath. Each breath of life that we take, from the first to the last. The breathing of wind, of trees; the green breath that gives us our own breath. Song and speech, whispers of love and shouts of revolution. Air off a waterfall, air of the forest at night, air on a hot summer's day. Air for thought, for clarity, for the fresh and new.

Water. Water that nurtured the beginnings of life and our lives, each day. Rain and lake, stream and ocean. Tears. Blood, sweat, saliva. Our watery bodies, our watery planet. Water of life. Clean water to drink, a privilege. Enough water, a luxury. Tides like our emotions, washing in and out. Water, where one thing merges into another, the edges lost, like love. Water for healing, for cleansing, for restoring life.

Earth. This planet. This body and this earth. The trees, mountains, animals, and rocks; all made from earth and returning to earth. Earth our mother. Earth that grows our gardens, our children, that feeds us; earth as flesh and houses and money and every single thing we pick up and hold. Earth for the material world, for the body.

And spirit. The fifth element, sometimes called aether. That which touches all and is everywhere and in everything yet has no fixed form. The center where all the elements meet, the circumference that holds them, the intangible where we become ourselves; our truth, our essence. Spirit, the divine unknowable and the divine expressed within the physical, marked and met by our animal senses. Spirit for blessings, for communion, union.

• • •

The words *elements of magic* can be considered a different way, with *elements* referring to the basic building blocks of skills, understandings, and practices that underpin effective magic and ritual within our tradition. Grounding ourselves, casting a circle, trance, visualization, working with breath, raising energy, charging an intention—these are some of the essential skills in the practice of magic. Within this book you will find exercises guiding you through these fundamental practices. When creating a ritual, spell, or other working, we usually thread numbers of these things together or layer them one within another, weaving our magic in a careful—or sometimes spontaneous—tapestry. Understanding these fundamental threads and achieving not just competence but coming to understand our own flavor, strengths, and inclinations within these sets of skills is part of learning magic.

Reclaiming offers WitchCamps, public rituals, and its core classes worldwide. For an event to be under the Reclaiming umbrella, the organizers and the event need to subscribe to the Principles of Unity. Where teaching is involved, the majority of teachers will be Reclaiming trained. All Reclaiming events open to the public are drug and alcohol free. We keep to this guideline to be in solidarity with people in recovery from drug and alcohol addiction. We make a conscious choice that our magic and ritual be conducted from a place of grounded presence, without the aid of external substances.

The elements of magic are just the beginning—but they are a beginning that even very experienced practitioners return to again and again. These pieces of our magical practice are not something we learn once and then move on from; rather, they are at the core of it all. With each deepening or growth or development of our skills and understanding, we still base our magic on these fundamentals and in relation to the elements of earth, air, fire, water, and spirit. Thus returning to them again and again renews and strengthens our relationship with the source of our own power. Time and energy devoted to the elements of our magic may act as a renewal, an inspiration, a consolidation, and a deepening of the journey.

The elements of magic are available to everyone. Every person can reach down and touch the earth, gaze at the sky or observe the life of a plant from seed to seedling to seed-bearing, recognize the preciousness of water, become conscious of the power inherent in each breath.

Each person can form an understanding of the sacred, begin to work with self-knowledge, imagination, transformation, and change, and come to increasing levels of understanding about our relationship to this world. Some of us do magic with silver chalices and polished crystals, others of us pick up a stone from the ground and a leaf or flower from whatever grows around us. Some work in groups, covens, traditions, or partnerships, and others—by choice or necessity—work alone. Age, gender, race, sexuality, and wealth are not the determining factors of access to or success in magic. Breath, will, focus, and daring are more relevant.

All five elements are always with us. Our bodies are made from this earth, literally from its molecules and chemicals. We cannot live a moment without breathing air. The fiery sun heats our planet enough for life to flourish; it is the single star we see by day, though at night we see many more. We are continually with water—in our blood and saliva as well as the water we drink and bathe in. Spirit we take to be that animating force within us that links us to the Mysterious Ones, to each other, and to all the worlds. We can do magic wherever we are because we always have these things with us and within us. The special stone, beautiful feather, wand, chalice, and an image of a deity may live on our altars and be invited into our rituals, but we recognize these are symbols, sacred as everything is sacred and yet not the essence of our magic.

Earth. Air. Fire. Water. Spirit.

In this book we invite you to find these elements of magic within yourself, to learn and experiment, strengthen your skills, and find what works for you. Section by section we will explore magic through the journey of the elements: pairing earth with embodiment, activism, and nature; air with breath, sound, communication, history, and lore; fire with power, creativity, and transformation; water with trance, self-knowledge, and healing; and spirit with divination, soul purpose, and working with spirits. In this way we learn, allowing elements of magic to be both the fundamentals with which magic is created as well as the elements which make up life and everything we know.

The Reclaiming Tradition

Elements of Magic is central to the Reclaiming tradition. It is the name of a course in magic and witchcraft, one of the core classes of Reclaiming that is taught all over the world. It commonly runs over six weeks, one evening a week, and is offered publicly to people who feel they are witches, who are drawn to magic and ritual, or who are curious about earth-based spirituality and the meeting of spirit and politics. They come together, usually with two teachers, to learn the foundations of magic and ritual and to encounter the elements. The course is also taught over four or five days at a WitchCamp, a magical intensive offered by the Reclaiming tradition in the United States, Canada, England, Europe, and Australia, or it is concentrated into a weekend. Elements of Magic is taught to people of all ages from all walks of life and with a variety of magical and non-magical backgrounds. Worldwide, Elements of Magic is offered many, many times each year.

Every time it is taught, Elements of Magic is somewhat different. This is because of the circumstances of where it is taught—the different communities and their needs as well as the different teachers and their interests, skill sets, and teaching styles. Most people within Reclaiming attend Elements classes many times, recognizing not only the need to revisit the roots of our connection to our own magic, and to the tradition, but also the wide variance that exists between, say, an Elements class that focuses on teaching ritual skills, one that orients itself toward activism and ecology, and one that emphasizes spiritual sovereignty and self-growth.

Even with all this variation, all Elements of Magic courses share vital commonalities and material. They all teach the basics of ritual and magic in the Reclaiming tradition. In recognizing each person's spiritual autonomy and ability to participate in ritual and spirituality, they all offer empowerment to the participants. Each Elements class introduces the magics and mysteries of earth, air, fire, water, and spirit. During the course some experience of creating ritual space, trance, of energy sensing and raising, and of group ritual is offered, as well as the history, values, and context of Reclaiming.

An Elements of Magic course is an invitation into the realms of mystery and magic. Within the Reclaiming tradition—and many other contemporary witchcraft traditions—encountering the elements and learning the art of magic are intertwined and cannot be separated. We pair each element with skills and practices relating to its nature and symbolism.

It has been said that Reclaiming is a cauldron that stands on three legs known as magic, healing, and activism. Further, there are four roots that hold the earth firm upon which the cauldron stands. These are the traditions and practices of witchcraft, particularly Feri, ecofeminism, anarchism, and psychology. Elements of Magic is found at the nexus of these things.

The Reclaiming tradition is often cited as beginning in 1979 when a young woman named Starhawk published *The Spiral Dance: A Rebirth of the Ancient Religion of the Great Goddess*. This book was Starhawk's poetic and striking interpretation of traditional occult lore and witchcraft mythology and technique passed to her by her own teachers, both human and otherworldly. In *The Spiral Dance,* traditional Feri and modern Wiccan teachings met with the countercultural movements of feminism and Goddess spirituality. This book is often regarded as the central text for the Elements of Magic course. The following year, in 1980, Diane Baker and Starhawk taught the first Elements of Magic class to a group of women in the San Francisco Bay Area. It became one of the catalysts for the birth of the Reclaiming tradition.

The roots of Reclaiming-style witchcraft are in the Anderson Feri tradition. This was spelled "Faery" in *The Spiral Dance,* and that spelling is still used by some groups in Anderson-derived traditions. Some of our core magical techniques and tools derive from this potent tradition, as well as the way in which ritual space is created, a focus on the raw elements of life, and the basic cosmology of the Great Goddess being all things, from whom we arise and to whom we return. While Starhawk has written that in her view witchcraft is the Goddess-centered initiatory tradition of Europe and the Middle East, Reclaiming does not rest on a single or specific culture. At the time Reclaiming began, the San Francisco Bay Area was a melting pot of many thriving cultures and schools of magic, and there have been direct and indirect influences from the Yoruba traditions, Hoodoo, Gardnerian-style Wicca, and other witchcraft traditions including Dianic, Celtic folklore, and Feri, which is itself a syncretism of various cultures and customs.

The Reclaiming tradition is also grounded within principles of ecofeminism and anarchism. Ecofeminism is the theory that society's treatment of and behavior toward the feminine and women is parallel and related to our relationship to the earth and her ecosystems. This analysis, interrogation, and philosophy deeply impacts Reclaiming's ethos and practices. Reclaiming—and many of the community organizing tools and principles we are guided by—also arises from the anarchist activist practices connected to the anti-nuclear Diablo Canyon protests in 1981. These three roots—witchcraft, ecofeminism, and anarchism—meld with the psychology and mythic movements in which stories and myths become entry points for personal and cultural exploration. Inside this cauldron Reclaiming is brewed.

The elements are acknowledged, invoked, and worked with in many magical, witchcraft, and other traditions. Often they are associated with particular directions. This can change depending on what tradition you are working in, which hemisphere you are in, or your particular location or purpose. Sometimes we turn to the center, the place where all our consciousness derives and dwells—some might say the belly of the cauldron—to honor all the elements. In Elements of Magic we consciously seek or invite relationship with these elements, discovering that all things are made of them, including ourselves. "Earth my body, water my blood, air my breath, and fire my spirit" is a modern Pagan chant whose words underlie our spirituality, ritual, magic, and communities.

Magic, according to influential British occultist Dion Fortune (1890–1946), can be defined as the art of changing consciousness at will. It can also be described as the practices that allow us to consciously participate in the change-making, mystery-opening powers of life, death, decay, and rebirth. Learning magic is learning how to change oneself and change things outside oneself. It is the subtle cunning of weaving strands of fate. It is radical evolution and deep spiritual insight in one. Magic is how we become as the gods, how we access our divinity and consciously act and exist from that place. Magic is the fruit of the Tree of Knowledge, and there is a primal risk that comes with eating that fruit. The risk is one of relatedness and intimacy, and the dare to realize and act from and with our own divinity.

The backdrop of our understanding is not just magic as practiced or understood through European and Western colonial histories. It is also the practice of witchcraft, sometimes referred to today as the Craft. Witchcraft, as we name it in the West, is the revival and inheritance of the ecstatic—some would say shamanistic—healing, mystic, and sorcerous traditions of Europe, Northern Africa, and the Middle East. Witchcraft lives in faerie stories, folklore, superstitions, legends, rituals, and spells. Its gods are the Old Ones who come out of the stars, the land, the mountains, seas, and caves—the ones we meet at the crossroads or in the twilight, in all the liminal times and places of our lives.

Over time Pagan and magical practices associated with witchcraft were maligned by the state, the church, the medical profession, and those whose minds became devoted to only reason and rationality, cut away from primal instinct and human intuition. Witches listen to wild nature and seek direct and intimate relationship with its forces and spirits. Witchcraft never died. Many of its traditions and rituals may have been revived and reconstructed, but its spirit has been expressed time and time again in every generation through artists, dreamers, healers, and teachers. It has been kept alive by people who are drawn to faerie stories, folklore, curious superstitions, and ritual, and who—in their deepest dreams—know they are full of magic and destined to practice its ancient and ever-living arts.

If you have picked up this book and read this far, you are probably one of them.

HOW TO USE THIS BOOK

. . .

Elements of Magic contains writing by some of the most currently active Reclaiming witches, priestesses, and teachers. It includes essays by fifteen teachers from the United States, Australia, Canada, and England. In particular, the essays presented at the beginning of each elemental section—by Paul Eaves, Gwydion Logan, Raven Edgewalker, Rose May Dance, and Dawn Isidora—contain essential understandings and content that form the backbone of the Reclaiming Elements of Magic class. These contributors are strongly identified with the teaching of and commitment to this core class, as well as the continuance and deepening of Reclaiming as a magical tradition.

Each elemental section also includes two further essays containing content that potentially could be part of an Elements class, although not all of this material can be included within any single class. Rather, an Elements class might contain, for example, an emphasis on healing (as outlined in Willow Kelly's essay in the water section), be slanted toward work with breath, sound, and song (as described in Suzanne Sterling's essay within the air section), or encompass activism (as discussed in Ruby Berry's essay in the earth section). Each Elements of Magic class is unique, as each person's journey through this book will be unique to them. Some of these essays may call strongly to you to continue or develop your learning and engagement within that area, whereas others may be informative to read or confirm material you are familiar with or not resonate with you at all.

Thirty-five spells, processes, rituals, practices, and exercises are included in this book, spun out of the dynamic and diverse cauldron of Reclaiming teachers. These contributors are current teachers of Elements of Magic within their home communities and at WitchCamps. Here they have offered practices that they use when they teach. Every Elements class will definitely include some of these exercises, such as the Tree of Life Grounding and Casting the Circle, while many classes will include some of them, such as Aligning the Three Souls, Wish Birds, and Trance to a Place of Power. Even so, each teacher may offer the exercise slightly differently, so the flavors can range widely. Some spells and processes included here are very particular to the individual teacher; for example, Preston Coyote Vargas's Creating a Wand with the Spark of Life, SusanneRae's Rotting Body Meditation, and Lisa Lind's Trance to Meet Our Ancestors Through Our DNA. This cornucopia is a wealth of knowledge, experience, and wisdom from an international movement known for its radical inclusiveness, grounded approach to the mystic, and deep relationship with divinity.

At the end of the book you will find a glossary, where words and phrases that you may not be familiar with are explained. There is also a resources and recommended reading section, where titles mentioned throughout the book are listed with their authors and publishing details. This section is divided into Reclaiming material and then by each element. At the very back of the book is an alphabetical list of all the contributors and their biographical details, often including a way to contact them or discover more about their work.

Elements of Magic is an invitation, not just into the world of ritual, spellwork, healing, and celebration, but into your self, your true self—the one you were born into and have spent all this life yearning toward—the self you are becoming.

For some people, taking an Elements of Magic course confirms what we always knew and maybe what we always have done, but we never knew anyone else did it too, or at least had never met them, let alone worked magic and ritual in a group with them. For some of us, it adds another piece to skills and knowledge we already had; perhaps we have studied shamanic traditions or technique, ceremonial magic, another witchcraft tradition, an eastern religion or permaculture, healing, divination, or any one of dozens of other disciplines. Perhaps we are parents or farmers or bush walkers or scientists or artists and we have a sense of these things or work in these ways without having language to put around it or a framework of magical technologies.

Elements of Magic teaches skills—of casting circles and invocation, of working with energy, of entering and leaving trance states, of raising power using breath and song and music, of the components of spellwork. This work asks for trust—of our intuitive selves, of each other, of spirit or the divine. It also activates and empowers our creative critical prowess, our discernment skills, and our capacity to be self-nourishing, fierce, and draw boundaries. Elements of Magic has within its ambit the formative pieces of the Reclaiming tradition: ritual and magic, personal development and political empowerment and change. Thus its study can support those on an inward path of self-knowledge and healing, those seeking skills to work with community in ritual and circle, and those dedicated to activism and social change.

This is a book that can be worked by yourself in the time-honored tradition of the solo magical practitioner or with a small group or with one other person. One of the reasons this book was written was so that this core Reclaiming class could be available anywhere, to anyone. It can be worked with your partner or family. You might be part of a group that is looking for a workbook with activities and thought-provoking material to do together. Your ritual or magic group may be seeking structure, instruction, or just inspiration. You might be wanting to honor the elements and explore nature-based spirituality or find a way to empower yourself in a world where religion and belief are dominated by churches and institutions that place power and authority out of the hands of the seeker.

Elements of Magic is a workbook. We have arranged the material to be approachable and comprehensive, travelling through the journey of the elements one by one in the order we, the authors, most commonly use: earth followed by air, fire, water, and spirit. The final segment of this book is where all the elements are brought together, culminating in the traditional ritual that makes up the final piece of every Elements of Magic course. It's traditional in that we always do it; what is *not* traditional is the content of that ritual. That is composed entirely by you, the person or people who have taken the course or worked through the book. The ritual is an expression of your own learning within Elements of Magic.

You may choose simply to read this book or to read it all the way through before doing any of the exercises or processes included within each section. You might read it once before going back to the beginning and then starting to work through it section by section. You might read one section at a time, then sit with it or meditate on it before transforming it into your own working, using the exercises as given or in your own way. You might be someone who works best dipping in and out of the book as a whole, doing a piece here and there as it suits you and when the time seems right. You might undertake it as a group working, reading the sections privately, then coming together for each element to spend a day or several evenings undertaking the exercises together and discussing the themes of that element. There are probably as many ways to work with this book as there are readers.

It is possible to do the work in this book over a weekend or over a course of six weeks, one evening or afternoon a week. That is a traditional approach to Elements of Magic and how it is most often taught. If you plan to do this, especially over a single weekend, it would be invaluable to read through the book first. Another time structure, and one that we recommend, is to work with the book over six months: one month per element and one for the final section. This allows a far deeper working with and understanding of each element and of the overall journey. If you do this, you can align your working with the

Wheel of the Year; you might start at one of the solstices, for instance, and work all the way through to the next solstice. Or you can align with the moon, beginning each month's working at the dark, new, or full moon and waxing and waning through your journey with each element along with the moon. On the other hand, six months might seem too long a period to remain mindfully diligent to the work; in that case, choose a briefer time frame.

Each of us will receive and integrate information and experience a little differently; hopefully one of these time structures will work for you. We believe that attending a live Elements of Magic class, if and when you have the opportunity, will deepen and enrich your experience. This may occur alongside your work through this book, beforehand, or afterward.

An Elements of Magic course can change your life. The way it will change your life will be different for each of us each time we turn up and do the work. The invitation the course offers is to connect with your spirit deeply and to learn the tools of magic and ritual within the Reclaiming tradition of witchcraft. In doing this, we find a place of empowerment within this world, a place that verges on the edges of the tangible and the intangible within that realm we call magic. Elements of Magic is a journey through the elements—a magical journey.

Let it begin.

EARTH

. . .

Earth is the name of the planet we live on. It is also one of the traditional elements in a four-element magical system of earth, air, fire, and water; five when we add spirit. In this book we place it first of the elements for several reasons. On a mythic level, many creation myths speak of all things, but especially humans, being formed from earth, dirt, or clay. This comes first, before those figures are given breath or spirit. As a scientific observation, this planet existed before it had an atmosphere—before what we call air was here. From the earth, life emerged, or the organic processes that led to life. Without the gravity of the earth, water would have no way to coalesce into the oceans and rivers. Fire is present in the stars; here on earth it needs organic matter such as wood, wax, or other substances to burn.

The Elements of Magic class traditionally begins with the element of air. Perhaps this is an inheritance from ceremonial or high magic. Some Elements classes begin with spirit instead, and they can begin with any of the elements. Sometimes they are taught along broad themes and all the elements are incorporated throughout the teaching.

In Australia, most of the time when we call to or acknowledge and honor the elements within a cast circle, we begin with earth. This aligns us with earth-centered spirituality, earth-focused traditions, and modern Paganism. It is an acknowledgment to the sacred land we work and live upon. What we have learned, and continue to learn, from and with indigenous cultures is a tremendous reverence for and deep relationship with the earth—not so much the generalized whole planet Earth, although that too, as the local earth, the place where we live and make magic. It is partly in our acknowledgement of these traditions that we place earth as the first element.

The grandeur and power of nature is immediately apparent as we work with earth. We come to understand that we are intrinsically a part of nature, living and dying within a vast network of all other life forms; we are not separate from or outside nature. We are intimately connected with earth, not just with the food we eat, the water we drink, and how we clothe and house ourselves, but in every way. Every breath we take is part of a planet-wide exchange between those who breathe oxygen and those who breathe carbon dioxide. We acknowledge that all our spiritual experiences occur within the context of living in this body. In this way we learn that body and spirit are not separate things. Therefore, we might surmise, the actual earth and the spirit of earth are not separate; they are the same. The Goddess is the earth, alive, and we are part of her.

This brings us to activism. When we understand we are part of the earth—not just in a practical way, that we rely upon her water, oxygen, plants, and animals to survive, but literally that our bodies are a part of her body—it is much harder, maybe impossible, to stand by while the Great Barrier Reef in Australia is destroyed by global warming, sand-dredging, shipping, coal mining, and agricultural runoff, the rivers and seas are polluted, and the Amazon rainforest being cleared and lost, forever destroyed, to pick only a few of the environmental atrocities currently occurring on our planet.

Perhaps we come at it from a different angle. Once we realize all human beings are equally part of the Goddess, how can we allow some of us to be treated as less than others of us? How can we tolerate racism, sexism, the class system, the deliberate impoverishment of whole nations? How can we bear to exist in a world where we don't raise our voices against forced prostitution, child soldiers, and hate

crimes committed against individuals or social groups for simply existing as themselves in this world? Earth is a call to action.

When we are in right relationship with the earth—when we are
nourished in every basic way directly from the land, the rivers, the
plants, the animals, the sea—we become obliged to defend her in all
her forms and aspects from senseless destruction. To do this, we might
first stop, consider the powers of the magician or the witch, and *be
silent*. Embodied as earth beings, we can leave our houses and find a
place to be on and with the earth—and listen. Our work begins with
silence and listening.

The elements are sacred. Earth is sacred.

Earth Is Sacred
Paul Eaves

• • •

The earth is a living being and it is sacred. It is a source of sustenance that feeds all life. Its beauty nourishes our souls, and the diverse beings that inhabit the planet with us create a rich fabric of interdependent existence. Through recent millennia ideologies have developed that view the earth and its resources as commodities, creating a world in which many, if not most, humans do not regard the earth as sacred. Instead, it is viewed as being there for our exploitation and the consequences are passed on to future generations. Our continued health and well-being as individuals and communities, as well as the diversity of life on this planet, depend on humans reconnecting with and invigorating our relationship with the earth.

The earth has a spirit that is both within and beyond its physical self. This spirit is immanent and weaves an energetic web that connects all life on earth. The web is fed and nourished by the spirits of all beings on earth, be they trees, wolves, rivers, whales, spiders, mountains, or humans. The earth is a spiritual whole that is greater than the sum of its parts and enhances the physical links between itself and the beings that call earth home. Divine is its nature, with names such as Goddess, Gaia, and Mother Earth. As we seek to deepen our relationship with the earth, our actions and devotions are rooted in both the physical and the spiritual.

One way of making sense of our human lives is through the concept that our souls have chosen to live in a physical form during this lifetime, continuing the eternal cycle of birth and death and rebirth. We are born with an immense capacity for pleasure and love, creation and connection. It is one of life's challenges to embrace these marvelous possibilities. Modernity and all its devices have done much to distract us from the wonder of this. Some religious teachings have tended to minimize our physical existence and demonize the body. Learning to live as an embodied presence in all the magnificence and fragility of our bodies is an excellent pathway for learning to be in right relationship with the earth.

Embodied presence is a key component of Reclaiming magic. Each ritual or gathering starts with a grounding activity. In many of our rituals we encourage folks to engage their bodies as much as they are able. What does stillness and silence feel like in your body? How is it to move exuberantly and make sound with abandon? We encourage folks to quiet their minds and listen, smell, touch, taste, and see. Eating is an act of devotion. All acts of love and pleasure are rituals, as it says in the *The Charge of the Goddess*. As we learn to love, accept, or at least open to the sacredness and potential of our bodies, we may also sense our own spirits, the divine within, which deepens our capacity for relationship with other beings as well as with the earth.

An essential skill to further this path of being present is known as grounding. It is often referred to as the most important skill in Reclaiming. To be grounded means that our conscious awareness is fully present in our bodies and the now. Its primary components are breath, a relaxed body, an integrated connection to earth and sky with an awareness of where we are, and, if we are with a group, who we have gathered with.

Grounding serves us in ritual and other forms of magic in many ways. It encourages us to let go of distractions that are not relevant to the task at hand. There is a time and place to worry about work, what the kids are doing, school assignments, the state of the world, or our beloveds. Fully tuning in to the magic of the moment increases our capacity to later be creatively present to those things. Rituals can bring up difficult personal work, which may create opportunities for healing if we are able to stay with the feelings that arise. We can increase our capacity to remain present and allow these emotions to move through us in the moment. Perhaps noticing them is enough. If we choose to engage them and need assistance, when we are grounded we can be clearer about what we need and who our allies are. If we need more energy, we can draw up energy from the earth. If we need to release energy, we can send it into the earth as compost.

We encourage people to bring grounding and other magical skills home with them. As important as grounding is in ritual, it can be even more useful in our day-to-day lives. Ground before you speak in a group or if you are sorting out a problem with a friend. It is very helpful to ground when we are involved in political actions. If you are out for a walk on a beautiful day and distractions keep getting in the way of fully being with these lovely moments, ground and breathe. Grounding helps you relax and stay present, as well as connect with the earth as an ally. A regular practice of grounding throughout the day is one way of integrating this tool into everyday life.

There is a saying that until we know and love ourselves, we can't truly know or love another. As we deepen our ability to love and know our own bodies, to open to our own sacredness, we can more authentically open to a relationship with the earth. In Reclaiming we have learned that developing a connection with a specific place or places is a key part of beginning or deepening this relationship with the earth. Regular connection with a place fosters familiarity, an intimacy much like and also different from those with human beings. This place may become a beloved.

Your place could be a tree, a spring, a river, somewhere in a city park, or a room in your apartment. It could be one of your current favorite spots, a place a friend has mentioned that sparks your interest, or one you read about. It may take some time and exploring to discover it. Use your imagination. Remember to employ magic. Be patient and allow for luck and synchronicity. When a place calls to you, ground and center from a state of humility and gratitude, open your senses, and listen. Come back to it on a regular basis at different times of day. Notice the impact of the changing seasons on the plants, the animals, the landscape, and your senses. You might ask yourself how the energy of this place is different in the moonlight, a thunderstorm, or a winter day.

With your senses enlivened, observe or at least open to its spirit or the mystery that is present in this space. Challenge yourself to discover what it really means to be in relationship with the earth here.

Like many relationships, the growing familiarity with this place may deepen a commitment to it and its well-being. To me, the sensory experiences are their own reward. Your place may become a teacher for you in the physical, emotional, and spiritual realms. It may ask if the intention you have of developing a partnership with this place, the earth, is genuine. Open to the possibility that as you get to know a place intimately, you may take on the joys and obligations of protecting it. My personal places are my home and gardens that I tend with my marvelous spouse, a sacred spring called Coldwater Spring, and several spots along the Mississippi River near where I live.

Centering is another skill we teach in Reclaiming. It can facilitate the authentic relationship with our place as well as ourselves. While grounding is primarily a work of the physical, centering is a skill that integrates our minds, hearts, and spirits with our bodies. Our bodies are not separate from who we are. We are all of our parts—a whole. Centering deepens presence as well as connects us with our core worth. Core worth is the phrase we use in Reclaiming to refer to the intrinsic, innate value of each and every being in existence. We all possess it; it is never greater nor lesser and it is never more than or less than anyone else's worth. It assists us to know or at least open to who we truly are and what our path is in this lifetime. Ideally we are able to set aside the voices and obligations that don't serve us and be engaged with our magic and lives by conscious choice. A centering practice in a ritual or workshop may be the beginning of a process or a consistent affirmation of our core worth that we have anchored and revealed in our bodies numerous times. Our experience of our core worth is usually not static but evolving as we wend our way through life experiences. It also holds a consistent thread of connection that emanates from within us, from our souls.

To learn and practice centering offers us the possibility to be fully engaged in the moment, embodying our core self in magical workings as well as personal and professional relationships. When we are in our center, we are able to assess what is asked of us and what is right for us and know if an action is something we are truly called to participate in. We are able to bring our gifts and inspirations forward in service to ourselves and the group magic from a place of authenticity. In ritual: Do I support this intention? How do I serve the magic of this moment? In our daily lives: Is this a relationship that I am truly drawn to or am I just settling? Is this job part of my life's work? If not, what steps do I need to take?

With the skills of grounding and centering, it is possible to be genuinely engaged in our actions in the world and deepen our impact and sense of fulfillment. We can stand in intimate connection with our sacred places and open to the wider webs of life and the cycles of the earth and find our genuine relationship with them.

Opening to, acknowledging, and celebrating these cycles as individuals and communities can be a pathway of healing the human relationship with the earth. An initial step is to notice the earth cycles you are aware of, how you engage them, and how you are impacted by them. As your awareness of these phases starts to formulate or become clearer, allow your intentions for being in relationship with them to arise. What are the ways you and your community can honor and celebrate them?

One of the cycles I have found most accessible is the cycle of birth, growth, death, decay, and regeneration. This is the cycle of the seasons, which all beings—from plants to mosquitoes to birds to bears and us humans—are dependent upon for our continued well-being. I live in a place with four seasons and the plant cycles emerge from them. As a gardener, I am engaged with this cycle and intimately aware of what the plants are doing throughout the year. In my community we celebrate eight seasonal holidays that are relevant to us because of the distinct nature of our changing seasons. We honor

each turning of the Wheel of the Year that literally creates our sustenance as well as impacts our personal and community spiritual, emotional, and energetic well-being. Depending upon the desires and the
needs of our community, these rituals can range from the deeply personal to a broader community focus.

One of these seasonal rituals is Samhain, popularly celebrated as
Halloween, when the veil between the worlds is thin and we seek to
connect with our beloved dead and our ancestors. Our relationships to
ancestors are often overtly acknowledged at this time in community as
well as personally. Honoring our ancestors is also a consistent practice
throughout the year for me and many folks in my community. Our
bodies stand in the continuing cycle of life, death, and rebirth. We look
backward in time, recognizing and often thanking those who have
come before and the gifts and challenges they have bequeathed us. It is
important to remember that our ancestors may not be just of blood
but anyone or anything that has passed from this world and influences
us. As we stand in the present, how do we acknowledge, honor, and
learn from them? What must we do to make amends for mistakes they
made? As we ponder the future, each one of us can ask how our
actions as individuals and communities impact and form the world
where our descendants will live one day, the world where we will have
become ancestors.

One of my personal forms of earth magic is the creation of labyrinths. Labyrinths have served many purposes over time, such as a way
to journey between the worlds, opportunities of personal inspiration
or calm, and healing, as well as community celebration and prayer.
They have been a part of cultural traditions all over the world for
thousands of years. I have found from my own work with labyrinths
that they can be a means of facilitating communication between the
earth and humans and a way of deepening relationship with the land
on which they are located.

I was recently part of an indigenous water ceremony, a Nibi walk,
that honored the cycle of the Potomac River in the Eastern United

States. We gathered water at the river's source in the mountains of West Virginia and walked this water for 12 days and 320 miles to the river mouth at Chesapeake Bay. Each step of this walk was an offering to the spirit of the river and an expression of our desire to heal the relationship between humans and the river and all waters. When we reached the river mouth, we poured the source water into it, saying to the spirit of the river: "This is who you are, this is who you were before human beings polluted you. We seek relationship with you. We love you. We respect you. We thank you." This ceremony was part of a series of river walks that originated from visions of Ojibwe women and their desire to bring their spiritual work with water into the wider world. I met them through our shared commitment to a sacred spring and the Mississippi River. This was a traveling water ritual through the heart of the United States and one of the most deeply moving experiences of my life.

When we are rooted in our core worth and in intimate relationship with a place, we connect with the cycles of the earth, the network of all beings, and our interdependence. We may be called to act in support of them. The Reclaiming tradition has a strong component of activism: social and environmental justice work that also informs our spiritual practice. Being an anarchistic tradition, it is left to each of us to determine what those actions will look like. With these actions we create our own cycles, intertwining our fate in our physical forms with the well-being of all life on this earth.

In Reclaiming we come together to consciously choose our place in the greater cycles. We infuse our values, our ethos, into our interactions, rituals, and gatherings. In our Principles of Unity we address some of these challenges with these words: "We strive to teach and practice in ways that foster personal and collective empowerment, to model shared power, and to open leadership roles to all. We make decisions by consensus and balance individual autonomy with social responsibility." Evolving from this statement, there are several ways that many Reclaiming communities integrate these values into our ongoing practices.

We work with intentional magic, which means we express clearly why we are doing what we do. Embedded in each intention are our ethics, our values, and the focus of the magic. Magic sets in motion cycles that have impact and consequences. Stating our intention allows individuals and the community as a whole to ask questions such as: Can I truly engage with this intention? How does it serve community? Am I open and willing to accept its impact? We have found that when a community affirms an intention at the beginning of a ritual, the magic is more powerful because all participants are more fully engaged in the group magic.

We recognize and respect that each of us is a unique individual as well as a community member who is vital to the success of the whole. Our primary teachings come from our own experiences in our lives and relationships with each other, the spirits, and the earth over time. We are our own teachers. We are responsible for taking care of our own needs. As individuals, we are also in service to community, to a larger magic than just ourselves. We ask that folks be aware of and responsible for how their individual actions impact the magic of the group and the community at large.

We encourage community members to set and respect boundaries. We seek to create space where participants are physically safe for our magic. Because of the deep work we often engage in, this does not mean we are always comfortable. To create a safe space, we ask participants to know their limits and express them as needed. While we will ask folks to stretch their limits, we also insist that others respect a boundary when a participant expresses it. A key boundary is confidentiality. This means that participants may talk about their own experience and what we do generally as a group. If someone wants to talk about another person's experience, they need their explicit permission.

We ask folks to look at our time together as a communal brownie and to be mindful of how much they are eating and to be sure to leave plenty of time for others. Brevity with impact is also referenced, which means to ask ourselves: What is essential that I want the group to hear or witness from me in this moment? Our human societies are beholden to clocks and schedules, so we don't have an infinite amount of time for our gatherings.

Other Reclaiming members may highlight other agreements or cultural ethos. The guiding wisdom is that we live our values and integrate them into our individual and community lives. We strive to consciously create human relationships that more authentically integrate our human cycles with the wider webs of life on this planet.

As human beings, we are of the earth. The earth is of the stars in a continuing, evolving journey over time that our imaginations can barely grasp. Plants, mammals, reptiles, birds, soil, mountains, and all the other beings that live on this earth with us share a similar cellular makeup. We are all interdependent. All living beings' survival and ability to thrive over time is rooted in respecting this profound connection. Humans have had an immense impact on the planet and all beings who inhabit the earth. As individuals we are relatively insignificant, like grains of sand on a beach or one star out of billions in the night sky. At the same time, each of us is the center of a multiverse whose every breath, every heartbeat, every step impacts the whole in a miniscule yet profound way. Holding this paradox, it is essential that we come together as a species, stand fully in relationship with this earth, and create magic that touches and changes all of the worlds.

Practice: Tree of Life Grounding
Heidi Marian

Time: 10 minutes the first time you do this;
  afterward, 2–5 minutes

. . .

Grounding provides the foundation for magical or healing work. We ground to connect our life force with the ever present and nourishing earth that sustains, enriches, and gives us life. The deeper we ground, the further our spirits can journey. This exercise appears simple, and in practice it is straightforward. It can be deeply profound and is the groundwork from which we build our magic. Most, if not all, practices, processes, and rituals in this book begin with grounding. We often return to a simple grounding on completion of a magical working.

Starting a ritual or magical working with grounding, we might notice the tendency to jump right to the journeying or trance piece of the ritual or working. We witches are travelers, and this is a natural inclination. I have been in many circles where, as the grounding begins, we close our eyes, sway, hum, or even drum a slow trance rhythm. This is exactly the opposite of what we seek to accomplish with a grounding.

In a grounding, what we aim to embody is a powerful presence in our physicality and all of our senses. We seek to become aware of our surroundings and our own state of consciousness, while at the same time resolving momentarily anything that may be distracting us, and letting go of thoughts and feelings that might hinder the work at hand.

Centering is a related practice, and often grounding and centering are done together at the beginning of magic or ritual. To center ourselves, we mindfully bring all of our attention and awareness to the center of our bodies, at least for a moment. For some people, the center of their body feels like the midsection; for others, it may be slightly lower or higher. Sometimes we place our hands on this part of our body while we are doing this to reinforce the experience of centering.

. . .

Begin in a simple neutral position, either sitting or standing, as suits your body. Remember to keep your eyes open during this exercise.

Breathe deeply. Roll your shoulders and your head. Rub your hands together.

Begin to move your awareness from your body down into the earth, like the roots of a tree. Allow your energy to become the roots of the tree.

Your tree roots communicate and connect with the mycorrhizae, the seeds and Mysterious Ones of the soil. Your roots extend deeper still, deeper into the earth.

If there is any part of you that feels fearful, reticent, unsure, over-stimulated, anxious, or another emotion you wish to release, you can send those feelings, thoughts, and ideas into the roots. The roots take them and offer them to the earth as compost.

Your roots journey down until they are solidly anchored in the earth, as if you and the earth are one body. Breathe again, and allow yourself to feel fully the experience of deep connectedness.

In another breath and with full awareness, through your roots draw up the energy of the earth. Draw up resilience, strength, clarity, or inspiration. Whatever you need, drink it up through your roots and into your body.

Move that energy up through your rooted body into your arms. Hold your arms up to the sky.

Your arms become branches as you reach toward the heavens. Greet the sky and bring that starlight down into your body.

Allow the two energies to meet and mix within you, earth and stars.

You are the tree of life, stretching deep into the earth with your roots and far into the heavens with your branches.

Center yourself by focusing on the center point of your body and bringing all of your attention and awareness to that place for the space of several breaths. You might like to place one or both hands on that midpoint of your body.

Having established grounding and centering will assist you to return to feeling grounded and centered later during the ritual or during your day, often with just a mindful breath or two.

Blessed be.

Ritual: Connecting with Spirits of the Land
Zay Eleanor Watersong

Time: 1 hour

You will need: your journal and an offering such as
a water offering, a handful of nuts, a song, a stone,
a strand of hair, or other biodegradable gift

• • •

When Reclaiming witches create sacred space, in addition to invoking the directions and deities, other allies may be invited to join the circle. Often the spirits of the land are acknowledged and welcomed. But who *are* they?

The spirits of the land are the crawling ones, the flying ones, the trees, the plants, the winds, the four-legged, and all their kin that call a place home. They are the ones who are there, the ones who used to be there, and the ones yet to come.

They are the ancestors, Mysterious Ones, and deities of place, and they deserve our recognition and respect. By acknowledging them, we acknowledge we are in their space. To be able to name and honor them well, however, requires taking time outside of circle to develop a relationship with them.

To do so, our first task is to listen.

By *listen* I mean with all our senses, not just our ears. Information can come to us as words or impressions, as visual cues, as waves of emotion or feeling, as changes in temperature or energy or some other sign. The key is to practice being open and receptive, and to notice these subtle forms of communication.

This can be done anywhere and should be done briefly whenever we are in a new place where the spirits of the land are unfamiliar to us. However, it is best to start close to home or where we practice magic, as these are the spirits most relevant to our work.

* * *

Go outside.

Take a moment to bring yourself fully present.

From that gut-level of sensing, find a welcoming place to sit, prefer-ably on the earth rather than concrete.

If you find yourself called to the base of a tree, stop at the edge of the tree's canopy and ask permission of the tree's spirit. Convey your desire, and then let it go and listen for your answer. If you receive any sense of no, accept it with respect and see where else you may be called.

When settled, drop your roots down into the soil. Reach out and feel those roots intertwine with the others below you.

Soften your gaze, but keep your eyes open. Quiet your mind. Reach out, listen with all your senses. Let impressions flow over you. Who calls your attention? What do you notice?

After a time, introduce yourself. Ask the question, verbally or non-verbally: *How may I be in right relationship with you?* Notice the answers.

When you are ready, thank those you have encountered and leave your offering.

Take some time to record your experience in your journal.

Remember to implement what you have learned!

* * *

In my experience, in England the spirits of the land spoke English in my head. In my home woods of New York we communicate more in images and feelings. In New Zealand the wildness of the spirits of place was foreign and fascinating to me.

The sense of connection and gratitude this work can bring is pro-found. Connecting with the spirits of the land also allows me to work politically and with integrity in support of my Onondaga Nation neighbors. They know I have my own tradition of relationship to the land, and I am not inclined to appropriate their traditions out of a lack of my own.

In demonstrating respect and gratitude, we gain it as well. Therein lies the magic.

Practice: Casting the Circle
GEDE PARMA

Time: 30 minutes the first time you do this;
afterward, 5–15 minutes

• • •

The circle in the Reclaiming tradition is considered to be one of the primary ways that we step between the worlds, orient to the sacred, and create a container and cauldron for our magic.

The circle can be cast in multiple, perhaps infinite ways. This particular method is useful for those beginning in the arts of the witch and magic-making.

Customarily, the five elements are aligned with the seven directions. Reclaiming emerged from the San Francisco Bay Area, so the usual correspondences for the northern hemisphere are north/earth, east/air, south/fire, west/water, above, below, and center/spirit. In the southern hemisphere we usually still follow the sun's movements through the sky—which appears to move in an counterclockwise direction—and so the correspondences become south/earth, east/air, north/fire, west/water, above, below, and center/spirit.

In this exercise the elements are not associated with the directions. If you wish to assign elements to directions, however, this is your circle. The practice of casting the circle usually gets swifter and pithier the more practiced we become. Although later we may choose to cast a circle with a wand, knife, or other tools, in this exercise we simply work with our bodies and voices.

• • •

Ground and center. You might also like to align your three souls (see page 229).

Turn to the direction that the sun does not pass through in your hemisphere; this will be north in the northern hemisphere and south in the southern hemisphere. If you live near or on the equator, you can begin from the center; this is what I did when I lived in Bali, where the sun seems to travel directly overhead.

When you are facing the north, south, or center, deepen your sensitivity to your grounding and your souls. Drop your focus into the direction you are facing as a source of power. With your breath, will, and presence, draw in the power from that direction. You might like to do this with your receptive hand—for most of us, our left hand—and feel that power and life force moving up through your hand, up your arm, across your chest, and then down your other arm into the dominant hand.

Walk out to where you perceive the eastern edge of the circle to be. Depending on your hemisphere, this may be to the right or the left, but the sun rises in the east no matter where we are on this planet.

Gazing into the east, think and feel into the dawn. Access your memories of being awake at that time. What sounds, scents, images, and symbols connect you to your dawn experience?

When you feel full to the brim with this, draw a pentagram—a five-point star—in the air in front of you, facing the east. We often like to begin at the top of the pentagram and then draw down to the bottom left as we are looking at the symbol. We follow on from there in a continuous line of power and light, or flame, to the top right point, then across to the top left, then down to the bottom right point and back up to the top point where it all began. Some of us will then draw a circle around the points, and, when that is sealed, move our hand, witch's knife / athame, or wand intentionally through the center of the pentagram to activate the symbol. We do this both to draw in the power of that direction and to bless and seal this quarter of the circle.

Continue on from there in either a clockwise direction (if you are in the northern hemisphere) or counterclockwise direction (if you are in the southern hemisphere). We do this to follow the apparent direction the sun travels. Going with the sun is a ritual action common to many cultures. In Reclaiming and in many forms of modern witchcraft and Paganism, we draw inspiration from Celtic folklore and stories. To go with the sun is to bring blessings and good luck upon you or those assembled.

So when I am in Australia, I would continue on to the north and fill my awareness with the noonday peak of the sun's arc in whichever season I am in. I imagine myself standing or lying under the midday sun; I feel the grass or stones or roots against my back, and I recall the sound of the birds and insects of the day. I then draw the pentagram and activate it. In the northern hemisphere, this would all be to the south.

Then we turn to the west, where the sun sets, and go through the same process—accessing our feelings, memories, and experiences with the twilight of dusk and the setting sun, drawing the pentagram, and activating it. We now return to the direction where we began, either south or north—this is the place of midnight, the place the sun does not pass through the sky or where it goes through the underworld to be reborn—and repeat this process. In the center of the circle, we then repeat it again with above—dark, pregnant space filled with iridescent stars—and below—the roar of the underworld sea and the throb of the heart of the planet—and then we return our attention to the center itself. The circle is a sphere emanating from the center into six directions.

When in the center, we might wrap it all up with words—for example:

"By the center which is the circumference, the circle is cast and we are between the worlds. What happens between the worlds changes all the worlds."

And so it is done.

When we are ready to release the circle we've cast, after our ritual or magic, we might travel backward from direction to direction, beginning in the center and unwinding all that we did in the casting, or we might just stand in the center, bring our whole attention to the whole space, and dissolve the circle, releasing it to the directions and elements it came from. I like to send the circle out as a blessing to the spirits of the land.

The Web of Life

FIONA MARIPOSA

• • •

Life is a wondrously complex web of connections. Atoms formed in the furnace pressures of supernovas—building blocks joined together in an infinite number of possible forms—an unimaginable diversity of life—biodiversity. The dance of existence perpetually weaves connecting strands of the web between each form, for it is through relationship that life occurs.

Each breath taken is an exchange between animal and plant. Each death feeds more life. The cycle of water turns, connecting us all across time, for the water in our blood and tears is the same water that formed gaseous clouds in Earth's atmosphere at the time of her birth. This water has been passed between fungi and fern, from trilobite to dinosaur, from tree to soil to river to sea to cloud to tree to mammal to creek to bird, over and over and over again.

Whenever I eat, minerals that were once in the soil become part of my body. When I die, my flesh will become the food of bacteria and insects and my bones will decay slowly, releasing calcium and phosphorus back into the soil. The roses in my garden, with their sweet perfume and delicate, fleshy flowers, inspire me with their beauty and cheer me up when I am feeling depressed. The ancestors and family of these roses have inspired poetry, tapestry, and all manner of beautiful art. They have helped humans express and celebrate love, and for some people they symbolize gratitude and mourning.

Each dance of existence woven into the web of life has its own pattern. Some patterns are ancient, having withstood the test of time, and are repeated over and over. Some patterns are variations on other patterns, and some are brand new. Yet all of this joins living beings in connection. When we breathe, we are in relationship. When we eat and drink, we are in relationship. When we are born, we are in relationship; and when we die, we are in relationship. It is through this intricate tapestry that we exist together in the vast community that is the web of life.

One of the primary outcomes, and perhaps even purposes, of our journey with the elements is an extension of our perception of kin and community. This enables us to go beyond purely intellectual understandings of our place in the web of life and open ourselves to deeper relationships with landscapes and other beings. As we learn from each of the elements, we deepen our understanding of our place in a diverse community. More importantly, we begin to reclaim our human animal birthright—learning we are not alone in this world and that our lives are supported by a myriad of relationships with other beings.

Knowing that the oxygen in the air our mammalian bodies crave is produced by the green-blooded beings around us and that these beings breathe in the carbon dioxide that our bodies expel offers us a sense of wonder. The understanding that the iron in our blood—an essential mineral for mammalian life—comes from the rocks and soils of the earth and enters our bodies via the plants and herbivorous animals we eat can become a source of awe at the complexity of connections that are woven into the web sustaining our individual lives. Yet these scientific understandings may ultimately remain abstract to us if we do not also take steps to establish emotional connections with other beings and landscapes.

This deepening emotional perception of the ecological relationships between us and other beings within the elemental cycles can expand our sense of community and kin. In broadening our understanding and experience of who our family and community are, we widen the sphere of the ethics and values that underpin the ways we live our lives. When we feel connected to other beings, we are far more likely to take care of them and treat them with respect. When we feel connected to others, we are much more likely to take actions to ensure their well-being or to protect them from threats. Intellectual understanding alone rarely gives us a strong enough impetus to act in such ways. It is emotion that drives us, motivating us to move beyond comfort and complacency for the sake of others.

To live with a sense that we are kin to the fruit trees who provide us with food can inspire a longing to show gratitude to those trees by tending them and marking their cycles through celebration. To live with a deep knowing that the small, lively birds called willie wagtails are members of our community can motivate us to plant and care for shrubs that provide protection and nesting sites for wagtails.

As I sit writing this, my attention has been captured by a black wasp busily visiting the flowers on the pomegranate tree outside my window. An internet search for information about this wasp reveals little to me—a number of photos that almost match its appearance, possible species' classifications and taxonomic information, yet nothing about this wasp species' relationship to pomegranates. Nevertheless, my own observations over the years since I planted the two pomegranate trees in my garden have taught me that these black wasps with their orange-striped abdomens are particularly drawn to pomegranate flowers, and that they and their bee cousins fertilize the fruits on my trees every year.

I never see these wasps at any other time of year, so to me they seem intrinsically linked to pomegranates. The flowers they pollinate grow into large, juicy fruits that are enjoyed by my daughters and me as well as by our human friends and family, dogs, blackbirds, rats, possums, and a variety of insects. All our bodies take in nutrients and energy from the pomegranates, so that for the season of pomegranate fruiting every year, we each become made, in part, from the stuff of pomegranate. Through the simple act of eating we are linked in relationship to each other, to the pomegranate trees, and to the wasps and bees who pollinate their flowers. When I eat the pomegranates, I feel a sense of gratitude to the wasps. They may not even be aware of my presence or role within the community of the garden, but I am certainly aware of theirs.

This expansion of our concept of kin can come about through observation of our local environments and the ecological communities dwelling within them, as well as direct participation. While studying Elements of Magic, it can be helpful to build a practice of spending time outside observing the plants, fungi, and animals who share our local area. Taking notes about these observations can help us to gain a better sense of our local nonhuman community over time.

Indigenous peoples around the world have always had broad concepts of kin. In many indigenous cultures, animal and plant totems and kinship groups define a community's identity or an individual's identity within a community. They describe and regulate relationships with other species and taboos around what is eaten, hunting practices, and even marriages.

All of us have ancestors who were indigenous to particular lands at some point in time. As someone who lives in a different land from most of my ancestors, I am interested in learning from both the land and the beings who live in the place of my birth, Australia, as well as from my connection to the species and lands embedded in the cultural heritage of my ancestors from Western Europe, Scandinavia, and the British Isles.

In Scotland, a land where many of my matrilineal ancestors lived, clan members traditionally wore clan badges, otherwise known as plant badges, to identify themselves as a member of their clan. These badges were sprigs of a plant local to the lands of each clan and were worn or carried. They were symbols of connection to land and place, demonstrative of clan members' essence of kinship to each other, their homeland, and the plants that grew there.

Such emblematic links between human communities with the animals and plants who share the lands where they live can be found throughout human history. It could even be argued that the contemporary animal and plant emblems of nation-states or countries are a vestige of the understanding that our relationship to place is closely linked to our relationship with our animal and plant cousins. Knowing that my ancestors in Clan Campbell could identify kinship connection through their relationship with the bog myrtle or sweetgale, *Myrica gale*, helps me to more deeply understand my own sense of strong emotional connection to river redgums, *Eucalyptus camaldulensis*. These majestic beings dwell on the farmland where I grew up. Their bodies became the playgrounds of my childhood, and their huge, supportive limbs gave me a sense of being held and loved by the world. River redgums have gifted me with many lessons and insights about ecology, generosity, and gratitude. Out of all plant species, I feel a closest sense of kinship to them—they remind me of who I am, the land of my birth, and my place in the world.

Our human ancestors often led geographically localized lives. Although trade enabled human communities to somewhat diversify their food and materials for clothing, building, and tool-making, for tens of thousands of years, most of the resources our human ancestors used would have come directly from the local environments they dwelt in and the species who shared those locales. Regardless of ethnic heritage, our ancestors hunted, gathered, grew, and farmed almost all of their own food. They would have partaken in planting and harvesting, milking and killing. They participated in the death of the animals and plants that became their food, clothing, and medicine. They harvested grasses, bamboo, and willow to weave baskets and gathered stones and shells to fashion tools and jewelry.

The close proximity in which they lived with the landscapes and other living beings who sustained their lives would have undoubtedly given them a sense of connection and relationship with their nonhuman community. Who would fail to feel gratitude toward goats for providing you with milk if you were spending time every day herding and milking them? Who would forget to acknowledge the mountain who yielded ochre for paint or stones for your tools if you had walked to that mountain yourself?

For many of us living in urbanized, capitalist societies, it is no longer the case that we know where our food, clothing, or building materials come from. Most of us do not grow our own food. In fact, most of us know little of where our food comes from—the land it is grown on or the processes used to farm, hunt, or harvest it. Our food is not born from seeds we have planted with our own hands. We know nothing of the lives or deaths of the animals and plants that we eat.

Living this way, many of us feel little or no connection to the other beings who sustain our existence. As a species we have a tremendous capacity to seek connection through empathy, but it seems that this is far more easily done when we are in face-to-face contact with others. Food production, for example, is now largely removed from urban life. In these days of global markets, many urban societies source their food and other life-sustaining materials off-shore, from other lands altogether. It is not surprising that many people who live in urbanized societies feel no awareness of the real-world ecological relationships between themselves and other species, even though they eat them and their products, as well as wearing clothes made out of their fibers, skin, wool, and fur every single day.

Learning with the elements is not an invitation to begin beating ourselves up. We have little choice about the cultures we are born into. We do, however, have the power to make changes in our lives and in the world. Even those changes that are seemingly small can create ripples that combine with others to form magnificent, transformational waves.

Although I was raised on a farm, I now live in the large urban metropolis that is Melbourne, Australia. I am fortunate to have garden space and an understanding landlord, so I have been able to plant many fruit trees, berries, and herbs over the years I have lived here. I also keep bees and hens and thus supplement my family's diet with fruit, eggs, and honey produced in our simple garden space. I have friends who do not have their own gardens but make use of pots on balconies and community garden lots to produce some of their own food. Other friends actively seek out locally grown produce markets and visit farms to pick fruit. All of us, in our own ways, are seeking to deepen our relationships within the web of life. We yearn to reclaim our human heritage as beings who are fully immersed in our ecological communities and are nurtured by the feelings of connectedness we gain through this immersion.

We can all look for opportunities to deepen our relationships with the beings who provide our food and create our environment. Many of us are raised in cultures that cheat us of a sense of connection to the natural communities to which we belong, but when we take steps toward breaking down this alienation, the results can be incredibly healing on both individual and societal levels.

The understanding of the importance of re-establishing a sense of connection to nonhuman beings and landscapes underpins much of the work of Deep Ecologists Joanna Macy and John Seed. One of the processes they co-created—the Council of All Beings—is a lengthy ritual specifically designed to help participants enter into feeling relationships with other beings. When we deepen our empathy and compassion for others, we are much more likely to act in caring ways toward them. It can be relatively easy for most of us to put ourselves in the shoes of another human being, if we make the time to do so. This can be much harder to do for nonhuman species with whom we have no relationship or understanding of. The Council of All Beings process aims to break down some of the barriers we humans have in relation to empathy for nonhuman species.

A structured outline of the Council of All Beings process can be found in *Coming Back to Life* by Joanna Macy and Molly Brown. The process is often taught as an exercise in imagination and empathy, although it can also be more shamanic in form, incorporating some degree of possessory spirit work, or aspecting, in Reclaiming terminology. In the Council of All Beings, the human participants take on speaking for, or sometimes speaking as, a variety of nonhuman beings, within a council meeting where they may discuss various issues or how they are feeling and experiencing life. For example, participants might take on the roles of different beings within a local forest ecosystem and speak with each other about the current state of that forest. As this process can utilize trance states or even aspecting in Reclaiming contexts, it is advised that facilitators have experience and a clear understanding of the nature of this work.

In being open and willing to listen to what is being communicated by others, we are both demonstrating respect and increasing our opportunities to learn from them. Ritual processes such as the Council of All Beings remind us of the importance of, and give us a forum for, listening to the most marginalized voices of all: the nonhuman members of Earth's community.

Our life is born from, and sustained by, an intricate, complex web of connections and relationships. Yet, for many of us, a sense of our place in this web is at best an abstract scientific understanding, while within our society a general sense of alienation from nature prevails. But we humans retain an amazing capacity for empathy and an ability to see and feel the relationships between ourselves and other beings and landscapes. This is a gift we have inherited from our ancestors. Our magical journey through the elements, and particularly with the element of earth, encourages us to open ourselves more fully to these natural abilities. Striving to move beyond purely intellectual understandings of our place in the web of life, and to re-awaken to our human-animal propensity for deep connection with other beings and landscapes, is part of our magic. It is time to reclaim our birthright—a feeling sense that our lives are supported by a myriad of relationships with other beings. We are never alone, for we are embraced and held by—and are active members of—the great web of life.

Exercise: Ecstatic Breath Work with Plants
Riyana Rose Sang and Chuck

Time: 15 minutes

You will need: an offering of water, milk, honey,
or a song; journal or Book of Shadows; a pen;
essential oils or herbal incense (optional)

. . .

One of the most basic, elegant examples of witch's work with plant allies is the interdependence we can connect to in every breath: the simple experience of the oxygen that blossoms in our lungs and brushes against our hearts as we breathe in, and the carbon dioxide that streams out of us and sustains the lives of the greenbloods as we breathe out. This dance of interdependence happens in every second all around the world, in gardens and rainforests, on snowy mountaintops and in the oases shoals of the desert. By tuning in to it with intention—and ecstasy, if we dare—we remember our connection to the plants and heal any illusions about disconnection with the earth that we may have.

. . .

Begin by taking a few grounding, centering breaths. Breathe very deeply into the belly, allowing it to be full and round, and then sip up a little extra air into the heart. Release your breath. Take three of these full, expansive breaths, making sure to exhale fully each time to release any mind chatter that may be keeping you from being fully present.

Next, choose a plant to connect with. You will need to be next to the plant physically. It can be an ancient redwood or a tiny bean sprout, a weed growing up through the cracks in the sidewalk or a rose blooming in a botanical garden. If they are derived from the plant spirits you wish to connect with, this is also a great working to incorporate essential oils or herbal incense into.

Sit and allow yourself to simply be with the plant you have chosen. Next, make an offering of water, milk, honey, or a song, and ask the plant if it would like to spend some time connecting with you. Most plants really love this as they are our friends and loving ancestors, and they've been waiting for humanity to wake up and remember our ancient bonds. Wait for a sensation of yes in your body or heart before moving on. If you receive a no, either choose a different plant or return to this exercise at another time.

Once you've received the yes, begin intentionally breathing and exchanging energy with the plant. Breathe in through your nose, allowing the breath to dance in your heart for a moment before breathing out through your mouth. As you exhale, imagine your love, intention, and hope being carried on your breath to the plant. As you inhale, imagine that the medicine and energy of the plant is beaming out of the plant and streaming into you. You may be able to see this, in your mind's eye, as a figure eight of light and connection between you and the plant.

With each breath turn up the sensations of your heart and body through the power of your imagination. Encourage yourself to feel as beautiful, good, sweet, and wonderful as you possibly can. You can take this exercise deeper and add a rush of ecstatic communion by pulling up with your root chakra or perineum and tightening your abdominal muscles as you inhale, taking in the energy of the plant, and then deeply relaxing the root chakra and belly as you exhale.

Finish by taking three grounding breaths with your hands on your heart. As you drop your hands and finish your third intentional breath, whisper a prayer or blessing for the plants and the earth.

Jot down any notes or messages that you want to hold on to in your journal or Book of Shadows.

Spell: Magic Herbal Sachet for Protection
Riyana Rose Sang and Chuck

Time: 1–3 hours

You will need: a small piece of fabric, herbs of your
choosing, sea salt, needle and thread, and altar items
for directions or elements

• • •

Spell work is the manifestation of the ethereal through the material. When we engage in spellwork, we enter an altered state of consciousness through alignment with both the earth and the transcendent before performing a symbolic act to bring about change. Although the particulars of this process vary from spell to spell, all spells contain the steps of connection and alignment, a symbolic act, and an intention that directs the energy raised in the spell-work process.

• • •

Since the intention of this spell is for protection, find some cloth that you experience as protective. It could be a piece of an old T-shirt from a time in your life when you felt safe or a shiny-shimmery reflective fabric. Choose something that resonates intuitively for you.

Harvest or gather the herbs that you will use to fill your magic sachet. Be sure to only collect a wild plant if it is growing abundantly and you feel confident that you can follow sustainable, respectful wildcrafting protocols. The plants you use must be dried, so harvest at least two weeks before you plan to work your spell. Plants that are commonly used for protection by witches of European traditions are rosemary, sage, lavender, basil, bay, nettles, cedar, yarrow, wood betony, and vervain. In your bioregion there may be other powerful plant allies that are more relevant.

Create an altar for your spell with items for the different directions or elements and any protective deity or ally that you are working with. It might feel right to work at the time of the waxing moon to forge a new long-term protective relationship with a deity or plant ally. If there's anything to shed or release as part of the process, you might choose the waning moon.

Begin your ritual by taking some time to ground and center. We can do this through breath work, triple soul alignment (see page 229), or connecting to the earth's center and aligning ourselves with the divine guidance that lies deep within the earth.

Cast your circle, call the elements and directions, and invoke the energies and allies that you are choosing to work with for this spell.

Within your sacred space, begin to craft your magical bag. Start with a round, square, or rectangular piece of cloth. Fold the edges of fabric to meet each other and sew them together, leaving one seam open for now. With each stitch, visualize or sense a strong web of protection around you, weaving organically. You may want to chant or sing as you sew to charge your magical working and hold the focus of your intention.

When the sachet is ready, add the herbs and salt while you breathe and realign with the earth and your intention. Offer thanks to the plants and ask them to release their protective energy through this spell. Hum, sing, or whisper words of gratitude as you fill the bag with the herbs and salt.

When the sachet is full, sew it shut or create a drawstring to close it. During the final stitches, again visualize or sense that strong circle of protection around you. Take the bag in your left hand and charge it with energy of protection, then place it on the altar. Say aloud as you place the bag on your altar: "It is done. So mote it be."

Offer gratitude to the plants, your allies, and the energies present in the spell as you devoke.

Then, with a breath, open the circle and release the spell into the world.

Meditation: Rotting Body
SUSANNERAE

Time: 30 minutes

You will need: a journal, a pen, and water

• • •

This guided meditation developed from the Buddhist *Maranasati*, or mindfulness of death, is powerful in developing a deep understanding of our true relationship with the earth, with our body as part of the earth's nutrient cycle.

Be aware that strong images, emotions, and sensations can arise when working with death. We can more easily choose to undertake this type of provocative work, even knowing we may be deeply affected by it, when we practice good self-care. This might look like scheduling this work when we are rested, fed, and have allowed for some time afterwards to integrate or just sit with our experience. If you are uncertain about doing this meditation by yourself, find a friend to share the experience with. You may also choose to ground, cast a circle, align your souls, invite allies to be present, or invoke the Goddess before you begin.

You can record the instructions first and then listen to them as you go through the meditation, or you might prefer simply to read them through a couple of times and then lay them aside, trusting that your meditation will contain what it needs to. An alternative is to work with a partner and take turns reading aloud to each other. Allow long pauses between the sentences.

• • •

Find a place where you can lie or recline comfortably, where you won't be distracted or interrupted.

In your journal, record the time and date you are doing this work.

Become aware of your breathing and allow it to soften and slow as you let go of the outside world.

Become aware of the weight of your body on the floor or chair where you are. Allow yourself to feel the heaviness of your flesh and bones.

Feel the breath in your body as the rise and fall movement of your chest or abdomen.

Breathe in and soften, breathe out and release…let your thoughts drift. As you go deeper and deeper, feel yourself becoming softer and softer…heavier and heavier…until breath is all there is.

Imagine that you are lying on the earth, somewhere safe outside. Feel the air and listen to the wind. Smell the soil and feel the solidity of the ground below you. You are safe, at peace.

The breath is coming and going, moving the body, rising and falling. This body of flesh, of bone, of blood is animated by breath. Breathing…heart beating…blood pumping…

Take a moment to appreciate this breath, this thread of life, this sustainer of your existence.

And then…one day…it stops!

No more breath…

It stops, and with it stops the beating of the heart. All is still…all is quiet.

Feel the heaviness of the body as it comes to stillness, as it sinks toward the earth and then softens into the ground.

The body begins to change. There is expansion as gases fill the body. Cell walls begin to dissolve, and fluids leak and mingle. The body spreads, expands, and dissolves, becoming a slimy mush.

Bacteria released from the gut begin to gobble up the juices—they transform and digest the soupy ooze. They delight as they grow in number and strength.

The smell of rotting flesh draws animals. Worms and insects come, ants and flies—they feast on the dissolving flesh. Larger animals, too, take parts of this glorious notorious meal, scattering bones…

Grateful birds take hair to line their nest. Tendons and sinews dissolve. Bones fall apart.

Here is death and here is life.

And then all that is left is bone and hair, scattered across the ground, covered in leaves and debris from the earth. Tiny creatures make homes in the now hollow bones. The body is now a rich layer of compost, broken down into its chemical parts. What was borrowed from the earth is now returned.

Wind blows and rain falls.

The seasons change and tiny seeds begin to sprout, to push their way through the soil. They bring with them the nourishment of chemicals once contained in your body, to create stems and leaves, flowers and seeds.

The seedlings grow taller and stronger until one day the plants themselves fall and begin to rot. Here is silence…here is stillness. Here is death…here is life…here is earth.

Take a deep breath and start to bring your awareness back into your body.

Become aware of the sounds around you, the sounds of this time and place.

Move your body. Sit up and pat your body. Be aware of its solidity.

Look at the paper with the time and date on it. Say your name aloud and read the date of today that you wrote earlier.

Drink some water and spend some time writing of your experiences in your journal.

Earth Activism

RUBY BERRY

• • •

I am an activist. I am an activist because I love the earth. We are beloved and gently held. Think not? Try jumping off the ground or even raising your arm into the air. The earth calls us back in so many ways. Our Earth—who we are part of and deeply in love with—is our paradise, and we're not looking to go anywhere. This is home.

The Charge of the Goddess, written by Doreen Valiente, teaches "My law is love unto all beings." I take this to mean that the charge is to find all the ways to love the earth, to every day actively love and care for her, to recognize and work to heal and mend the damage the culture of domination has wreaked. It calls on us to be conscious of how we live, of the need to be places where our actions are strategic and have influence on a larger than individual scale, to take on direct responsibility and stewardship.

The Reclaiming tradition sees responsibility in this love of the earth, which is why I was first drawn to this particular tradition of witchcraft. I had been an activist for many years, inspired by my recognition of social injustice and the ways in which that was supported and condoned, even created, by the Christianity of my childhood. I had come to believe that spiritual practice had no place in my life and was not in touch with the inherent spirituality in caring for the world around me. The commitment to political change and activism was so central, vital, and varied to the Reclaiming priestesses I encountered at British Columbia WitchCamp that I was drawn to explore the sacredness and spirit of all I had come to care and fight for.

Reclaiming WitchCamps are intensive retreats for the study of ritual and magic, usually held in a campground setting for about a week. Connecting with spirit at this camp deepened and enriched my activism and introduced a deeper meaning, as well as bringing a whole raft of additional tools to my activism. I felt spiritually supported to engage in the potentially more stressful work within my activism. Utilizing the intuitive, grounding, sensing, and weaving skills I developed in my magical practice strengthened my ability to stay centered and focused in my political action. I found access to resources that continued to pull me out of despair. At the same time, my activism deepened, widened, and enriched my spiritual life. As witches we learn to practice within all the realms, the physical being as powerful and as relevant as the mystical.

The Reclaiming Principles of Unity begin with our commitment to earth activism, seeing responsibility in our love of the earth. We are dedicated to her care and the beings who are part of her: "The values of the Reclaiming tradition stem from our understanding that the earth is alive and all of life is sacred and interconnected. We see the Goddess as immanent in the earth's cycles of birth, growth, death, decay, and regeneration. Our practice arises from a deep spiritual commitment to the earth, to healing, and to the linking of magic with political action."

For some witches, the progression has been the other way around. Many of us are drawn to witchcraft and magic through the mystic and then discover that love of the earth inspires action. Just as we would respond when a dearly loved person is wounded or hurting, so we feel the call to act in response to the wounds of the earth. Developing our relationship with the sacred elements, we grow into our connection with the earth with each other and our deepest selves, becoming more aware of the deep pain and trauma the earth is suffering at the hands of the current culture, of which we are a part. We are challenged by the power of the dominant culture—also known as the patriarchy, the overculture, capitalism, oppressive culture, and corporate control—which feeds on separating us from our web of connection. We are taught and encouraged to put ourselves first and not care or even notice who or what gets hurt in the process. We are separated from the consequences of our actions. The message is that we are inadequate and incomplete, and that the only way to success and happiness is to constantly purchase whatever trendy remedy is on offer. Individualism reigns, and the more inadequate the individual can be made to feel, the more successful the scarcity and consumer regime become.

My spiritual practice reminds me that I am part of a magnificent web, strong in diversity and connection. Creating and maintaining vibrant, healthy communities is likely the most difficult and most important work, as the dominant culture teaches individualism and dominion over each other, people and cultures different from our own, animals, and all living beings—over the earth herself.

We are a web and interconnected; we are not the rugged individuals that the overculture wants us to believe we are. The cultural paradigm is not simple to change, so we're in need of all kinds of change action. Living a life in alignment with the earth is commendable and can be an example to others. Our activism becomes much more powerful when we develop strategies to grow and work in collaboration with others. Connecting with our web of allies—human, plant, animal, earth, ancestral, elemental, and magical—our work for change can be significant.

As my activism is infused and inspired by my values, so I must recognize that I am living and practicing on stolen land as part of a settler culture that has and continues to devastate and impact the indigenous peoples, cultures, and land. Yet I am witness to the enormous generosity of those whose lands and lives have been stolen, who continue to be willing to attempt reconciliation and continued hospitality. It is incumbent upon those of us who are settlers to learn about and listen well to the people of the land, take direction for our support and restitution from them, and put an end to continued persecution. This will mean very different things in different places and so it is important to practice deep respect and attention.

As a descendant of settlers and an immigrant to this land, I have a responsibility to educate myself in the ways we have contributed to and colluded in ongoing oppression and cultural appropriation. Scrupulously assessing and acknowledging my own privilege and complicity in oppression is essential. My own journey in this involves searching out and listening carefully to indigenous voices and finding a circle of other settler folks to work through confusion, shame, sorrow, and right action that doesn't perpetuate the damage. This is very hard work, as it always is whenever I truly confront and seek to understand the impacts of the dominant culture. My witchy skills, such as dropped and open attention, support my ability to stay focused and present in this learning process. Working with altars as well as grounding and centering allow me to move through the sometimes extreme emotions this work brings up so that denial doesn't stop me from acting.

I find it refreshing and satisfying to find ways to build the world I envision, as so much of the time a call to activism begins with alarm or concern about harm that is being done. My initial response is to want to name the wrong and make it stop. Permaculture offers ways to engage in creating rather than tearing apart, and it has become an important practice for many Reclaiming witches. Developed in the 1970s by Bill Mollison and David Holmgren, permaculture is a system of agricultural and social design based on observing and replicating natural earth patterns and processes. It calls for care for the earth, care for people, and a return of the surplus. It is the art of designing beneficial relationships reliant on the power of cooperation. It teaches how to design human systems and relationships so that we are not depleting and working from a scarcity model, but working as nature works— creating sustainable abundance. I think of it as practical witchcraft.

Permaculture is a useful design tool for communities and also political actions, built on indigenous concepts of survival and living in concert with the earth and her cycles, garnering the most effect with least impact, working with, and valuing, diversity. As the biodiversity of the earth corrodes, so we lose our collective resilience. Permaculture teaches that increasing our circle of inclusion and enshrining diversity is the path to manageable, lasting abundance. If we are able to be a community that values the gifts and differences of all members without casting outsiders as others, a community within a network of different communities, we become who we are meant to be: a web of life, living our power, love, compassion, and support.

Ecofeminism links the oppression of women and what has been considered feminine with the harm humans wreak on the earth. Ecofeminism sees this oppression as disenfranchising all that gives life, all that nurtures our wild, natural selves. This particular articulation of feminism calls for a recognition of the intersection of gender, the environment, and socioeconomics and the ways they are all oppressed and vilified. There is an understanding that as life flows from women, so the earth brings forth life. Recognizing this connection, we understand that it is vitally important to value life in all its forms. The ecofeminist movement was born out of the need to remember the value of the female and the primal connections between earth and women. Its desire is to redress the imbalance resulting from millennia of patriarchy.

The rise in goddess traditions in modern times paralleled new understanding in the environmental movement; the resurgence of the Goddess in the West opened the door to re-linking spirituality with this planet, empowering relationships between each other and all life. In many parts of the world, it was a revolutionary idea to name the earth as alive, although indigenous people everywhere have always understood this to be fundamental.

The circle is cast. We are between the worlds, and what happens between the worlds changes all the worlds. Thus we begin our ritual work. We practice this understanding that we impact our mundane physical lives and culture through our work with magical realms. Intention is important here, as it is in all the worlds. The tools offered in the pages of this book are often used in service to protect and heal the earth. When we invoke the sacred circle in this manner, it has a number of results. We focus our own energy and intention on the work at hand; our effectiveness is increased by combining our efforts together; we engage the help of our spirit allies, the Mysterious Ones, and the energy we raise is concentrated and then released in service of our intention. The patterns of the earth teach us the power and resilience of diversity. If we're striving to change the cultures of our world, redirecting energy that is flowing relentlessly to the destruction of the earth and all that we love, we must do everything we can think of, everything we can imagine. Commonly ascribed to the Sufi mystic and poet Rumi is the phrase "There are hundreds of ways to kneel and kiss the ground."

The paths to social change are numerous. Practically, I find ways to reduce my carbon footprint, protect wild places, recognize the wild in my home and in myself, walk lightly on the earth, use and consume less, recycle, educate, make art, and raise the children I know in earth-loving spiritual feminist traditions. I attempt to scrupulously examine my own relationship with privilege, racism, and oppression. Imbuing these practical acts with intention and energy to engage the larger magical realms strengthens and clarifies them. So I am no longer simply washing the dishes as I set an intention that the waters run clean, free, and wild.

I do all that I can think of to help, heal, comfort, and prevent harm. Balancing a life that strives to be imbued with our values while engaging in activism intended for social change with a strategic plan and collaboration can be difficult. Organized activism can take many forms—blockades, civil disobedience, writing, political campaigning, boycotts or preferential purchasing, flash mobs, rallies, street marches, strikes, occupations, and hunger strikes. For each of us, finding our own balance of action, personally and communally, is a necessary part of the work. I'm not an effective agent of social change if I don't take care of myself both physically and spiritually. My best tools are attention, listening, connection, and acting together with others both human and spirit. The practice of witchcraft offers many opportunities to hone these tools. Lessons from seasons and stages of growth help to see this commitment as a continuum, perhaps a spiral, with each of us contributing differently at different moments of our lives. We act in magical and practical ways, using the tools at hand as well as others we discover.

Dion Fortune, beloved ancestor of spirit, wrote "Magic is the art of changing consciousness at will." It is hard enough to change our own dearly held beliefs, habits, and consciousness, but what activists intend and hope to change is the consciousness of a neighborhood, an institution, entire cultures, entire paradigms. If I think that it isn't appropriate for a fast food place to be built next to the schoolyard, I may choose to protest the building permit. As I get more involved, however, I may be drawn into a lifetime of advocating for organic foods, nutritional literacy, food security, labor equity, eradication of poverty, animal rights, climate crisis awareness, radical community planning...the list goes on. When I recognize the issue I have noticed is a symptom of a larger-scale issue, I'm challenged to become more actively involved. My understanding of the problems and my capacity for engagement will determine where I direct my energy.

Grounding and centering is always important and incredibly helpful amid the excitement and chaos of a rally, public demonstration, direct action, or act of civil disobedience. Magical skills I regularly take to an action include shielding, grounding, connecting energetically with other witches and magical allies, protection spells, good chants, and friends that can sing loudly and carry a tune. I also like to bring chalk for sigils and runes, a drum, and plans to fit in a spiral dance if the occasion calls for it. I get the itch for a spiral dance whenever I'm in a group of fifty or more people. The spiral dance can be very powerful in a public event. At a gathering that was called to support the Women's March on Washington and protest growing misogynist political legislation, the inclusion of a spiral dance allowed eye-to-eye contact, linking people together with a common intention. Walking the spiral, a sacred pattern, provided focus and direction for our collective energy, bringing us closer as a community and imbuing the action with sacredness. It moved us beyond theory and ideology to include emotion, spirit, and connection.

Reclaiming WitchCamps are meeting grounds for emotion, spirit, and connection. They also offer a cauldron in which to experiment with living together according to our values and practices, working with the intention of creating the world we want to live in. We are in intentional community for that time, learning and practicing magical skills, mediating power, challenging each other, celebrating, making powerful magic, replenishing our energy, and working with resolving conflict and exploring our edges both individually and as a community. Similar community learning and growth occurs in Occupy settlements and other protest actions and blockades where people gather for a common purpose. These temporary communities often include talking circles, consensus decision-making, nonviolence training, and meditation practice, as well as the development of new group tools such as the people's microphone. This is a method for a speaker to reach a large crowd simply by people close to the speaker repeating their words so those behind can hear. It's a powerful example of communal problem-solving. These exercises in building and maintaining connections are both magical and practical. They provide hope and reassurance that we can indeed learn to live together.

In these times of great change, when we seem to be moving closer to the edge of planetary destruction, it can be easy to become overwhelmed and depleted. Taking on the overculture and challenging its right to dominion over us and the earth is not a simple matter. It is hard work to protect a waterfall or be an ally to your indigenous neighbors or stop the strip mining of a mountain. One action or campaign is not likely to make all the changes needed. We need to pace ourselves and care for ourselves as part of the earth. How frail we sometimes feel in the process! In our tool kit we have healing spells to support each other, spells that create safety nets—to channel anger, for example—psychic and invisible connections, and many shared meals.

We remember to celebrate, to rest, and to support each other. We love the earth by also loving ourselves. Connecting to the land refreshes and heals us. For me, healing is consciously and physically remembering my earth love. When I'm worn out, despairing, confused about what to do next, and need to recharge, I put my hands in the earth in my garden or immerse my body in a body of wild water. Even something as simple as having a bath or standing barefoot on the ground will help, as will snuggling with my favorite cedar trees. I listen to the plants and the elemental beings and look for direction and inspiration from the patterns and rhythms of the earth. I find that both my magic and my political work are more powerful and more satisfying when I align with the seasons and cycles of growth and decline.

I have learned that it is not possible to ever know your full impact. A small move may result in a massive change for all kinds of reasons; thus is the nature of energy. Perhaps cycling to work inspires someone to think of transportation choices and impacts that they've never considered. Perhaps your brilliant editorial letter did not change fisheries' policy, but maybe it did motivate someone in another community to take the issue one step further. It is a powerful, courageous act to change the way we live. As we strengthen our spiritual practice, our activism is strengthened.

Activism in service to the earth takes many forms, limited only by our imaginations—which, when aligned with the mysterious, are infinite. Art in all its forms is a very powerful tool, touching hearts and minds, and is well-aligned with the magical realms. The culture of domination is pervasive and social justice issues are complex, so our understanding of their dynamics is continually changing. The dominant culture is in a particularly pivotal time of disruption and change right now, and our skills as listeners, observers, learners, questioners, and educators are crucially needed. As lovers of the earth, we are called to recognize and work to mend or hopefully prevent new damage. Witchcraft teaches that we are all an inherent part of the interconnected web of life, inseparable from all around us. We are an active ingredient, the leavening agent. We can make change.

Practice: Anchoring to Core Worth
Kellie Wilding

Time: 25 minutes

You will need: somewhere comfortable where you won't
be disturbed; you may wish to prerecord the exercise
and play it back

• • •

Embodying and remembering core worth can be a radical act in a
world that often seeks to have us believe that our worth has to be
earned and so easily can be taken away. Somewhere within your being
there lies an innate knowing—a thread, a pool, a memory that reminds
you—that you are, in fact, divine.

You are stardust. No less, no more than anyone or anything else.
You are shimmering immanence in motion. Sometimes we forget this.

• • •

Stand, sit, or lie comfortably. Ground yourself and allow some time to
release any distractions that come. Begin to sink deeper into yourself.
Breathing in and out, settle yourself into your most comfortable
relaxed state.

On your next in-breath, find that right-sized place in you that sits
pivotally between an inflated and deflated state of self. It might be
connected to a joyful, easy moment in your life. Perhaps it is simply a
felt sense of the most embodied comfortable expression of yourself. If
this does not come easily, just imagine what that sense of right-sized-
ness and ease might be like.

In your own time, fill your lungs fully with a sense of well-being,
ease, and deep, deep relaxation. As you do this, expand this deep relaxation throughout your entire body, through every single pore. Begin to
sense, picture, or imagine your whole being vibrating and resonating
with relaxed, potent life force. This is the essence of you stripped back,

divine. Spend some time here, immersed in this energy. Call back any threads of yourself that have forgotten this immanence within.

What shape, form, color, smell, or sound does this divinity take? Are there any moods or feelings that come with it? Does it have a particular location in your body that is most noticeable?

Bathe in this state until it leaves an indelible, tangible, and memorable imprint in you. Allow it to radiate through every cell and every space in your being. Let it seep through all your energy bodies, including your aura. This state of being is inherent in you always. It cannot diminish or disappear.

When you sense that it has reached its fullest expression, find a way to anchor and moor it within so that you will be able to easily seek it out when you next lose connection to it. Find an image, a word, and a literal gesture—for example, the image of a rose, the word *worth,* and touching your heart—that will help you access this remembering of core worth when circumstances in life pull you out of alignment. Combine this image, word, and gesture and take some time to repeat them until they feel embedded deeply. This is your anchor. In order to access this anchor and the experience that goes with it, recite the word, make the gesture, and imagine the image. Seal this anchor with three slow, full breaths in and out, with some toning or whatever feels right for you.

Then, knowing this state is ever present, slowly shift your attention. With another breath, begin to bring your awareness back to the knowledge of yourself in the physical space surrounding you. Feel where your body touches the ground, move your limbs, and open your eyes if they were closed.

Practice using this anchor in your interactions in everyday life. Take regular notice of when you drift out of embodiment of core worth and use this anchor to return, so that accessing this inherent state becomes quicker and easier over time.

You can read more about core worth in *The Twelve Wild Swans* by Starhawk and Hilary Valentine.

AIR

• • •

Air is what we breathe, an intricate combination of nitrogen and oxygen with some argon and a little carbon dioxide thrown in. We breathe between twelve and twenty times per minute. If we stop breathing, or if we start to breathe in a substance that is not fairly close to our usual mix, we die—quickly. All of the four traditional elements are vital to us, every minute of every day. With air we breathe, speak, hear. Air is the wind that moves the clouds through the sky; it is the realm birds fly through. We associate air with music and song, with thought, ideas, and intent. With each breath we can be conscious of communing with the green world, accepting the air they have expelled and drawing it into our lungs, then changing it inside us to become air that they need and will, once again, breathe in. Air draws us, each second, into this web of life on earth.

We often work magic while focusing on breath. Counting the inhale, holding, exhaling, and holding of a single breath is used in various meditation and relaxation techniques. With our breath we reach into the earth, imagining our roots and the layers of rock, soil, water, and even fire beneath us; with our breath and our imagination we reach up toward the stars, calling down starlight and remembering our connection to the cosmos. We consciously slow and deepen our breathing to enter a trance state. We might breathe deep and fast to support our singing voices as we raise a cone of power, and then, after the energy has been sent out into the world or down into the earth and ourselves, we often drop our breath with our bodies, down to the ground.

Every breath we take, every single breath, means we are alive. Alive right now, breathing and holding the potential to speak aloud, to make a choice, to become conscious of our thoughts and actions. Each breath can be a blessing—another moment of life, and what will you do with this moment? And this one? And this?—and each breath can be a prayer of hope or gratitude or a call to action. When we bring our awareness into this micro level of breath, each word holds meaning and choice, each thought takes us in one direction or a different one. We work with intention all the time in magic and ritual; we form it into words, we speak it aloud, sometimes we turn our intention into a song—we breathe it. We can choose to live each breath with intention.

Every word, communication, and thought is fueled by air. Thus we link air in an Elements course with the ideas and beliefs underlying Reclaiming, in particular the Principles of Unity. What do you believe or hold as immeasurably sacred, irrevocably valuable? What values are important to you? What principles do we hold as a group, and when we consciously try to put those into practice, how do we do that? How would that look? We may all have different opinions on many things— do we share enough to make it worthwhile to do the hard work of communicating, word by word and meeting by meeting, to begin to create the world we want to live in? In Reclaiming we take a deep breath and say yes.

Air is associated in our tradition with the power *to know*. As witches and magic workers, we desire to know the hidden—the occult—ways and mysteries of the plants, mountains, gods, ancestors, spirits…We might wield the witch's knife, the athame, and see that it cuts both ways though it comes to a single, precise point. Knowledge is a type of power. It opens the mind as much as it focuses our thoughts. With knowledge we may become precise and pointed with our language, with the words we are able to speak by virtue of vibration through air.

With our words we weave spells, we make promises, we enter relationships, we draw boundaries, we say yes and no, we express and order our thoughts and feelings with each other. With a knife or with our intent we cast the circle and step between the worlds. As we breathe we become more and more aware of how we may participate in the Mystery.

The elements are sacred. Air is sacred.

Air Is Sacred
Gwydion Logan

· · ·

Air. Our first breath as we emerge from the birth canal; our last breath as we transition from this life to death and into the next.

Air. A mixture of gases in decreasing concentration: nitrogen, oxygen, argon, carbon dioxide, neon, helium, methane, krypton, hydrogen, and xenon, where nitrogen and oxygen make up 99 percent.

Air. We breathe in, we breathe out. We humans take over 23,000 breaths per day. Our inhalation brings in oxygen. Our exhalation releases carbon dioxide. Hemoglobin in our blood transports oxygen to the cells throughout our body and carries that carbon dioxide waste product back to the lungs to be released. We breathe, our cells breathe. In and out.

As animals, we need many things to survive, but first and foremost we need air, and in particular, we need oxygen. Without it, we decline rapidly. In many modern Western occult traditions, air is often the first element invoked or acknowledged when crafting a ritual or working space. In Reclaiming we usually associate the witch's knife, or athame, with the element of air, and the circle is often drawn and demarcated with this tool. It becomes natural to some witches, who might take up their knife to trace the circle, to begin with air.

We associate air with the dawning of a new day, the rising sun, the springtime, the buds, with new life. It is the birth of life as we terrestrial creatures know it. Air is the word of a poem or protest chant, the note of a song, the sound generated by a musical instrument: sound travels through air. We use air to create vibrations across our larynxes as the air moves in or out of our lungs. It is the sound of these vibrations that gives us voice and allows us to communicate with one another. Air is also the wind that blows off the sea, over the mountains, and across the desert. It is the gentle breeze that cools a hot summer day and the cold wind that chills to the bone in winter. It is the rustling of leaves in the forest and the swoosh of the winged ones around us, altering the air currents with their wings and allowing them to fly.

As witches we work with our breath to ground and center. We wield air to focus our attention like the edge and point of a knife or a laser beam. We channel air through our voices as we call, sing, or chant to the elements, the ancestors, the Goddess, the God, and the Mysterious Ones. We move energy with our breath, much like a practitioner of martial arts uses breath and sound to focus their movement. In aikido and karate this is known as the *kiai*. Its effectiveness can be explained through physics: force is equal to mass times acceleration, or $F = M \times A$. The mass of a hand or foot in motion remains constant, yet we can use our breath and sound to focus our intent, allowing us to increase the motion or acceleration of the hand or foot. This increases the force of the hand or foot in motion in a martial arts movement and results in a greater impact. Magically we use our breath and sound to accelerate the energy we raise so that we too will have a greater impact in our actions.

Air is connected to our thoughts, our intellect, our ideas, our collective agreements, our values, as well as our knowledge and learning. Air evokes the challenge "to know." This comes from the Four Powers of the Sphinx, found in many witchcraft and Western magical traditions: "To know, to will, to dare, and to keep silent." In Reclaiming this is sometimes referred to as the challenges of the elements. I like to add "to be" as the challenge of center or spirit. The air challenge—to know—reminds us of the importance of knowing our history as witches, the history of our traditions and covens, and the names of those who have come before us.

My first interaction with Reclaiming was in the mid-1980s. I was a teenage witch venturing into San Francisco from the suburb where I lived to check out the metaphysical shops. In a shop called Curios and Candles I found the *Reclaiming Newsletter*. It was filled with articles and poetry by people with exciting names like Raven Moonshadow, Pandora Minerva, and M. Macha Nightmare. I loved the connection between magic and politics present in the newsletter, and I kept returning each quarter to that little shop to purchase the latest issue along with my candles, incense, and herbs. Its stories of nonviolent direct action politics inspired me to participate in my first demonstration, against apartheid in South Africa on the UC Berkeley campus in 1985, while I was still attending high school. In 1989 I attended my first Reclaiming ritual, quickly followed by taking an Elements of Magic class taught by Raven Moonshadow and Pandora. In that class I developed friendships that continue to this day. That same year I volunteered to do production work for the newsletter, finally putting all of those years of student publishing in high school and college to good use. A year later, after more classes and volunteer work, I was asked to join the Reclaiming Collective.

When I first found the *Reclaiming Newsletter*, I was struck by the Reclaiming Mission Statement. It moved, excited, and inspired me.

> *Reclaiming is a community of women and men working to unify spirit and politics. Our vision is rooted in the religion and magic of the Goddess—the Immanent Life Force. We see our work as teaching and making magic—the art of empowering ourselves and each other. In our classes, workshops, and public rituals, we train our voices, bodies, energy, intuition, and minds. We use the skills we learn to deepen our strength, both as individuals and as community, to voice our concerns about the world in which we live, and bring to birth a vision of a new culture.*

This statement has appeared on every copy of the *Reclaiming Newsletter*, later the *Reclaiming Quarterly*, since its creation in the early 1980s and appears today on the reclaiming.org website. While it had been reviewed periodically for potential revision, it has only once been edited, to remove a reference to San Francisco Bay Area in 1997. This simple five-sentence statement has summarized Reclaiming effectively, as a community and a tradition, for over thirty-five years.

Today, I would propose that the phrase "Reclaiming is a community of women and men" could use an update to be more gender inclusive and thus more reflective of the many practitioners of our tradition. For me, the proposed wording from longtime Reclaiming member Captain Snowdon resonates strongly: "Reclaiming is made up of many overlapping communities that spiral in and out of each other. We are non-binary, genderqueer, trans*, women, and men of many different places and paths."

Why does this matter? Why do we need to update our language? Why not just be gender neutral and replace "women and men" with "people"? Because language is important; language holds power. As we learn in our studies of the element of air, our language needs to be specific; it should be precisely focused on the intent of our magical working. So too our language in community can be equally specific and focused on the intent of our community and tradition. While this may seem cumbersome, this precision and evolution of our language is perfectly in alignment with our mission statement as well as the intersection of our magic and politics. In Reclaiming we are deeply committed to the politics of inclusion, even when it means having hard conversations about our differences and challenging the many forms of our comfort and privilege. We don't just do it once and call it good but instead keep coming back to it to re-evaluate, adjust, and improve. This is the practice of discernment, of precise focus and intention, one of the important lessons of air.

Reclaiming began in San Francisco in 1980 when Diane Baker and Starhawk offered a women's class that would give people the tools they needed to do their own ritual work. They decided that the class would be co-taught to model a different approach to power. When we co-teach, no single person has all of the power. Different perspectives and even opposing views can be presented by each teacher, demonstrating that there is not a single one-true-way to do something. The students of that first class wanted another class, so a second and then a third class were constructed. New teachers were recruited from these classes, and Reclaiming's first teaching cell began. After Elements of Magic came the Iron Pentacle and then a class called Rites of Passage. These classes, along with the Pearl Pentacle, came to form the four core classes of Reclaiming. (In 2012 at a Reclaiming Dandelion gathering in Oregon, it was decided that there would be a fifth core class teaching the skills of mediation, communication, leadership, and participating effectively in community.)

In 1981, while a Spiral Dance ritual was being planned to celebrate Samhain, a Celtic-inspired festival of the dead, a blockade was called for at Diablo Canyon. Pacific Gas and Electric, an energy monopoly in California, had announced plans to begin building a nuclear power plant at Diablo Canyon on California's central coast, near an earthquake fault. Many of the planners of the Spiral Dance ritual went off to the blockade, while other community members stepped in to finish the planning. When those who had gone to the blockade returned, they brought back more experience with collective process and the use of consensus decision-making, as well as models of non-hierarchical group structure.

After Diablo Canyon and the Spiral Dance ritual, many of these folks formed a loose-knit community and started meeting under the name Reclaiming Collective. With this and the teaching cell, Reclaiming was born. Classes and rituals continued, and soon the community began publishing the *Reclaiming Newsletter* to advertise these events. The number of people attending Reclaiming rituals grew.

The first summer intensive was taught by the collective's teaching cell in San Francisco in 1985. Reclaiming taught two additional camps, both in Mendocino, California, the following year, in 1986. In 1987 a Reclaiming WitchCamp was held in Vancouver, Canada, thanks to the work and dedication of Pat Hogan. The same year there was also another Northern California WitchCamp in Ben Lomond. Up until this point Reclaiming had been very much a San Francisco Bay Area phenomenon. Through Starhawk's books, traveling, and lectures, and the WitchCamp in Vancouver, that geocentric focus began to slowly shift.

In 1989 a WitchCamp began in Germany. Soon after, a Midwest WitchCamp was organized and held in Michigan, eventually relocating to Diana's Grove in Missouri. Diana's Grove was founded by Midwest WitchCampers Cynthea Jones and Patricia Storm as a mystery school and land sanctuary. When I student taught at my first Witch-Camp in 1993 at British Columbia WitchCamp (BCWC), there were only three or four WitchCamps in existence. The following year that more than doubled with the addition of Winter WitchCamp in Wisconsin, Vermont WitchCamp, Tejas Web in Texas, a mid-Atlantic WitchCamp that eventually became known as SpiralHeart, and a return to having a WitchCamp in Northern California.

There have been WitchCamps in Maine and New York in the United States; Wales; England; Victoria and Queensland in Australia; Alberta and Ontario in Canada; and Spain, as well as several family camps in the Northern California redwoods and other places. Some camps have dissolved while new ones have sprouted up, and others have gone through cycles of hibernation and re-emergence. These camps brought many people into the Reclaiming tradition and broader Reclaiming community who were not living in the San Francisco Bay Area or part of the Reclaiming Collective, its cells, or local community. Mostly we were connected by common spiritual and political values.

But not everyone shared that connection. For some Reclaiming Collective members, this shift away from the San Francisco Bay Area focus of our tradition created unease, a tension that can occur naturally with change. Questions arose. Who could call themselves Reclaiming? Did they have to take all of the core classes? What made a Reclaiming witch? What, exactly, were our shared values? In 1996 the Reclaiming Collective went on a retreat with an agenda focused on discussing and deciding what its role should be in the growing broader Reclaiming community. Two-thirds of the Reclaiming Collective were actively participating in Reclaiming WitchCamps all over North America, while the other third focused their work within the local San Francisco Bay Area community. We invited Keith Hennessy, a respected community member, artist, and activist who was not part of the collective, to come to our retreat as a neutral facilitator. In the end, we could not reach consensus. It was clear that we could not come to such an important decision on our own.

I recall Keith asking the group, What are the principles of unity that unify us and bring us together in this tradition? That phrase sounded magical. We brainstormed a list of what we thought these values might be. Starhawk suggested that we divide into groups of two and go off and hold charrettes. A charrette is a creative process used in architecture to incorporate multiple viewpoints. Each charrette allowed us to get input and feedback on these different values and to seek ideas toward our organizational structure. For an entire year we held charrettes in groups of four to six in the San Francisco Bay Area and with WitchCampers. Words that reflected shared values transformed into phrases and sentences. Over and over we heard that the collective should transform and become a more open body, modeled on the spokescouncil framework used in direct action politics. Rather than the core group of long-term members in the Reclaiming Collective, a spokescouncil utilizes a representative model where members rotate in and out over time. This would dissolve feelings of exclusivity, being left out, and cliquishness by creating a more inclusive organizational structure.

In November 1997 the Reclaiming Collective held another retreat. What had evolved into phrases and sentences from that original list of words was woven beautifully into what we now know as the Reclaiming Principles of Unity. Vibra Willow, a longtime Reclaiming Collective member, summarized the outcome of the retreat in a *Reclaiming Quarterly* article (issue 76, fall 1999) a couple of years later:

The Principles of Unity is a statement of core values in the Reclaiming tradition written by the Reclaiming Collective at that retreat. Fundamental value is placed on reverence for the Earth, the natural cycles of life and death, individual autonomy, nonviolence, feminism, and responsible activism.

At the 1997 retreat the Reclaiming Collective dissolved itself, creating basic suggestions and guidelines for the structure of Reclaiming in the Bay Area which exists today, consisting of the Wheel, various working Cells, and the Advisory Council. Reclaiming Witches in other places organize themselves (or not) as they will. There is no central authority and all Witch Camps are autonomous.

As Vibra stated, there is no central authority in Reclaiming, not any individual nor group. We aspire to be non-hierarchical, while acknowledging that differences of power do exist within our tradition and in our communities. Every time a priestess steps into the center of the circle to teach a chant or lead a trance, they step into power, into a position of leadership. While some of these differences in power are earned, some are unearned. As the Principles of Unity state, "Our feminism includes a radical analysis of power." While it is easy to critique the dominant culture, in Reclaiming we also turn this mirror on ourselves, examining how we contribute to structures of power in our relationships, our communities, and with each other, even when it is uncomfortable and challenging. Our conviction toward shared power requires that we trust one another, but these things do not come easily. To do these things, we can sharpen our blades of discernment and focus our intention like the point of our athames. We center, ground, and focus; we must breathe. Something will always come along and knock us off our center; this is part of living. But as we learn in martial arts, when we are centered, grounded, and focused, it is harder for us to lose our center. We are able to recover more quickly, perhaps to roll with the energy, perhaps to duck underneath it or quickly twist and turn and see things from another perspective.

In November 2017 the Reclaiming Principles of Unity will be twenty years old. It still resonates as deeply for me now as it did in that weekend retreat twenty years ago when we read it aloud for the first time. It captures not only the core values of Reclaiming but also our vision for our tradition, our community, and for the earth.

The Principles of Unity state that "we are an evolving, dynamic tradition." In the twenty years since it was first written, we have come to realize that while we intended to be inclusive and reflect the diversity of our community, our language needed to evolve. In a decentralized organization it can be difficult to make such updates: who has the authority to endorse such a change? In Reclaiming there is an international gathering of Reclaiming witches known as the Dandelion Gathering that occurs every two to four years. This is different from a Witch-Camp in that it is specifically a gathering to discuss intercommunity logistics, thealogy, and values. At each Dandelion Gathering there is also a meeting of BIRCH, the Broad Intra-Reclaiming Council of Hubs, which is a cross-community spokescouncil decision-making body.

After much discussion, online and in person, leading up to the BIRCH meeting at the 2012 Dandelion Gathering, the statement "Honoring both Goddess and God, we work with female and male images of divinity, always remembering that their essence is a mystery that goes beyond form" was rewritten, by consensus, to better reflect the gender diversity of our community. It was replaced with:

> Our diverse practices and experiences of the divine weave a tapestry of many different threads. We include those who honor Mysterious Ones, Goddesses, and Gods of myriad expressions, genders, and states of being, remembering that mystery goes beyond form.

It is said that knowledge is power. So too does language hold power. We need to be precisely focused equally on the intent of our magical workings as well as our language within our community. In Reclaiming, we value tradition and hold the Principles of Unity to be one of our sacred documents. And we are an evolving tradition unafraid to look inward and make changes as we grow. The change to the Principles of Unity reflects this and allows us to be more precise and inclusive, to more accurately reflect our values and our communities.

Air. Air is life. When we center, ground, and focus, when we breathe with intention, when we listen, when we dare to know, our actions, our words, and our songs can breathe life into the dreams and visions we hold for this world. May the Mysterious Ones, goddesses, and gods bless each of us, our breath, and our work. Blessed be air.

Exercise: Exploring Your Relationship to the Principles of Unity
Preston Coyote Vargas

Time: 1–2 hours

You will need: note cards, a journal or Book of Shadows,
a pen, a copy of the Reclaiming Principles of Unity
(this can be found on page xix), a glass of water

• • •

When I made my path to witchcraft, I arrived with a belief system. These beliefs were from my religious upbringing and from my social culture of origin. I clearly remember preachers warning me against questioning God or God's appointed leaders. I was also trained not to rock the boat by keeping up with the Joneses and maintaining the status quo.

Decades after becoming a practicing witch, I still catch glimpses of these old beliefs secretly swaying my thoughts. Though I may have outgrown those beliefs, it is tough to break the habit of accepting dogma. Every now and then I need to exercise my witchiness by investigating my beliefs. What is my relationship to the Principles of Unity? Am I in agreement with them? Have I simply accepted the Principles of Unity as entrance into this community and tradition? Where do I find complexities, paradox, and challenge with them?

There is a Reclaiming saying that "You are your own spiritual authority." I understand this as an invitation to critically investigate what we are doing and why we are doing it. Witches ride the edges and dance in the liminal spaces, but we gain this power by exploring, questioning, and challenging ourselves and the world.

• • •

Read over the Principles of Unity.

Run your fingers across the page. Hum and sing the words to yourself. Whisper it again and again.

Allow yourself to discover what sentence or phrase of the Principles of Unity is holding a charge for you today. This sentence might be a part that you tend to skip over or ignore, a part that feels less certain to you or that you don't resonate with, or something you disagree with or object to. What part does your body respond to? Take that part of the Principles of Unity and write it out on a note card to begin your exploration.

Create your ritual space. State an intention to reside in the paradox of liminal spaces, the space without certainty, of not knowing. Place the note card with the written part of the Principles of Unity in the middle of the space, where you can see it.

Write on each note card a different identity you hold, or part of yourself. For example: *parent, African American, steelworker, witch, healer, queer*. In addition to including your younger self and your future self as parts of you, remember to include your shadow or hidden self. The shadow self often reveals an inner voice we are reluctant to acknowledge. You may choose to have thirteen identities. This could be your inner coven.

Arrange each of these cards around the circle as if they were all sitting at a round table in equality with one another. As you place each name tag down, call out aloud what is written on it three times. Invoke that part of yourself to the circle.

When all the parts of you are present, take up your journal.

Stand near one of the name tags. Envision that aspect of you present in the space. Step into that part of yourself. It is, after all, part of you.

Ask that part some of the following questions and record the answers in your journal.

- What are your thoughts and feelings on this phrase of the Principles of Unity?
- How might this phrase of the Principles of Unity benefit you, your community, and the world?

- How might this phrase of the Principles of Unity challenge you, your community, and the world?
- Is it time to explore evolving this phrase of the Principles of Unity with your Reclaiming community?

When you have answered these questions, step out of this aspect of yourself. Physically shake your body. Drink some water. Take some breaths deep into your belly to ground and center.

When you are ready, step into the next part of you and ask these questions again. Continue this process until you have completed the round table discussion.

Afterwards, review what you wrote. What you have created is the beginning of your own witch's code of conduct. Remember, "I don't know" and paradoxical answers are valid and can be wonderful invitations to keep asking questions.

The goal of this exercise is not to have all the answers but to remember to keep exploring the edges of our growth. The Principles of Unity is an entity that evolves over time. As you evolve, the invitation remains to interrogate your relationship with the Principles of Unity and how it is supportive, challenging, and everything in between.

Practice: Creating Ritual Space with Visualization
ABEL R. GOMEZ

Time: 20 minutes

You will need: a wand or athame (or just your finger),
enough space to cast a circle, and purification
incense or an alternative

• • •

Visualization is an important skill in Reclaiming witchcraft. We may visualize when grounding, in trance work, during invocations, and as a component of spellwork. Visualization is usually connected with the element of air. It is one of the tools introduced in Elements of Magic, and we continue to extend and develop it. If visualization is not one of your strengths, you may want to stretch into it with this exercise, allowing your other senses to contribute while continuing to invite visual awareness.

We practice visualization for several reasons. It offers a way to focus attention toward our magical intention. In spellwork it allows us to see, in our mind's eye, directing and focusing energy toward an intended result. When we visualize the goal, we begin to make it real. As a part of ritual practice, visualization is another resource, in addition to movement or song, to call elemental powers or deities.

Part of the effectiveness of visualization is that it allows us to tap in to the power of what Starhawk called Younger Self. Also called the fetch in some lineages of Anderson Feri witchcraft, Younger Self is the nonverbal, intuitive, imaginative part of self that is aroused by color, symbol, sound, and movement. In both Reclaiming and Feri it is said that the Younger Self facilitates access to the Deep Self, our innate divine nature. Through visualization, we arouse the Younger Self.

The following exercise draws on visualization as part of establishing ritual space. To focus your attention on visualization, use as few words as possible.

* * *

Begin by purifying the space of anything that might be creating feelings of discord or disharmony. As you carry the incense around the ritual area, visualize the space glowing with white light, transforming all energy that might hinder the work. You may want to say "I clear this space" as you visualize the space becoming clear and ready for ritual. When you feel the space is ready, say "So mote it be."

Next, cast a circle. Set your casting tool or your hand to the center of your space and begin visualizing blue fire gathering there. When you have that image firmly in your mind, lift your hand or the tool and see it holding that blue flame. Walk to the east and begin tracing the boundaries of your circle in a clockwise or counterclockwise direction depending on your hemisphere (See Casting the Circle, page 32), visualizing the blue flame following your hand or tool. When you return to the east, see that circle holding the boundaries of your space and say "So mote it be."

To invoke the elements, focus your attention on holding images of them in your mind's eye. Begin with earth. You may choose to stand in the north if you are in the northern hemisphere, the south if you are in the southern hemisphere, or simply stand in the center of your circle. Allow your mind to focus on images or scenes you associate with earth: a grove of trees, a mountain, or whatever it may be. When you feel the presence of earth, say "Welcome, earth." Continue around the circle to do this for air, fire, and water, holding in your mind a strong image that you associate with that element and chanting the name of that element. If you are in the northern hemisphere, you may be circling clockwise, or counterclockwise if you are in the southern hemisphere. You may choose to stand in the center of the circle throughout. When you return to your beginning place, try to hold in your mind's eye the representation of the elements that you worked with at each direction simultaneously.

At this point, you could invoke a deity. If you wish to do this, concentrate on the image of that deity at the center of the circle and chant or sing his, her, or their name. When you feel their presence, say "Welcome, (deity name)."

Spend as much time as you desire in the space you created.

To close or release the circle, begin by thanking any deity you invoked; say "Hail and farewell, (deity name)." You can visualize that presence dissolving from that space.

To thank the elements, begin in the west, imagining the image you held to invoke water dissolving. Say "Hail and farewell, water!" or, if you do not feel that you are farewelling the elemental presences in your life or in your being, many of us simply say "Thank you, (element)." Continue counterclockwise if you are in the northern hemisphere or clockwise if you are in the southern hemisphere, similarly thanking fire, air, and earth. You may choose to remain in the center of the circle throughout.

Complete this by returning to the east and with your casting tool or hand retrace the circle while walking counterclockwise. As you do this, visualize the circle of blue flame following your tool, just as if you were opening curtains. Affirm "The circle is open. So mote it be."

Practice: Burning Herbs Purification
SERAPHINA CAPRANOS

Time: 15 minutes (longer or shorter)

You will need: dried herbs (if you wish to gather them
yourself, see instructions below), lighter or matches,
and a flameproof bowl or plate

• • •

Burning herbs is an ancient plant medicine practice that crosses cultures, lands, and peoples. This fragrant art has been considered a holy offering to the gods, a practice of preparing one's body for a sacred rite, and a way of marking magical space while banishing unwanted energy. In some traditions it is considered a purification practice and is associated with the element of air. Before humans scientifically understood the antimicrobial benefits of fragrant plants, our ancestors were using them to fumigate sick houses. Old medicine is now new medicine.

Part of the beauty of this smoking practice is that it calls upon the earth element of the greenbloods, the element of fire, and that of air through the smoke itself.

The aroma of burning herbs can immediately bring us into the present moment, allowing us to let go of distractions. Following a fragrant inhalation, it can release tension with a big exhale. The aromatic medicine of herbs can transport a person into a holy temple or an ancient spell or conjure an important memory. Our olfactory sense is a powerful one.

Many of us may associate the practice of burning herbs with commercial incense sticks or the Native American practice of smudging. This is not what I am referring to here. Smudging, typically with buffalo sage, sweetgrass, or cedar, is a cultural practice that belongs to the indigenous people of North America, and it is not my practice to teach. And while there are environmentally safe incense sticks sold commercially, most are laden with toxic fragrance oils. I encourage you, dear reader, to go outside and connect with a fragrant tree or plant and ask it if it's willing to be used in your magical practice for clearing energy. You can even ask a local herb-witch to advise what herbs in your local bioregion would be suitable for a smoking practice.

An example of trees that would be suitable are those with aromatic leaves or needles such as pine, fir, eucalyptus, cedar, juniper, and bay.

Plants that work well for burning are rose petals, lavender flowers, sage leaf, thyme leaf, and rosemary leaf. These are just a few examples of an infinitely huge world of plant medicine.

If you are able to harvest them fresh, dry them first before burning. You can gather a bundle of chosen herbs, one type or many bound together, wrap with cotton or hemp twine, and light it aflame. Blow out the flame and it should slowly smolder, causing a dance of beautiful, fragrant smoke to arise. Alternatively, you can simply set a few pinches of dried herb in a bowl and light it.

. . .

Hold the bowl with herbs in your hands. Set your intention, silently or aloud, for burning the herbs. This could be something like "I desire to be free from the grips of grief and anxiety right now."

Take a moment and breathe in the magic of the plant aroma slowly, sensuously. Give gratitude for their body and spirit. Then, either standing still or walking around your space, silently or speaking aloud, name what you banish or what you wish to call in. These are the magical actions we usually perform in this kind of work.

Carefully, to avoid dropping the bowl or plate of herbs, allow the smoke to waft over you. You can use a fan, feather, or just the air to move the smoke across your body. Continue consciously breathing and releasing, allowing the herbal magic to bless your body and cleanse you of unwanted energies. As you breathe in the aroma of the herbs, feel or imagine their medicine working and healing your body.

During this practice I like to do a quick body scan, relaxing my jaw, then shoulders, chest, belly, sex, and legs, and exhale, releasing with my breath all that doesn't serve the magic I'm about to do after this practice.

Once you feel complete, thank the spirits of the plants and extinguish the herbs.

Blessed be.

Practice: Boundaries and Borders with the Witch's Knife
Tarin Towers

Time: 10–30 minutes

You will need: an athame, pen, or any knife with a point

• • •

Casting a circle is many things; in this practice we emphasize the protective boundary between your sacred space and the outside world, and cutting yourself away from the concerns of that world.

This act of cutting when casting a circle is why the magical tool of air is the athame, which represents the art of discernment. In making a decisive choice, we snip away what is not needed. Pens are also tools of air. When we make a mark or draw a line, whether to name something or divide two things, we're discerning what is and is not meant.

Boundaries, both psychologically and in magical practice, are both our physical edges and the emotional, cognitive, and psychic borders that mark where we stop and where the world and other people begin.

It's not always practical to pull out one's athame—say, at work or on the bus—to create a demarcation between one's own space and everyone else's. Being able to visualize such boundaries in different sizes, shapes, and consistencies is not only a good magical skill, it's great practice for being able to exercise and assert your boundaries when negotiating everyday situations with colleagues or housemates.

With sustained practice, you'll be able to assess a situation, say to yourself "Shields up," and immediately be able to let energies and emotions that are not your own bounce off those shields.

• • •

To begin a practice of boundary setting, ground and center yourself and cast a circle using an athame, any pointed knife, or a pen. Sense the difference in the room before and after the circle is cast.

Then sense a smaller sphere just around your body. How large is it, and does it have a color or consistency? Can you hold that sense of a sphere as you walk around the room?

Focus on this sphere and imagine or sense it shimmering until this personal bubble is the consistency and iridescence of a soap bubble. Do you feel larger? Safer? More exposed? Continue shifting how you hold the space around yourself by transforming your edges into the texture and quality of different materials. Some spheres to try inhabiting include Jell-O, clouds or fog, a cotton ball, a feather cloak, and the steam of a shower. After each successive texture, shake it off and reassume your natural boundaries, which may be a different size or color as you experiment.

Shielding is practicing with these boundaries, sometimes as heavy structures. To feel your boundaries solidifying and strengthening to become more protective, imagine or sense your personal bubble taking on the texture of a balloon. This membrane is much less permeable but still light enough to walk around in.

Heavier boundaries may be easier to grasp sitting or lying down. Imagine your balloon solidifying into a box-like wooden egg you can see through. Do you feel protection?

As you practice, see if you can build a house around yourself, with or without windows. Try encircling yourself in a brick tower. A strong spell of protection can be the careful, deliberate mental construction of a stone fortress with iron locks on the gates. Make sure you shake off heavy shields until your personal bubble feels again like your own space.

Walking around the world as a stone fortress isn't practical or sustainable, and it can foster a sometimes counterproductive emotional distance. Cultivating temporary shields you can call into being when you need them, though, can be a handy survival tool. Just make sure you practice not only calling them into being, but letting them go.

Remember to release the circle you cast at the beginning of this exercise.

Sacred Sound, Sacred Song

SUZANNE STERLING

. . .

Song and sound are sacred, and when we sing we can create magic. As a longtime Reclaiming teacher and ritualist, I have written many chants and participated in hundreds of rituals utilizing the power of collective singing. However, it was working with my co-founded non-profit organization Off The Mat, Into the World, which trains leaders in conscious and sustainable activism, that I gained a profound understanding of how song can be a universal language that connects and brings joy. For nine years I was the director of a project that raised funds for local organizations doing direct service work in Africa, India, Cambodia, Ecuador, Haiti, and the US. I also led humanitarian tours to work with those local organizations and support the incredible work they were doing in disaster relief, social justice, community empowerment, and environmental protection.

During one trip we worked at a tent city in Port Au Prince, Haiti, after the devastating earthquake of 2010. We were planting trees, marking tents for supplies, and more; but on this particular day we were asked to move a garbage dump from one place to another to make room for more shelters. This was hot and very stinky work, made even more uncomfortable by the fact that a large group of locals was standing along the edges watching us work. The situation felt more and more uncomfortable, and as much as we tried to engage, the local folks just wanted to watch us work and laugh at the crazy people moving their garbage.

At some point I remembered that one of my most memorable musical jam sessions was with five young boys around a fire one evening in Uganda. Because there were no drums available, these boys were playing rhythms on plastic jugs as we all took turns improvising short call-and-response nonsense chants and having a blast. So I picked up a plastic jug from the garbage pile and began to play a beat and sing a simple call-and-response melody with the others in my group. As we continued to sing, a few of the younger children who were watching started slowly coming closer in order to join in the singing.

As the song picked up momentum, the others very slowly began to join in. Soon the entire village group was dancing and singing with us in the hot sun in the middle of the garbage dump! This was unprecedented, and the staff and volunteers who worked at the tent city had never seen anything like it. By the end of the day, we had created a conveyer belt of members from our group mixed with villagers of all ages, and together we moved that garbage dump while laughing, singing, and dancing. This was a moment of awakening for me, as I saw and experienced the power of music to move beyond language and other barriers to create deep connection and spontaneous joy with others.

How do we begin to tap in to the power of sound and the voice? We begin with the breath. Take a deep breath as you read this sentence, expanding the rib cage in all directions and filling the lower and upper lungs. Allow your exhale to be longer than your inhale, and as you exhale make an audible sighing or humming sound. Notice what happens to your emotional and mental body as you do this. When working with the elements, we often begin with air and the breath because it is our most immediate human need; we each average 23,000 breaths per day. Breath holds the power to transform our experience profoundly.

Breathing is central to our autonomic nervous system, which acts largely unconsciously and regulates bodily functions such as heart rate, digestion, respiration rate, pupillary response and hormonal secretion. Breathing is also key to our overall health, stress release, and concentration. When we breathe deeply, and especially if we lengthen our exhale, we are allowing the heart and lungs to signal to the brain and body a sense of safety and calm. Conscious breath can assist us in stimulating the parasympathetic nervous system response, which is the opposite of the fight-or-flight response to stress. When the para-sympathetic response is stimulated, our heart rate can slow down, our muscular system relaxes, and our digestion and glandular activity normalizes. When this happens, we become less contracted and potentially more available to experience the truth of each moment in a relaxed and creative way. The quality of breath has the capacity to strengthen the entire energetic field within and around us.

Breath is fundamental to human life and vitality, but it is also one of the most important magical tools that we can employ. One very potent definition of magic is Dion Fortune's "art of changing consciousness at will." Humans across many cultures have been practicing and perfecting this for eons, and one of the main tools for changing consciousness is the breath. In ritual we use breath to assist us to ground and connect to the earth and all the other elements, to center in our own being, and also to raise and focus energy. We can use conscious breath to enhance or amplify our experience and to drop down and into states of deep concentration. Through intensive and very focused work with breath, we can utilize the breath as a fast-track tool for reaching many different states of consciousness. By turning breath into sound, we tap into one of the most ancient and powerful forms of magic available to us: our voice.

The human voice is composed of air and breath shaped into waves that move out into the world and affect, through vibrations, all they encounter. It is this vibrational initiation that causes sound to move matter. Sound waves or pulses can have an immense impact on the environment that they move through, and there are numerous examples of the physical effects of sound. In the science of Cymatics, which is the study of sound and vibration made visible, sound can be seen to organize particles into coherent and symmetrical patterns. The underlying frameworks in harmonics or musical relationships correspond to some key underlying frameworks in physics, chemistry, botany, astronomy, architecture, and more. In this way, sound and musical structures can be seen to have an inherent intelligence and coherence. An understanding of the profound intelligence and power embedded in sound can help us to see that the act of turning breath into sound, or singing, is a profound act of magic in and of itself.

There are numerous creation myths from many cultures that include teachings about sound being a causative force. The Egyptians speak of the god Thoth singing the world into being. Some Aboriginal Australians, who to this day have a complex and powerful relationship to the land and the songlines, say that their ancestors sang the world into being. Indigenous North Americans have practices that include songs being sung to land and animals, such as singing for the return of the salmon. These indigenous song practices demonstrate a deep understanding of interconnection with all beings. In many ancient Yogic teachings, the story of creation begins with the great void or ground of being. Within this void emerged the first event, which was the sound *Aum*, which subsequently gave birth to all the other vibrations of the universe. It now appears that modern science is beginning to understand and articulate what many earth-based cultures and magic practitioners have known for millennia. The world is alive and interconnected, and it is all vibrating. The world is singing!

Through scientific methods of observation and study, we now understand in a quantifiable way that the entire world we live in is composed of vibrations. At every level of existence there are multiple webs composed of particles. These particles become wave forms as they move through space at different rates or frequencies. All that we perceive to be solid is moving at rates whose motion we cannot perceive. There are, however, some vibrations we can perceive, including many vibrations within the spectrums of sound and light. We cannot perceive certain light frequencies such as ultraviolet rays, nor sound frequencies such as high frequency dog whistles or the low hum of elephants over many miles, but we do have a range of perception that allows us to see great variations in light and color and to hear even the subtlest differences in sounds.

Humans are very sensitive, much more than we often think, and we are constantly receiving vibrational information through the instrument of our bodies. We are like walking antennae picking up signals and responding in each moment, and our bodies hold all of our experience as energetic signatures that impact our hormonal, nervous, and brain systems. In the world today, many of us are vibrationally overwhelmed, and this is contributing to some of the trauma patterns that we see around us. Humans and other animals are designed to express what impacts us, both positive and negative. If we do not express what impacts us, then we hold on to those vibrations, experiences, and emotions as stress, which over time can become tension, injury, and disease.

So many of the current trauma responses and coping mechanisms such as addiction, depression, anxiety, post-traumatic stress disorder, eating disorders, isolation, and violence are due to long-term buildup of stressful impacts and little or no way to respond or process these. In the field of somatic experiencing, there are studies that show discharging or rinsing these stuck energies from the body can be extremely effective for recovery. This discharge can be physical such as shaking or stomping, but it can be even more effective when use of the voice is included because sound vibrates us from the inside out and moves stuck energy patterns and strengthens vital life force.

On a purely physical level, when we move energy through the body and the voice with physical practices like yoga asanas (postures) and pranayama (a breath technique), dance and singing, we help to remove blocks to the natural life force and increase our ability to heal and respond creatively to life. In nature and in human bodies, a healthy system is one in which the energy is moving. When we remove built-up stress, habitual holding patterns, or calcified energy signatures, the body naturally responds by bringing itself into a state of balance and health. Just as sounds are vibrations that can deeply affect matter, self-expression is one of the keys to healing. We can use our own voices to remove blocks, awaken the body as an instrument, and respond to our lives with the full range of our emotions, life force, and creativity.

Earth-based healers of many cultures had and have strong wisdom teachings about vibrational healing and the use of sound and the voice as medicine. In many cultures, breath, sound, and sacred song are still utilized as primary tools of healers and shamans. Often the healer will read the energetic signature of the patient and sing sounds or songs that can bring the entire energy field back into balance, wholeness, and harmonic resonance with itself. When this kind of conscious sound healing is done in sacred space, either with a healer or by oneself, the effects are far more powerful. It is possible that the effects are enhanced as a result of connection to community and to the sacred that is intrinsic to many rituals.

While sound healing is gaining acceptance and widespread use in the scientific and medical world—such as with sonograms, sonic surgical techniques, sound healing for all manner of bone, organ, and brain healing, even removal of pre-Alzheimer-related brain plaque—it is also being used destructively. Military sonar testing has been proven to be related to huge beachings of whale and dolphin populations as well as contributing to behavioral changes such as cessation of vocalizing and foraging for food within these species. Sonic and ultrasonic weapons that can injure, incapacitate, or even kill are being developed at an alarming rate, and currently police forces are increasing the use of sound cannons against protestors, most recently at the Dakota Pipeline protests in South Dakota in 2016 and 2017. It is my hope and intention that we understand the power of sound in our world and reclaim that power for healing and connection.

Humans are hard-wired for expression. Just watch the sheer amount of sound and song that arises in any young child at play. The spontaneous expression of sound is natural to humans, and in the context of ritual it is possible for us to tap into even the preverbal parts of us that require expression. Throughout history cultures have created specific times, places, and rituals that allowed for the primal human impulses and emotions to be expressed. They had—and some still do have—times for grieving, for expressing terror and anger, and for celebrating and coming together in community. They had rites of passage marking the ages of their lives; rituals that gave them ways to understand the human experience in the broader context of the mythopoetic and universal truths of being alive. But through religious and cultural oppression and colonization, perhaps driven by our need to control the wildness of nature both within us and around us, the natural forms of human expression have come to be seen as dangerous at worst and silly at best.

Mechanistic thinking and controlled behavior has taken precedence over the intrinsic wisdom of the body and served to suppress the very thing that has the power to help us be whole and to feel connected to each other and the world. We have come to value what can be proven and measured over the forces of mystery, magic, and imagination. As a result, our expression and creativity are suppressed, devalued, and seen as accessible only to professional artists rather than as the birthright of all humans.

So many people have been told that they should not sing or even speak their truth. Many of us were raised in environments of violence, fear, and excessive criticism, and some of us even now would be unsafe if we spoke and lived the full truth of who we are. When we are unsafe or when we internalize external judgment, we can shut down completely; we can become afraid to be seen and heard in any way, and for self-protection we are forced to silence the very creativity of our soul. If we live within this prison of silence, we are safe but also unable to feel the full range of our experience and the inherent creativity that is central to all humans. With no expression allowed to move from inside us to the outside and loss of a way to connect to others, we may even lose our ability to experience deep intimacy.

Part of the healing available to us in finding our voice lies in understanding the idea that living our truth is a creative act. In order to find our authentic truth, we must go beneath the conditioned thinking of our particular upbringing and take on the challenging work of healing the wounds and cycles of violence that we have inherited. Once we can tap in to the inherent wisdom of our own truth and give it voice, we often have experiences of liberation and joy. When we express and create, and especially when we do so in community, we invite the childlike self that is always within us to be part of our experience and that inner child is directly connected to our deepest self, our purpose and our joy. Participatory ritual asks us to engage with our deep creativity, expression and ability to connect with others and to focus those gifts in ways that are beneficial to ourselves and the world.

Sound and singing are so intrinsic to effective ritual because of the principle of sympathetic resonance. Resonance is the synchronization of two or more frequencies of vibration, such as sound waves, light waves, or electrical frequencies. When this synchronization happens, the overall vibration is amplified and intensified. One example of this is the shattering of a crystal glass when exposed to the right musical pitch or its resonant frequency. This is an important concept because we can find resonance chambers in the body. The empty spaces in the chest, back of the throat, and nasal and brain cavities can be utilized to access vocal power and richness. There are also certain places that act as resonance chambers, such as caves, cathedrals, and even sacred sites, that are built specifically for acoustic amplification. Perhaps even more importantly, resonance naturally happens in groups of humans.

When groups of people meditate, move, breathe, and especially when they sing together, there is an amplified group resonance, or vibrational pattern, that creates something greater than the sum of its parts. In the past twenty years, a series of scientific studies from Harvard, Yale, Princeton, and other universities have shown a distinct correlation between large groups practicing advanced meditation and a significant drop in suicides, violent crimes, and even acts of war and terrorism. One particular study conducted in Lebanon and published in Yale University's *Journal of Conflict Resolution* in 1988 found that when the group of meditators was large enough, the war in Lebanon stopped.

When groups of people sing together, their heart rates and brain waves begin to synchronize, endorphins and oxytocin hormones flood the body, and often people have a sense of being connected to all beings and the web of life in a visceral way. Imagine a group of people blending their intentions and voices together and the profound impact that the amplified vibration could have, not only on the participants but also on the world as the sound expands outward.

Just as most spiritual teachings include sound as a primary force, many also state that our words have tremendous power. In some languages, certain words and chants are specific formulas for taking us to particular states of consciousness, and magical practitioners often spend many years learning and perfecting the use of these word spells. In many magical traditions, the essential teachings were only passed on orally, and the priestess or priest became a living library for these lineages. In both Latin and Hebrew, there is a similar linguistic root for the words *poet, singer,* and *magician.* In Egypt and other cultures, the chanters were highly treasured and revered for their spiritual contribution to the community. In modern ritual arts, we create invocations; translated, it means to call upon with the voice. We also use incantations, which are magical, often-rhyming phrases that imbue and seal a spell with power. Chants are deeply significant too. These are repetitive magical formulae with melody and rhythm and form a strong part of Reclaiming magic. Our vast body of chants and songs holds much of our lore and culture.

The use of songs and chants in ritual allows us to embody sacred archetypes, strengthen our connection to nature and community, and tap in to our own spiritual authenticity and authority. When we combine our passionate voices in song, we are amplifying and raising energy toward a collective vision, and that collective song can become a spellworking that has the power to heal us and create change in the world. This is one exciting potential of collective singing and ritual. So while song and singing is a magical tool for each individual, the effect of singing in groups in sacred space is some of the most powerful spellwork available to us. In fact, it is revolutionary!

Songs and singing have been part of many revolutionary actions, including the liberation songs of the anti-apartheid movement in South Africa, the singing revolution that took place in the Baltic nations of Latvia, Lithuania, and Estonia, and numerous current day actions in the streets. In the Reclaiming tradition, drumming, song, and chant have been deeply embedded in our rituals and social justice actions from our beginnings. We recognize that in dangerous and even violent situations, sound and singing within a ritual context can serve to diffuse escalation and shift the collective experience away from discord and toward connection.

The magical use of the voice encompasses many layers. We can begin with breath and sound as tools for shifting consciousness. Then we can remember that the world is interconnected via vibration and that sound moves matter. As we reconnect with the natural sound within us, we can release trauma from our bodies and allow our vibrational sensitivity to deepen. As our own personal and inherited wounds begin to heal, we can give ourselves and others permission to know, speak, and live our authentic truth. As we become fluent in our own truth and creativity, we can create powerful individual spells as well as rituals that focus the enhanced energetic resonance of the collective on a vision of the world we wish to inhabit.

For many years now, I have been co-creating rituals for connection, community, and transformation. I have been blessed to work with incredible colleagues and communities, remembering and reinventing the myths and stories that give our lives hope, meaning, and a deeper connection with source. In each of these situations, singing and song have been deeply unifying forces. I have seen thousands of people dance and sing in the streets in unified prayer for peace and justice; I have heard voices raised in grief and sorrow, in joyful ecstasy, and in heartfelt devotion. I have sung with birthing mothers and dying fathers. I have sung in garbage dumps, orphanages, rescue shelters, and in the streets; in kirtans, soup kitchens, and church services; onstage at huge public festivals and around fires in shimmering temples deep in the woods. I know the power of the collective song, and I can imagine a world where we remember that singing is our birthright, as natural as breathing.

Exercise: Writing and Singing Chants

IRISANYA MOON

Time: up to an hour

You will need: paper, pen or pencil,
an audio recording device (optional)

• • •

Song. Chants. Music. Harmony. Melody. Rhythm.

There are songs and chants that are stuck in my heart. They have clung to me and reached into me to show me where healing begins and what the gods are trying to tell me. And there are songs that have sung me, too.

Whether you want a song for a personal ritual or a public ritual, tapping in to the creative energies of the gods and the local lands is where chant writing can begin.

• • •

You might start by creating sacred space. Invite into this space the creative expansiveness of possibility and open yourself to inspiration. You can write down the intention for the ritual if that is already created, and think about how those words might inform a chant.

Then begin the process of collecting the ideas that are already lingering in and around you. Write down all of the things that the ritual is going to do and start finding phrases that stand out as important and juicy. You might write for a few minutes, then close your eyes, and then go back and circle the phrases that stand out.

Be willing and brave; write down everything you can. This is a time for bringing as many ideas out to play as possible, knowing that some will stay and others might be simply introducing themselves as future chant possibilities.

You might turn on an audio recording device to help track what you find as you're creating, or you might want to have your pen or pencil and paper ready to write down what you create.

A great way to begin to write a chant is to look at the list of ideas you have and start singing them. You can use tunes you already know from other chants or you might just start singing to see what emerges. Sing until you find something that makes your heart jump a bit. And when that moment happens, write it down and sing it again. And then sing it again. Recording it at this point is ideal so you can focus on creating rather than remembering what you created.

Some other ways to create a chant include:

- Going for a walk in the land where the ritual will take place. See what is there and sing about it.

- Thinking about what needs to be healed in the ritual; for example, the tired activist hearts, the land, or the local community. Write down a chant to focus into a spellworking with this purpose.

- Singing along to the words of the intention. Very often, you can find a chant in the intention itself, without moving too many words.

- Starting with a tune you already know and adding new words to it or shifting just a few words to better suit your ritual needs.

The key to discovering and opening up to a chant is to sing until you move past the inner critic, past the place of *How is this going to sound?* and *Are people going to like it?*

Sing and write and sing until the song emerges. Write it down and share it with someone who you know will support you and sing with you. Sing loudly and boldly if you like. You too are a song that is emerging. You too are a song that needs to be sung.

Spell: Wish Birds
PHOENIX LEFAE

Time: 15 minutes

. . .

The wish bird is a piece of Reclaiming magic going back to the origins of our tradition. It can be done at any time and there are many different ways of doing it; this is just one of them.

In this piece of magic, we create an energetic bird that carries our wish or desire out into the world to help manifest what we are working toward. Each time you do this, your wish bird may be a different bird or some other flying creature, or you may discover that you have a darling magical friend that helps you every time you need assistance.

. . .

Before beginning this exercise, you will need to think of a wish. What is it you want to call to yourself right now? What is the thing your heart longs for? Once you've settled on a wish, set that aside for a moment.

The wish bird is best done while standing. You will need space to move around undisturbed, but if that is not comfortable or possible for your body, you can sit. Close your eyes and take at least three deep, cleansing breaths.

Continue to breathe deeply and as you do, feel your connection to the earth below you. Begin to pull up the energy from the earth, pulling it up through your body. With each breath, pull the energy higher and higher, allowing it to fill your entire body. You might also chant or dance to strengthen your focus.

As your body becomes filled with this energy, allow it to flow down your arms, into your hands and your fingers. Filling up with this energy may bring through a desire to move, to sway, to shift your hips; allow your body to move as it feels called. As the earth energy begins to flow out of your hands, let your hands begin to move. Use this energy to create the shape of a bird or some other sort of flying creature.

You may be able to see this bird coming into existence, you may feel the energy as you shape it with your hands, or you may just trust it is there. Continue to draw the energy up, as if drinking from a straw that goes from your body into the earth, and continue to use your hands to build the shape of your bird. Use your breath to blow energy into the bird that you are creating. Allow the bird to take the shape that it wants, as big or as small as it needs to be. Try not to force a shape or change your bird into something else. It will take the shape that it needs to hold.

Once your bird is fully formed, take a moment to connect with it. Usually we do this process with our eyes closed and look at the wish bird with our inner eye. Take notice of its size, shape, color, and even its temperament. When you feel that connection, when you know all of the details of your bird, hold it close to you and whisper your wish to it. Make sure that you name your wish aloud to your bird.

When you have finished speaking your wish, release your bird. With your inner eye, watch as it flies off and away. It is headed out into the world to manifest your wish, to bring it to fruition.

Now is where the hard part comes in: release any excess energy, let go of your wish, and open your eyes. You have to have faith and trust that your wish bird is taking care of it for you. Let it go, and stop thinking about it.

Communication and Conflict
Gerri Ravyn Stanfield

. . .

Before you speak…

Something dynamic stimulates your brain's motor cortex and neurons begin to fire.

Your breath arrives and exits. The exhale tickles your vocal folds to make undulating vibrations. This air wafts upwards toward resonating cavities inside your head.

Your resonators behind your teeth, sinuses, and nose give form to the sound that will be born inside your mouth.

Your soft palate lifts high, a yawning cavern of potential.

Your tongue and lips give the sound a shape and it emerges, a word, like magic.

What were your first words?

My first words were *bye-bye*. Why did I want to communicate this? I wonder if I repeated the sound that went with one of the most familiar gestures, an adult taking my squishy baby wrist and making me wave at people as we ended a visit at their homes. Maybe even in those early years I needed to assert my independence to parents who would struggle to control me until I left home at the age of seventeen. Or perhaps I was an intuitive infant preparing for the torrents of farewell that I would soon experience. *I am leaving. I want you to notice my departure. I desire to tell you this. We will meet again someday. See you later.* Or *This is the last time we will see each other. It's important that we ritualize this. Goodbye.*

Communication is both a shining jewel of our human nature and a ceaseless weapon of destruction. It begins with a desire to express something that lives inside; your heart pulses against your rib cage as you think of it. Or perhaps it begins within the song that the stones and the trees make together, the spell of the living planet that everything sings to everything. The tongues we speak, the ideas we reveal, the stories to which we listen.

Communication is composed of listening and speaking. This includes our tone, pitch, vocal cues, throat sounds, as well as sign language that uses our hands, and ways that many people with vision impairments read with their fingers. Humans have the amazing ability to shift back and forth between modalities of communication almost without effort, speaking, then writing, then reading. Although many other animals vocalize, humans are the only ones to use our tongues and lips for articulation. Our writing is nothing less than a miracle. I place one letter in front of the next, just one line and then a circle and then a curve, and somehow you read and understand me.

Every human is a storyteller. We have a desire to communicate with each other, to tell the truth and relate and grow closer, to express our consent and negation, our attraction and repulsion. We speak directly or indirectly to the story of our own needs. We want to communicate the yes and no of us. Sadly, the world around us does not always honor an honest voice.

Our voices become pledged to the dominant culture's ideology very early in our development. The groundbreaking book *In a Different Voice* by feminist psychologist Carol Gilligan uncovers the subjugation of the authentic voice to the systems of patriarchy and oppression. Her research shows that boys are compelled to become suspicious of their mothers, the tender parts of themselves, and anything feminine between the ages of four to six. Their communication styles change drastically, essentially burying their most truthful voices. Girls tend to keep their ability to be candid for several more years, until between ages nine to thirteen. Sometime during this period the messages to behave in ways that are inhibited and unchallenging become so overwhelming that young women bury their authentic voices in order to survive.

It's time to restore the loss of our voices.

Sticks and stones may break my bones but words will never hurt me; this is a rhyme I recited as a child. It is not true. We can all think of words that someone spoke to us that are unforgettable. I know you have favorite words and words that you never want to hear again. I know that people have said things that called a spark up your spine or put a boulder in your belly. Communication lives in our bodies. Our very skin can grow numb to insulate against the words that might extinguish us. Blocked communication can form that bump in the throat to hold back all the unspoken emotion. That lump impedes anything that you know you must say but still seems unspeakable to your body.

When did you stop telling the truth about your feelings?

I once loved someone in secret for many years. Out of respect for our other relationships and to protect my own tender heart, I kept sacred silence. I didn't want to hurt anyone, but I could not make my feelings go away. I never used words, but I told him with my rapt attention during his stories. I told him with the sweetness of my touch, never inappropriate interactions for friends but full of the love that surged in me. Secrets can survive forever if they are fed and nourished, but with time, the pain of an unrequited crush transformed itself into an unbreakable appreciation. My love became something rare: a friendship that would never die.

One night, inside the complete honesty brought on by many beers, I told him that long ago, I had been in love with him. I wanted nothing in return. I found out he never knew that I had a crush on him. He asked me why I finally told him when we were not going to act on it. I replied that I had a strong desire to express something that had lived inside me for years in my own voice and without any need to control the outcome. Sometimes the impulse of truth needs to rest on the tongue, pass through the lips, and be communicated.

As vital as the need to speak is our need to listen, reflect, and synthesize the information taken inside. Often, the listening part is how we form relationships. To be heard and understood is a basic human need. Many of us think we are good listeners but when asked to repeat what is being communicated, we realize that we have missed important pieces. This inability to listen can erode healthy relationships.

Pauline Oliveros, an American composer, musician, and visionary, taught deep listening as an investigation of "the difference between the involuntary nature of hearing and the voluntary, selective nature—exclusive and inclusive—of listening." This kind of listening to music, natural soundscape, or even human speech requires us to be cognizant of sound vibrations and the tiny noises beneath the sounds. There are noises that reach our ears first because of dominant volume or rhythm. For a deeper kind of attention, we must learn to hear the sounds beyond the sounds.

The world is alive with sound. Remember that everything sings to everything in our vast web of life. There is song that rises from the cellular signaling of coral reefs to the wings of crows stirring air, from the splash of frogs slipping into water to the battle of the bands between crickets and cicadas. Humans have always noticed this natural orchestra; the Celts named it the *Oran Mor*, the Great Song, and saw it as part of divinity on earth. Some linguists theorize that our first words as a species may have been attempts to imitate or pronounce sounds around us. From listening, we learn to speak.

Angeles Arrien (1940–2014), an author and educator, named the power of communication as one kind of authority held within a community that is celebrated by indigenous peoples all over the planet. Those of us who can articulate through speech or writing have the ability to verbalize arguments and concepts in order for others to understand. It is said that history is written by the winners. The person who writes history has enormous power. This is how stories are formed, how culture is remembered and passed forward. Whose voices are heard most often? Which stories remain untold? If it seems that we are not telling all the stories that need to be heard, how do we change this? Meaningful relationships are created through truly hearing each other.

One way that we work to achieve this hearing of all the stories in our communities is to have a verbal check-in when we begin our classes or meetings. This can be an emotional weather report. It asks everyone in the group to look inside themselves and to scan how they are feeling, what their bodies are saying, and what their expectations are. Then we make space for each person to speak out loud and check in with the group. In these processes we ask people not to speak while someone else speaks, a behavior that we call cross-talk. Even though this is quite natural in a conversation and often encourages exchange, we ask that, in this context, full attention be given to the person talking.

The check-in is also where we challenge some of the habits that people who process either externally or internally bring to the group. Folks who are wired to think and talk at the same time can unintentionally take up a lot of verbal space, as they don't always know what they are going to say until it comes. Others feel they need a lot of time to consider what they will say before speaking in front of the group, so they can rely on comfortable patterns of listening and keeping their opinions to themselves. We may give people a prompt and ask them to write for a few minutes about what they would say to check in. We can also use a timer to ensure that everyone has a chance to speak for one or two minutes so the verbal space is shared equally. This builds trust, especially in larger groups where it can detract from the group's energy if one person speaks for a long time and no one acknowledges this is happening.

Often, our most important communication in the world ends up taking place within meetings, whether it be governments, universities, community activists, or multinational corporations. Margaret Mead (1901–1978), a cultural anthropologist, reminds us to "never doubt that a small group of thoughtful, committed citizens can change the world; indeed, it's the only thing that ever has." Whether we like it or not, our meetings of small groups are where lots of decisions happen. Facilitated discussions make the difference between whether much work gets done or we belabor points so long that no work gets done. Communication in meetings can make or break us when it comes to projects and making our dreams manifest. These can be the opportunities where we come together and problem solve or discover what the community thinks and feels beyond the individual's needs. Meetings are places where we hope for change, where many of our basic needs in community can arise, where we can actually connect with each other and build our visions. These also can be places where we experience a storm of tumultuous conflict that can scare us away from community endeavors.

In every group of people trying to change the world, conflict will likely erupt. This is absolutely normal, not dysfunctional, as the folks who fear conflict would have us believe. Humans will always have disagreements and differing opinions about how things should go. Unfortunately, unresolved conflict can tear relationships apart and sidetrack all the goals of the group. People leave and try to find another community of people with whom they can better relate.

Because resolving conflict is so challenging, it often does not happen. Instead, other less direct forms of communication show up. Some people will smolder angrily for years rather than offer feedback about someone else's behavior. People may offer feedback to those who are not the person who most needs to hear the feedback and hope it somehow reaches that person through the grapevine. There are also folks who behave harmfully toward others in the community and then pretend that nothing has happened. Most of these behaviors can be collectively understood as passive-aggressive behaviors that attempt to influence outcomes but never directly address the issues. In these situations, others in the group may see the behavior but not know what to do or fear getting involved, so the hurtful actions persist. Differences in power, hurt feelings, an absence of agreed upon codes of conduct, and a perceived lack of support from other members of the community can effectively prevent communication about conflict or conflict resolution.

This inability of communities to help members resolve conflict is heartbreaking because we can see that restorative justice processes of speaking and listening are quite effective, even in correction facilities. In the Oregon prison system, people convicted of crimes that have clearly identified victims, such as identity theft, assault, rape, and murder, are offered the opportunity to reduce their sentence by meeting with the victim or victim's family in mediated sessions. Studies show that people who go through this process rarely return to prison; the recidivism rates plummet and stay low. Victims and their families also report higher levels of emotional resolution and mental health after going through restorative justice.

Conflict is a natural part of the community experience. There is the very real dynamic that in larger groups of people, not everyone's needs may be able to be met at the same time. A great example in our classes and rituals comes when we attempt to create space for emotions to be expressed. Often, there will be one or a small group of people who express feelings at top volume while other people become distracted or adverse to high levels of noise. Both the need for full vocal expression and the need for tranquility are absolutely valid. They literally cannot be met in the same space in the same moment.

We all know it is impossible to please everyone always, and yet it is hard to be the one who is displeased and irritated. Marshall Rosenberg (1934–2015), the creator of Nonviolent Communication (NVC), takes the focus off what other people are doing wrong and instead creates a system where we start by exchanging our self-judgment for empathy. When we offer ourselves empathy, recognizing the pain or discomfort of the moment, most of us find that we relax our judgement of others. Self-empathy soothes our inability to see the other person's perspective. Stepping away from judgement of ourselves and others helps uncover what we feel and need. This gives us clarity to communicate requests of others to move toward what we would like to see or experience instead. These NVC basics put us in better touch with our own vulnerability and awaken our creative efforts to ask for what we want.

I have heard it said that all conflict actually arises from feedback that has not been given. Many of us have experienced criticism in our earlier lives from parents or teachers or other authority figures. Often this criticism was not constructive and was designed to control our behavior rather than to help us grow. It can be all too easy to remember the critique and project that onto a current experience when someone offers us feedback. Some people react physically to any critique; the thought of giving or receiving feedback can trigger our fight-or-flight response. In Reclaiming we create opportunities for everyone to give and receive feedback on a variety of experiences so that we build some muscle tissue around taking in other people's perceptions of us. I like to think this practice of skilled communication has the clear intent to improve our work and prepares us for some of the feedback encounters we have with other folks in the world who do not possess the same skill level.

I have been working as a facilitator in the nonprofit world, at universities, in the arts, in Reclaiming and in various community activist settings since 1996. I have noticed in all of these settings that truly gifted facilitators are using psychic or energetic tools in their communication. They are reading the energy of the room, trying to get underneath what is actually being said, calling the group back from tangents that might not be useful and guiding people toward the goals stated at the beginning of the meeting or discussion. Facilitators are often good synthesizers, able to take a handful of disparate ideas and restate them in a way that makes sense. This requires the deep listening outlined earlier. Gifted facilitators blend intellect and intuition to generate ideas, as well as a balance of speaking and listening.

All of the skills we learn in our spiritual work benefit us when we apply them to facilitating meetings and even conversations in our personal lives. We learn to sense energy, to understand what is not being said aloud. We learn when to speak our truth and when to keep our mouths shut. We learn when to stir the room and when to step back from the conversation and encourage different voices to come forward. We learn how to be in our own power and not to give it away when there are other powerful people in the room with us. We learn to return to our grounded selves even when triggered and keep going or take a break to calm ourselves if needed.

The more we can develop our competence in working with our senses and our bodies, the more knack we have for developing talent in all the areas of our communication. You can check in with yourself and feel into the energy of the room or imagine what you are noticing about the group with your mind's eye. Maybe there is a topic that brings a feeling of heaviness or obscurity into the discussion or you notice that people are restless inside a conversation. Your body can help you know whether you need to introduce an ice breaker to make a shift or ask a question to go deeper.

There are thousands of other ways to address difficult topics in a large group. Many facilitators will break the room into small groups or use a fishbowl method where participants face each other in an inner and outer circle and then switch partners to hear a variety of thoughts. There are great sociometric tools such as spectrums, where facilitators identify two opposing views, draw or tape a line on the floor, and ask folks to place themselves on the line according to how strongly they feel about the topic. Marshall Rosenberg would always encourage facilitators to acknowledge the needs of the group and trust that disruption or dissent was about an unmet need of some kind. The best facilitation finds ways to address needs that aren't being honored and to repair what is broken.

As the world radically changes, there may well be more tough choices we have to make in workplaces, communities, and spiritual traditions. There are so many oppressive factors influencing all of our interactions that are not popular to discuss openly—race, class, gender, ability, sexual orientation, religion, politics, education, cultural differences, the environmental impacts of human choices. The hallmark of our thriving future may well be our ability to take on difficult topics and navigate through them in meetings and discussion.

Thousands of people report that they are more afraid of public speaking than dying. Standing in front of a large group of people to say something out loud arouses fear of rejection, ridicule, exile, even witch burnings. My voice teacher suggests that we must use our most true voices in these times. With these true voices we must stand in the place of fight-or-flight and, instead, we must choose to reveal even more of ourselves. I think this is the most courageous communication possible. To utter the unutterable. To listen to truth undecorated. Can we be that brave?

In Reclaiming we are determined to find ways to heal our communication and renew our trust in each other. Somehow, we must rescue our listening skills from the brink of extinction and reassociate with the Great Song of life. Whatever it takes, we must learn to reconnect with each other when we are in conflict, since this ancient problem is a root of so many wars. Our every attempt to liberate our genuine voices and make space for more stories to be told will result in the world we want to see. Our work is to restore communication to an art, a shared language to describe all our experiences, including our pain, loss, fear, rage, and despair, and find a way through it.

What were your first words?

What would you like your last words to be?

Exercise: Basic Interpretation of a Tarot Card
Tarin Towers

Time: 20–30 minutes

You will need: a deck of tarot cards or any other cards with pictures; you will not need the book that comes with the deck

• • •

The tarot is a rich system of symbols and archetypes you can work with to tell stories, seek advice, and feed your intuition. Rather than viewing tarot as fortunetelling only, consider that it is also a decision-making tool, along the lines of asking a friend for advice. You don't have to take the advice, but you may get to see your situation from a perspective beyond what you'd come up with by meditating alone.

Tarot cards and other forms of divination tap in to the watery realm of intuition, but they are also connected with the element of air because they're a magical tool of discernment, decision-making, and description.

It's not necessary to know anything about tarot to get or give a deep reading—in fact, familiarity with the cards is sometimes an obstacle to approaching a question without preconceived notions about how things ought to be.

Systematic study of the cards encourages a reliance on helpful shortcuts, such as using the numbers and suits of the cards to sum them up. But sometimes seeking the wisdom of the card—for yourself or a friend—means setting aside what things are assumed to mean and looking solely at what's pictured on the card. You might give yourself fresh eyes by using a colorful deck you're less familiar with.

Think of a question while you shuffle the deck. Then place the cards on the table and cut them, with your non-dominant hand, into three piles. Put the cards into one stack and turn over a single card, faceup.

If the card uses interpretive words, such as Sorrow or Courage, hold it so your thumb covers those words. For this exercise, disregard astrological symbols or other notations on the cards that prescribe external definitions. Either silently or aloud, describe what you see on the card. Start by naming things that jump out at you: people, animals, colors, objects, shapes.

Continue by describing the scene: Where does the action on this card take place? Is it a city, a desert, a sea or lake? What time of day is it? Do you see or feel a particular season? Is it warm or cold?

Use both your discernment and your intuition to focus on what parts of this card are relevant, right now, to you and your situation. Remind yourself of your original question. If there are people on the card, what are they doing? Do they remind you of anyone? Are their actions similar to things you do in your normal life? Think broadly. For example, if someone is tending a garden, that might relate not just to growing food but to raising children, teaching, or managing a project.

One-card readings can be used as meditative tools: walk around with the card in your mind's eye or leave it on an altar or another prominent place so you'll see it throughout the day and revisit what it might represent.

You can also use cards as clues. Pick out a card before you leave the house and ask "What allies are nearby?" or "What messages should I be open to?"

Reading for someone else is just the same. Have them shuffle, formulate a question, and then draw a card. Ask them to describe the card to you. Encourage them beyond official-sounding interpretations such as "butterflies mean transformation," and listen to what story they have to tell about the card so you can help them answer their own question.

FIRE

• • •

We come together at the fire. We gather as the candle's flame is lit; we circle around the fire to tell stories, share music, practice ritual; we gather in the kitchen and share meals cooked by fire. Sacred flames in temples, sacred hearths in houses, a campfire at night or a bonfire to burn the old—fire and humans have a long association. Flames and fire, however domesticated they might be in some of their forms, always retain a wildness, a wonder, a fascination. We talk about the dancing, flickering nature of fire as if it were alive; a fire that has gone out is referred to as dead. Fires on the hilltop—as beacons, as celebration, as cleansing—are a part of human history. Some of the Pagan or witch's sabbats are referred to as fire festivals—the Summer Solstice, Beltaine, and Samhain.

Like all the elements, fire in its unbounded nature is dangerous. Wildfire, forest fire, bushfires, and volcanoes are all raw embodiments of fire that threaten habitation, life, and agriculture. The forces of earth, water, and air can be equally dramatic if we consider floods and tsunamis, hurricanes and tornados, earthquakes and landslips, but it is often fire that is considered the most dangerous, unpredictable. We have fire fighters, trained people who go out to house fires or land fires in an attempt to control and extinguish them; there's no such category as water fighters or earth or air fighters. Fire must be an element we think of as controllable, somehow, by us—one that we fight, sometimes winning and sometimes losing—an element we are in conflict with. Fire is certainly an element that has radically shaped our consciousness as a species.

We use fire domestically and commonly; it's an element we learn a lot about. How to conjure it, how to work with it, how to guard against it. In magic we often associate power, life force, or energy with fire, and in magic we set out to learn how to conjure and work with energy and power. Just as fires come in small and large forms, from a candle flame or lit match to a raging wildfire, so energy workings come in all sizes, from one of us sitting by our altar, casting a circle, and creating a spell to a whole group of us gathered around a bonfire, raising energy to change the world. Just as we build a fire, we work at building our magic, adding pieces carefully to the structure, to support it and achieve the desired strength. We also work at building community in this way, studying effective structures of communication, interpersonal relationships, leadership, growth, and learning, and seeking to add them, piece by piece, to an evolving local, broad-based, or even international community.

Passion, sexuality, and creativity are commonly associated with fire, as well as the ability to burn away what is old, unused, or limiting. The flammable, provocative nature of all these things adds to the allure—and sometimes fear or avoidance—of fire as an element to work magic with. A common expression in Western societies is the cautionary *Don't play with fire*. We also sometimes speak about power or sexuality as a corrupting influence. In Reclaiming and in many other magical, Pagan, and witchcraft traditions, we embrace power and sexuality as the fires they are and learn how to allow the natural radiance to shine forth. We learn how to share power and be with our sexuality consciously, and we become skilled in drawing boundaries and praising our no as much as our yes.

Fire, and the control and use of fire, is considered to be closely linked with the history of humankind. In Reclaiming we sometimes speak of the life force and vitality inherent in all things with fiery language. We link the wand with fire as it channels that life force; we wield the power of the sun that is stored in the branch as well as our own power. Fire is the element that requires earth and air, and it is extinguished by water. It might rise up and simply burn out, lost to the ashes, or—if we learn how to wield the power *to will*—the fire might continue on, passed from person to person, time to time, in the coals and embers of our lives. How might you fan the flames of your life into a potent and holy fire?

The elements are sacred. Fire is sacred.

Fire Is Sacred

RAVEN EDGEWALKER

. . .

Fire, fire of the candle flame, fire of the bonfire, fire of the sun, fire of the heat of passion that burns in our bodies, fire the quickening of our spirit, fire that warms us, fire, fire, we welcome you.

Imagine hearing words enticing fire into the circle, imagine bodies moving in patterns evocative of flames, drums beating, fingers snapping, evoking the sounds of crackling, burning fire.

The element of fire is usually invoked into our circle after air has been invited. While we will often call fire or any of the elements with words, just as often our invocation will be made with sound, song, or movements intended to evoke the energy of fire into our circle in a way that is more embodied.

In the northern hemisphere, we most frequently call fire in the south, associating it with the heat of the noonday sun as it appears in the southern sky. In the southern hemisphere, while we often invoke the elements in the same order, it makes little sense to call fire in the south—that way lies the cold iciness of Antarctica—or to ignore the heat of the sun at our back in the north, so we often call fire in the north. Within Reclaiming, directional associations are guidelines rather than rules, and we aim to be aware of the land we are in.

We find fire in many forms: from the tiniest of candle flames to a cauldron fire, a hearth fire, a bonfire, a raging forest fire, a lightning strike, or the unimaginable heat of the sun's core. It was our ancestors' discovery of how fire can be deliberately created, controlled, and contained—to give light and warmth, to cook with, and then to craft metal—that shaped the path of human evolution. The gifts of fire have helped us evolve from primitive proto-sapiens into the richly diverse cultures of modern humanity.

We use fire in many forms to cook, heat, and create light, often as electricity. To us, fire is both an ally and a challenger—unexpected or out-of-control fires can wreak terrible havoc, burning all in their path indiscriminately. It is good to approach work with this element with respect and awareness that while fire and its energies will happily help us transform what we no longer need, it may also burn away things we are still attached to.

Along with the physical presence of fire in our lives, fire also has many correspondences. The colors of fire are yellows, oranges, reds, and gold. Objects that have those colors are also frequently associated with fire: crystals, plants with fire-colored flowers such as sunflowers or flame tree blossoms. Fire is associated with midday, the time when the sun is at its peak, and with midsummer. It's associated with Will, which we often capitalize to indicate we are talking about true will, passion, desire, sex, ecstasy, life force, and creativity.

Earth was formed in fire, a burning ball of gas and star-stuff that slowly coalesced into matter. Over millennia it cooled and solidified, the magical combination of gas, matter, and heat sparking the beginning of life. Still our planet contains a molten, iron-rich core that occasionally erupts to the surface as volcanic explosions and less violently heats water bubbling to the surface in naturally heated springs. The sun, the burning star around which we orbit, is a fire. It is easy, with all these mysterious physical manifestations, to see how so many cultures around the world worshiped and continue to worship fire deities who are often, but not always, also solar deities: Sulis (British), Amaterasu (Japanese), Hestia (Greek), Ra (Egyptian), and Freyr (Norse) are but a few examples.

Within Reclaiming we typically work with the wand as our primary magical tool of fire. We may use a wand to cast a circle, as well as to store, shape, and direct energy and focus our energy in alignment with our Will. We often use a wand to direct energy into our spellworkings and in healing work. Our wands may be made of wood, metal, crystal, or glass—whatever feels right to you. We may choose to make our own wands, often as part of building and deepening our relationships with the element of fire, or we may buy one that calls to us—or why stop at one? Some of us have a number of wands that are used for different purposes. We can also work with drums as tools of fire, since they also can be used to shape and direct energy.

Fire is essential for the survival of all life on this planet. Without the sun, the earth would be cold and life would be impossible. While we warm-blooded humans can generate our own body heat, we also need the warmth of fire to survive cold winters and grow our crops. Fire gives us the spark of life that runs through our bodies, which we also call life force.

Different cultures refer to the idea of life force in related ways: *ashe* in Yoruban West African traditions, *chi* in Chinese culture, *mana* from the people of the islands of Hawaii, and *prana* from Hindu traditions. Whatever we call it, we understand not only that energy moves through our bodies, but also that the matter of our bodies is itself energy held in a physical form. It gives us our spark of life and our consciousness. It is the energy that connects us, one to each other and to all other beings, physical and nonphysical, conscious and not conscious. This is the energy that connects us to the universe and to divinity.

Reclaiming is an ecstatic, embodied tradition of witchcraft, which also embraces life force as sex, and we sometimes use the words interchangeably. Sex is the physical act of sex between lovers, but so much more! It is the energy that created the universe and our planet, but also the energy that we use to create art, music, magic, science, and more. Each new project we start is fueled with a spark of life force and sustained by the continued flow of that life force. As witches we can learn to sense, raise, and shape energy—to be aware of life force as it flows from one being to another. With their permission, we can learn to send someone energy to help them heal, to support them from a distance.

Energy is a difficult thing to define. The closer we come to pinning it down to a short, definitive sentence, the further away from it we actually seem to get. It is easier to experience than to describe in words.

Before we can learn to share, move, and raise energy, we need first to explore how to sense it. For some it is easy, for others something that we struggle with, but with practice we can all learn to do this. It's good to remember that there are different ways in which we sense energy; no one way is right or wrong. Some of us will feel the energy that we raise in our bodies, perhaps as heat, the hair rising on the back of our necks, or our hands and feet tingling. Or we experience it as changes in temperature. Some of us hear energy as a low hum, static, or as a wordless chant that's right on the edge of our hearing. Others can see energy as it moves in streams of colors or auras around beings or objects. Then there are people who sense energy with what we might call deep knowing of how energy is moving. Most of us have a dominant sense that perceives, some of us more than one, and most of us can practice to open up our other senses to gain greater understanding.

Everything in the universe has an energy body, which extends beyond physical substance. This is also called an aura. When you rub your hands together rapidly until they tingle, you are charging your hands with energy. If you draw your hands apart, you probably can still feel the energy generated, often as heat. Extend your senses and see if you can hear or see anything as well. When your hands are charged like this, you can try to sense the energy of other things; a plant, for example. Extend your hands toward the leaf of a plant until you feel the energy in your hands connecting to the energy of the plant. How does it feel? Try the same thing with a stone or a branch of wood. Again, what do you notice? You may find it useful to recharge your hands periodically. As you become more practiced, you will need to do this less and less, until it becomes as easy and natural as reaching out to physically touch an object.

We can use the same technique to sense our own auras and that of other people. Our aura usually extends about an arm's reach away from our bodies and forms an egg shape around us. The size will vary somewhat from person to person and also depends on how we're feeling—our aura tends to shrink if we're cold, tired, or sick, and expands if we're warm, happy, or excited. In the same way as we can sense the energy of an object, we can sense the edges of our own auras and those of others. This is one way that we can share energy with each other and, in doing so, learn to communicate energetically as well as with words.

As witches we are also able to gather and raise energy to magically honor or charge and give power to our ritual intentions and our spell-workings—a little like plugging them into a battery or a power outlet. Whether we are working alone or as part of a group, we can raise energy, gathering it in from the air around us, drawing it up from the core of the earth and down from the stars. Before we begin it is important to ground, connecting to the energy of the earth and to the stars, so that you are neither using all your own energy reserves, which would be exhausting, nor holding all the energy that is raised in your body, which would be uncomfortable.

Energy can be gathered and raised in many ways. What methods we choose depend on the nature of the magical working, as well as what is appropriate, what supports our intention, and what is easily accessible to us or the group we are working with. The simplest way of gathering energy is with breath. With each breath we are also drawing in the energy from the air about us. You can use the energy in your breath to direct into a spell you are doing (this works great with charm making) or breathe over your wand to charge it with energy so that you can use the wand to direct this energy.

The gathering and raising of energy into what we call a cone of power is most commonly and easily achieved with movement, sound, or a combination of both. We raise a cone of power to charge our intention within a ritual or magical working. The act of dancing, whether a circle-style dance like our classic spiral dance or more free-form ecstatic dancing, is one of the best ways of raising energy, as well as being fun. Combine this with sound—tones, animal howls, chants, rhythms, drum beats, and music—and we have a potent combination for raising plenty of energy for our magic. Raising energy is and should be fun, embodying the mirth and reverence from Doreen Valiente's *Charge of the Goddess*.

It doesn't matter if you're on your own, with a few people, or in a large several-hundred-people ritual, you can raise energy using one or more of these tools. Some are better suited to particular circumstances than others. It's up to you to experiment and figure out what works best for you and your style of magic.

Within Reclaiming, given our non-hierarchical ethos, raising energy looks a little different from other traditions because we don't have only one person who's in charge of directing energy. Often there will be a group of priestesses who have stepped forward to anchor different parts of the ritual. Some will tend the edges of the circle, some will hold the center. It's good to keep an eye on what these people are doing. Connect with them visually if you are able, mirror their movements if you find yourself opposite them in the circle, and notice if they begin to raise the tempo of the chant. We're all equally responsible for doing the work, and it's up to each of us to check in with each other as the energy begins to gather, to make sure everyone is included. It is especially important for people dancing to connect with those who are not able to stand or dance and who will often sit in the center of our circle along with any drummers that are present. We are committed to making our rituals and workings as accessible as we possibly can.

As the energy begins to gather, the chant will often dissolve into wordless toning, any drums will simplify their beats and begin to drop back, our bodies will press closer together, our arms raise, those tending the edge of the circle may begin to dance or run around the outside of the group in the direction the sun travels to help shape and encourage the gathered energy into a cone of power, while those in the center will work and guide the energy from there, sometimes stirring, sometimes pulling it up from the ground.

When the energy is close to reaching its peak, the cone of power will begin to lift, and now it can be directed with the intention of the whole group, using our voices, bodies, hands, or wands if we have them. The natural inclination of a cone is to shoot off, rocket-like, into the air before dissipating, which might be what we want—for example, if we are sending the energy out for healing around the world. We might, however, want to direct the energy into a spell or charm held in the center of the circle, down into the earth beneath our feet, or even into the bodies of those in the group. Usually we will have decided beforehand and communicated to the group what our intention for the energy will be. Once the cone of power has been released, it's good to take some deep breaths. Sometimes we bend down and touch the ground, releasing excess energy that we're holding in our bodies to bless the earth.

One of the reasons we raise energy is to charge our spellwork. Spell work is a huge topic, one on which many books have been written. Some rituals involve spellworkings, where others may be celebratory or devotional, when the energy raised will be released to honor rather than to charge.

A magical spell is a set of words or actions created with clear intention, directed with Will to manifest the need and desire of the spellworker. Spells can take many forms, limited only by your imagination. They can be written or spoken, they can be crafted with dance or stillness, they can be done quickly and spontaneously or over a long time. They can be complex, involve the gathering of many ingredients, and be carried out at a carefully chosen time of day in alignment with a supportive astrological event or moon phase. Or they might be simple; for example, a few words on a piece of paper. A spell might involve the creation of a talisman or amulet to manifest the need and desire of the spellworker. Spells can be crafted to manifest what you need—whether it be for healing or for enough money to pay the rent—for yourself, a loved one, the earth, or to effect transformation.

Many people have the idea that spells should only be used for really important things, when more mundane solutions have already been tried, and that's certainly one way of approaching it. As with so many things, practice is important. There's a reason why we call it spell crafting—any craft needs practice in order to achieve mastery. The more we practice, the better we're going to get, and it's usually best to practice in situations that are not critical.

Perhaps the most important part of spell crafting is the intention. When our intention is unclear, then the results of the spell are likely to be unclear and leave us with potentially unexpected results. If the intention is clear and well thought out, the spell is far more likely to succeed since we have a clear objective on which to focus our energy.

Along with intention, it is important to consider ethics. Reclaiming is a nonviolent tradition in both physical and magical deeds, an ethos that is detailed in our Principles of Unity. Within this framework it is important to consider the impact that any spellwork will have on both the recipients and the spell caster. Consider whether the spell may cause violence, intended or otherwise. Wiccan traditions, from which Reclaiming draws some inspiration, offer the following pieces of guidance. The Threefold Law, taken from the Rede of the Wiccae and often referred to as the Long Wiccan Rede, attributed to Adriana Porter by her grand-daughter Gwen Thompson, is "Mind the threefold law ye should, three times bad and three times good." Another piece of magical advice, known as the Gardnerian Wiccan Rede, is "An ye harm none, do what ye will."

Reclaiming witches tend to see any rule as a guideline, and it is your decision whether to adopt the Threefold Law as part of your ethical framework. It is important to remember that whatever energy you send out into the world will eventually return to you. These, along with the nonviolent ethos of our tradition, offer a useful starting place for figuring out your own individual ethics for magical practice.

My own preference is to hold the intention that my magical working will result in the best possible outcome for all concerned, both myself as the spellworker and anyone who will be impacted by the spellwork. There is great debate as to whether it is ethical to cast spells on behalf of someone who has not given their permission. Some believe very strongly that this is unacceptable. Others think it is acceptable in some situations; for example, casting a healing spell for someone who is unconscious.

The first step after deciding that a situation calls for spellwork is to craft a clear intention. Try to keep it short, simple, and to the point. Take time to refine it. You can use some form of divination to guide the crafting of the intention and the spell. Check that the intended outcome is supported by your individual ethics and those held in the Principles of Unity. It will help if your spell is about something you greatly desire or are passionate about and that you truly Will to happen.

Popular culture gives us stereotypical images of witches stirring ingredients into a cauldron while muttering incantations over the brew. In reality, spell crafting can take many forms, from the simple crafting of an intention and sending it out on the energy of our breath, through to spells that culminate in charging an item, through to more complex spells. Different methods lend themselves to some intentions better than others, and we often have personal leanings that will inform our choices. For example, if we already work with crystals or herbs, we're likely to be drawn to use them in spellwork.

The act of spell crafting is often, but not always, held in the container of sacred space. This creates a structure into which we invite the elements, deity, and other allies both physical and nonphysical to support our work. This structure also helps us raise and shape the energy that we need to charge our spells by containing it until we are ready to release it. At the point when we feel sufficient energy has been raised, we direct it into the spell so that it may do the work that we intend it to do.

From a spell's creation by the crafting of intent and the spell's substance and energetic charging, the element of fire infuses our process. From the microcosm of spell crafting, we can turn our gaze outwards again and notice how fire infuses our lives in so many ways: as fire in all its forms, as life force, and in the form of fire deities that we work with.

Without fire we would not exist. The magic lies not just in understanding how we can work with fire in our magical practice, but in learning how we can shift our awareness and deepen our connections to fire as an ally in all parts of our life, making the mundane magical.

Ritual: Building a Fire with Magical Awareness
Catherine Gronlund

Time: 30 minutes to several hours

You will need: a place to lay the fire (fireplace, fire pit,
large iron cauldron), natural materials to burn (logs,
kindling), natural dry tinder, lighter or matches,
water to extinguish the fire, dry herbs or other
natural material with magical properties that
support your intention (optional)

• • •

Fire is a paradox. It supports our lives in many ways, providing heat for
our homes, power to cook food, and power for most forms of transport. But fire is also a destructive force. When it is not contained, it
can grow into a raging inferno, devouring everything in its path. This
exercise is intended to provide guidance in building a fire to support a
magical intention.

Preparation is the key to working with fire. If you are lighting a fire
outside, prepare the physical location by establishing strong fireproof
boundaries that are large enough to hold the fire. Make sure you know
about and respect any fire bans that may be in place. Clear away all
flammable materials from the immediate area and extending out several feet. Organize the fire-starter, tinder, and flammable materials so
that they are not in immediate danger of combusting.

Prepare yourself magically with a strong will, clear intention, and
focus. You might like to ground and center, then align your souls (see
page 229). Think about your magical intention and the aspect of fire
that would support your work. These are the stages of fire you could
consider matching with your intention:

- Spark—the flash of potential.
- Ignition—the moment when the spark falls on dry tinder
  and ignites.

- Blaze—when the fire burns, limited only by the quality and amount of fuel and the strength of the boundaries that surround it.
- Ember—the stage where the fire has burned through the fuel and reduced it to coals.
- Ash—what is left behind after the fire is out.

For example, if you would like to invite the warming fire of passion into your life, you may wish to focus more of your attention on the Spark, Ignition, and Blaze phases. If you are at a transition point in your life, ready to let go and open up to something new, the destructive power of fire could support your work. Focus your attention on burning away what no longer serves you as you engage with the Blaze, Ember, and Ash.

· · ·

Once you have a clear intention in mind, tap into the magic of fire by grounding, reaching down with your awareness to the fire at the core of the earth, and extending your awareness to the fire of the stars. Bring the energy to center with an awareness of the fire inside you and your connection to fire above and below. You may wish to ask fire for support in your work.

Continue to focus on your intention as you build your fire. When you are ready to light it, remind yourself of your intention and the stage or stages of fire you have linked it to. You may wish to prolong a stage that supports your magical working.

Use pieces of wood to build the structure of the fire. A log cabin or cross shape will create a longer-burning fire.

Place a pile of tinder in the middle of the wooden structure. Focus on potential as you create the spark and ignite the tinder.

Place kindling over the tinder and across the structure logs, leaving space for air to circulate.

Continue to add kindling until all of the structure logs are burning. At this point, you may wish to add natural materials with a specific magical property to your fire. Continue to add wood until the fire has reached the size you need for your magical working.

Perhaps at this point you wish to speak your intention aloud or carry out a further magical working.

Continue to focus your attention on the fire as it cycles into embers and ash. Many traditions show respect for fire by having someone remain with the fire until it is completely out. This is also a practical way of keeping fires safe, especially when they are outdoors. If you do have to leave an outdoor fire, extinguish the remaining coals and embers.

Offer gratitude to the fire for supporting your work.

Practice: Wands and Energy

TARIN TOWERS

Time: 20 minutes

You will need: a wand, wooden stick, or wooden kitchen
spoon

• • •

The wand is considered the tool of fire in Reclaiming, in part because wood holds fire within itself. Having collected the sun's energy over the course of its life, a tree sheds a branch—which, when ignited, releases that energy back into the world in the form of fire. Until you've found or created your own wand, a wooden kitchen spoon is a perfect tool, as it's a tool used in practical magic: the transformative fires of the kitchen.

Fire transforms, and we use wands to transform energy, then direct it. Witches draw up energy into their wands, as well as their own bodies, where it mixes with the other energies present in themselves. We then focus that energy and channel it back through the wand into the world.

This beaming of energy from the wand isn't done willy-nilly; it is focused in an intention. Working with fire is working with will, and the wand is a way of making the embodiment of will both tangible and visible.

• • •

Ground yourself. Choose an intention to work with.

Pay particular attention to the way your body feels before you start, and then when your grounding cord drops into the earth. Pause before drawing energy up into yourself, and notice any difference in sensation as the earth energy mixes with your own.

Next, as you cast a circle to contain your work, let your attention gather in your hands as you move.

Before you pick up your wand, stick, or wooden spoon, focus again on your hands. Close your eyes and rub your hands together to feel the warmth of fire in them. Hold them close together, then far apart, and notice the sensations. Are your fingers tingling, and does that make your hands feel larger or smaller? Do your hands have a magnetic pull toward one another? Can you counteract that?

Rub your hands together again, and assign a color in your mind's eye to the energy created by that friction or let a color emerge. Bring your hands closer together until they are holding that energy as a ball. Let your hands feel this ball as having weight, and mentally adjust the weight and size of this ball of energy. Does the color change? Assign it a different color. Does the feeling or size of the ball change? Open and close your eyes as you play with this ball of energy.

Open your eyes once more, and with your hands still charged with this energy, pick up your wand, stick, or wooden spoon.

Point the spoon or pointed end of your wand toward the center of the earth, and—as you did when grounding—pull some warm, healing earth energy into your wand, stick, or wooden spoon. You may want to make a stirring motion as you do this. Pull the energy up your arm and let that energy fill your body and mix with your own.

Now, focus on sending this energy out toward your intention. Turn and face the direction where you imagine your intention might reside or come from. Point your wand toward that and make a small stirring motion with your hand as you let your energy and the earth's mingle in the wand. Notice a color collecting on or around the wand. When you feel you're ready, pull back your arm as if you're going to throw a ball over your head, and then cast your intention and your will from the end of the wand toward your intention, sending it a boost of energy.

Ground any excess energy by pointing your wand at the earth and letting it drain back out. When you're ready, reground and open the circle.

Practice: Playing with Your Energy Boundaries
CATHERINE GRONLUND

Time: allow 30–60 minutes for the initial exploration

You will need: a space with room to move and a few
obstacles that you can easily move past—you may
wish to have a private space the first time you
perform this exercise; a journal (optional)

• • •

Just as our skin defines the edges of our physical body, we have an energetic boundary that defines the edges of our energy body and interacts
with the universe. In our tradition we might even refer to two energy
bodies. The first, which can be perceived or sensed a few centimeters
from the surface skin, is the body of the fetch. Further out, past this
layer, is the body of the talker or shining one, also known as the aura. It
often looks like an egg-shaped luminous space. These bodies are parallel to the three souls, which are discussed more fully on page 229. If
you stretch your arms out to either side, you might even notice that
you feel the aura. It can be expanded and contracted consciously or by
feeling and emotion alone. We can control our energy with our awareness and attention to expand or contract energetically. We can change
the size, shape, and texture of our energetic boundary, shaping it in
ways that will help us move easily through the world.

This exercise is designed to expand your awareness and skills in
shaping your energy boundary. Consciously changing its characteris-
tics will help you attract more of what you want to experience in life.
You can also change your energy in a protective way to deflect, repel,
or soften harmful influences.

• • •

Stand in a relaxed way with your weight balanced equally on each foot
and with your knees slightly bent. Tilt your pelvis forward by tightening your butt muscles. Take a deep breath in and hold it. Imagine earth

energy filling your body. Continue to breathe until you become aware of your energy body, noticing how energy fills and surrounds you. Move your awareness to the edges of your energy boundary.

Holding an awareness of this boundary, begin to move through the space, noticing how it feels when you move close to an object or move where nothing is close to you. As you move, deepen this awareness of your energy boundary, paying attention to the size, weight, and degree of hardness or softness, color or brightness.

When you have a good sense of this boundary, you are ready to practice changing aspects of it. Do this while paying attention to any changes in the way you feel and the sensations you experience interacting with objects or, if you are around people, other individuals. Follow your instincts. If a change to your energy boundary feels good, you may wish to spend more time exploring that change. If a change does not feel good, you may wish to move on quickly to the next.

As you move, imagine changing your energy boundary in the following ways:

- Pull it in very close to your physical body.
- Expand it out as far from your physical body as you can.
- Return it to a comfortable distance from your body.
- Change the texture of your energy boundary to make it harder.
- Change the texture to make it softer.
- Change the texture to one you associate with power.
- Return the texture to one that is comfortable for you.
- Change the surface of your energy boundary to a mirror, reflecting everything away from you.
- Change the surface to a permeable membrane that allows in energy you judge to be positive.
- Change the surface to smooth and imagine it in the shape of the prow of a ship.

- Change the surface to a big fluffy ball that extends far from your body, surrounding and insulating you.
- Make your energy boundary appear brighter.
- Make it appear darker.
- Change it to your favorite color.
- Continue to change the shape, color, brightness, texture, surface, and other aspects of your energy boundary as you wish.

Using the information you have gathered in this exercise, continue to change your energy boundary as you move through the world in ways that feel best to you.

Transformation By Fire

PANDORA O'MALLORY

* * *

Every element is an element of transformation. The element of air transforms us through our thoughts and our meditations. The element of water transforms us through our emotions. The element of earth transforms us through our bodies. The element of spirit transforms us through our souls.

But fire, oh, fire. Destructive friend, it burns out the brushwood. It cooks us until we are done. It softens us until we are ready for the blows of the blacksmith's hammer, which will set our edges, strengthen us, make us useful. It transforms us through our wills and passions, and our wills and passions make excellent firewood.

If we use fire as our metaphor for regrowth, for our own personal metamorphosis, and if we use it consciously, we need not be afraid of it. It may burn through our lives—it does love to do that—but we will still be here when the fire has burned out, and though our lives will have changed, perhaps almost beyond recognition, they will still be our lives. All the crucial elements will be there. Not only will we still be ourselves, we will be more truly ourselves. The fires of transformation are not the fires of hell.

I speak out of my own experience and knowledge. I have walked through fire transformation several times and belong to a goddess who lives in fire.

Once, a long, long time ago, on the feast of Imbolc, sacred to the goddess Brigid, the goddess of the smiths, the poets, and the healers, I stood in the center of hundreds of my people and put my hands toward the Brigid fire, where it burned in the center of a cauldron filled with water, and said "yours." Since then I have belonged to this goddess of fire and water, and though I am grateful for the holy well, sustaining as it is for poets and healers, it is the smith's fire that has forged the most dramatic changes in my life.

If we want quiet conversions, we can give ourselves to the earth, which will hold us in its darkness and allow us to change slowly, slowly, slowly, or to the water, which will rock us through our changes. If we want intellectual shifts, we can give ourselves to air, and when our education changes our minds, we can watch our lives change in response. If we want easy transformations—well, I don't know that any transformation is easy, alas—we can certainly ask spirit to send us an easy change, a mellow cleansing, a sweet and subtle revision of our souls. And maybe that will work, as long as we are willing to actually change. If we are asking for an easy change because we want, really and truly, to get out of having to change at all, that will not, in the long run, work. Nope. But we can ask for easy and gentle change, if we believe that is what we can handle.

I don't find fire transformations easy. But I love them. And I trust them.

That's the key to fire transformation: trust in the process. Trust in the immense forces of love and power that hold us and give us the spiritual boundaries that we need to be safe while our lives become, at the very least, uncomfortable. Trust in whatever deities or ideas or higher selves we believe in, which guide us. Trust in ourselves, and that if we are led to throw ourselves into changing, it is for good reasons. Trust in the outcome, whatever it might be.

Trust is crucial to fire changes, simply because fire is so unknowable, unpredictable. Where it might go, what it might do, we cannot know. We have some ideas, perhaps, but we are, essentially, at its mercy once it gets started. When we choose fire as our metaphoric catalyst, as the magical element to which we give allegiance, we know that we choose mystery, and we have chosen to trust that the forces of love and power are working to our good, even if the process is sometimes scary.

I don't work with fire for little changes—the getting-in-shape changes, the figuring-out-how-to-get-things-done changes, the going-back-to-school changes. I wield it for the changes that require burning down the forest of my life as I know it, so that the new growth can appear.

Getting sober was that sort of transformation. There was no aspect of my life that had not been touched by my drinking. All of my previous life had to change; much of it is now entirely gone, but not all of it. Though many of the friends I had are no longer my friends, some are. Though I am not the person I was when I was drinking, the essence of me—my loves, my dislikes, my character, my humor—is still the same. The new forest is not the old one. But it is clearly an outgrowth of seeds that came from the old trees. It is, believe me, not only a healthier forest, a kinder and less annoying one, but a much more entertaining one.

In the decades since becoming sober I have been through other fire changes, and lately I have been going through yet another, moving into the last third of my life. For this change, not only did I walk away from full-time mothering, as is only right, really, when your child grows up and starts his adult life, but I walked away from my profession and moved across the country. Just attempting to re-root in the new home didn't work. I'd been stuck. So I realized it was time to once again burn away the underbrush and start over. Given how long fire transformations last before another one becomes necessary, this may well be my last one this life around.

Besides being dramatic and often painful, fire transformations can be scary. They can also be dangerous since they involve such sweeping changes. That's why we are smart to bring all our tools and all our consciousness to them. Otherwise we can get lost in our fire stories. Or they burn only halfway and leave us undone. Or we can come out of them having lost what should have been kept.

I have advice, a litany of what I do to move through fire changes successfully, by which I mean sanely and healthily:

The first thing is to notice that change is needed. This is harder than it might seem. It can take a while before the daily accumulation of small annoyances becomes a large enough pile to really be in the way.

But there's a moment when we are able to notice that we are in the wrong place or with the wrong people or doing the wrong things. Life doesn't fit anymore. It used to, probably. But the old structures need to be torn down and something new built. Luckily, there will be a lot of material from the old structures that can be reused! We won't know what those materials are, though, until we get them out of their current form. The entire job, when the fire transformation starts, is simply to understand that the transformation is necessary.

Then, we have to be willing to change. This is also difficult. Indeed, even after we know very well that it is time for a major change in our lives, we are likely to put off making it. Perhaps, we think, it will not really be necessary to change at all. Or maybe it will cost too much, emotionally, physically, spiritually. It might be too difficult. Also, it is highly likely that our best beloveds are not going to be happy about our giant transformation. It takes a lot of courage simply to come to the point where we are willing to change. Kindness is useful here. We are so very human. We get to be scared. Our courage lies in our willingness to move into a new life anyway.

If we decide we need to change, and we discover that we are willing to do it, and we want to work with fire, we need next to choose our fire imagery carefully. Are we using fire to burn out the excess undergrowth in our forests so that new growth can sprout? Are we using fire in a forge so that we are swords being forged by the Goddess through fire and water, our edges honed to a new usefulness? Are we using fire to create alchemical reactions, burning off our dross in the alchemist's chalice until we are clean, pure gold? Any of these will work, but how we react to them emotionally will be different for us all. Let us pick the fire metaphors that energize us, that can sustain us through what may be a long process.

When we have our fire metaphor clear, we can create rituals to empower our journey and mark our commitment to the process. Such a ritual needn't be a giant public one like my pledge to Brigid at the Imbolc feast. We might want a smaller audience. We might need for it to be entirely private. Whether we are alone or with others, it's best if there is an actual fire, a bonfire outside, a fire in the fireplace inside, even a candle. We can prepare our sacred space, we can invoke our beloved deities, we can stare into the fire until we are ready, and then we can hold our hands out, palms up, to the fire and make our promise. Fire will take us at our word, so let us choose our words carefully. We are promising to change, and we give ourselves over to the element of fire to help us do that.

We also have to be willing to do whatever the process demands of us. Once we know we are about to change, and we have agreed with ourselves that we'll do it, we will still, oh, humans that we are, try to figure out any way we can to make it easier, or smaller, or less obvious, or, or, or... But just as the new world is unknown, what will happen on our journey to it is unknown. It's not that we have no control over the process—there is much we can do in keeping our humor, being kind to ourselves and others, getting advice, learning all we can, practicing our meditations, making sure we get enough sleep and healthy food and exercise—but when we have chosen to walk through fire to transform, we of necessity cannot know what, exactly, will be happening, and where we will need to go, and what we must do. It's easier if we don't try to make deals with the process. If this is a process of health, if we are moving into sanity and joy and deeper connection with our world in all its glory, we can trust it. Going through it with the commitment to do whatever needs to get done makes the transformation much easier in the long run.

We can help ourselves by intelligently using the time of year or the cycles of our lives. Solomon tells us that "to every thing there is a season, and a time to every purpose under the heavens," and though that is true enough, it is also true that we can help feed our transformations by harnessing the energy inherent in cycles. I will often work with the winter when I need to move through some smaller change, allowing the Wheel of the Year to pull me down into the dark, where I can do my deep work, and then pull me out again in the spring, into which I carry what I have found or built or recovered in the dark of the year and my shadow self.

On a much larger scale, cycles such as our Saturn return can be very profitably paired with major transformations. They happen when we are around twenty-nine and again when we are around fifty-eight when Saturn, planet of limitations and boundaries, comes back to where it was when we were born. When it does, we come up against our own deep boundaries, fears, secrets; whatever it is that we are not dealing with, we meet outright. I got sober in my first Saturn return. I left a marriage, and eventually an entire life, in my second.

Believe me, though; what we need to know will be given to us, and we will find the tools we require. Believing in this helps because it makes us feel better, but it is also true. Sometimes this is presented as the saying "God never gives us more than we can handle," but that of course is a lie. Someday we are all going to die, which will very obviously mark a point when we were given more than we could handle. No, no. Life is very often more than we can handle. There are wars, there are deaths of loved ones, there are major illnesses, there are complete breakdowns. Eventually we will be leaving life altogether.

But though we will all meet things we cannot handle, what we are given, constantly and completely and truthfully, are tools to get us— moment by moment—through our lives until those lives end. Some of those tools we have with us before we walk into the fire. Some we gather along the way. Others will come to us in dreams or books or be told to us by friends and strangers, some will be overheard on the bus or be read in the signs of birds and leaves and clouds, some will be given to us by our spirit friends and guides. The tools are infinite, and they are constantly available. We are not without resources. If we miss anything when it is given to us, it will come back to us, perhaps in a different form, but it will come back. We will be given what we need to transform and change. That is simply the deep truth of the universe.

It is also a very good idea to get help. All the tools we need are available; we are not alone in this. Getting help from other humans is useful because it can shake us out of our usual stories about ourselves and what is happening to us. We need reliable outside voices. They might be in the form of spiritual counselors: a priestess, a shaman, a priest. Or therapists. Or self-help groups. Or our families and friends, if indeed our families and friends are part of our sanity. How do we know that these humans are reliable? Because they have what we want; they are in the place we believe we are moving toward. Because they do not harm us; they do not make us smaller, they do not abuse us. And if we find that they are not reliable, we find help elsewhere.

Then, we do what we need to do. We just walk through the fire. We move through the dark of the year one day at a time. We move through our Saturn returns one day at a time. We listen to trustworthy humans one day at a time. We practice our new tools one day at a time. We just keep walking. We don't know how long the transformation will take, and we don't know how painful or joyful or scary or hilarious it will be, but we do know that at some point it will be over, and things will be different. We keep walking.

Also, we assume that we will make mistakes. If we confuse making mistakes with being on the wrong path, we will be stuck forever and unable to find our way. We are going to get things wrong sometimes, even when we are on the right path. How could we not, when we are learning a new life, when we are walking a road we've never seen? It's best if we make it part of the journey. We are people who get things wrong sometimes. We are human.

Since we are making mistakes, we need to apologize when it's appropriate. We need some method to get through the mistakes and learn from them. Here is my method: we figure out what we ourselves did that we do not want to do again, ignoring what anybody else did; that's not our issue. We figure out what we need to change in our lives in order not to make that mistake again. We figure out if we have harmed anyone else in the making of that mistake. Then we say, to that human, if we can, without causing them further harm, that we are very sorry and that we will not be doing that again. And if we owe other amends—money, for instance, or goods or an announcement in the newspaper—we make those amends. Then we walk on, and we don't do that again. On the other hand, it's also important that we not apologize when we have not actually done harm. When we go through major changes, our friends and family are sometimes upset. That's okay. We don't owe amends for other people's feelings, just what we ourselves have done.

Next, when it comes up, we let go of people, places, and things that do not belong in our new lives. It is impossible to transform one's life without losing something; it is the nature of all existence that what exists leaves. Sometimes the loss will be grievous indeed. Relationships will be shattered. Beloved objects will disappear. Entire cities will be left behind. This was inevitable. We knew it. That's why we didn't want to come here. That's why, back at the beginning, we were trying to keep from changing. But this is the path. Let it go. Let it all go. It's good practice for the time when, at the end of our life stories, we let everything go. It is the nature of life itself. Things come into existence and disappear continually, continually. Let them go and walk on.

On the other hand, let it hurt, and mourn what has gone. Whoever and whatever we wore out or didn't need anymore or didn't love anymore or couldn't be with because that was too dangerous, it once had a purpose, and its place in our life is empty. Whatever we have lost was also ourselves, some integral piece of our beings. It's gone, it's all gone. I remember when my child was growing, I was always enchanted with the new person he became but was grieved for the loss of the earlier being. The toddler was adorably gorgeous and dreadful, but in acquiring him I lost the darling infant, who was then gone, lost to time. The depths of our sorrow for what is gone marks the depths of our love. It's an honor to mourn for what is gone. Also, if we don't mourn, if we don't mark our losses, we get very ill.

It's not all about loss, though. Hurrah! Not everything disappeared! Something remains. At the end of our fire transformations—of all our transformations—we come into a place that is recognizable, even when we have never seen it before. We knew it. We always knew it. Here we are. We are still ourselves. Indeed, if this was a true transformation, we have become more ourselves even than before. Besides, not all will be lost. There will be people, there will be souvenirs, there will be ideas and hobbies that remain. And there will be all the spirits who walked with us through the entire journey.

Finally, walk on. This wasn't the first transformation any of us went through, and it won't be the last. If we are lucky, we will get a little rest. Then we will do it all again.

Looking back on my list, I see that this is the advice I give, and the practice I follow, for getting through all of life, not just major transformations. It is my daily practice, writ large.

Well, then, I stand by it. Surely what gets us sanely and consciously through our days is what will get us sanely and consciously through our years. There is no life without transformation. Let us make the most of it. Let us enjoy it.

Practice: Flame Gazing
Seraphina Capranos

Time: 5 minutes or as long as you wish

You will need: a candle and a candle holder

• • •

It is recommended to remove eyeglasses or contact lenses. Make the room dark or dimly lit.

Think about the time when you last gazed upon the full moon—a bright, glowing orb, full of life, mystery, and brilliance. When the human eye gazes at a point of light, we are held in a moment. Distractions melt away, and our energy and attention become focused. Gazing into a flame is a great practice to center oneself. Using the power of fire can ignite your intent.

Some say that candles were brought to us from the ancient Egyptians, who began dipping papyrus wicks into animal fat. Candles have had a place in spiritual and religious traditions for ages. We light them for a blessing, after a tragedy, for vigil, and in ritual. They shift the energy in a room by focusing it. We call upon the spirit of the honeybee when using beeswax candles. It is not necessary to use beeswax; you can also use ethical soy candles or another vegetable-based candle. I do recommend using candles that are unscented and environmentally friendly, which means avoiding petroleum (paraffin) candles, as they release toxic chemicals when inhaled—even if you don't smell it.

Fire magic has been around for as long as humans have been engaging with this element. Gazing into a fire, whether a campfire, wood stove, fireplace, or candle, is hypnotic and can quickly move us into a state of trance. Being in a room lit by candles regulates the nervous system, coaxing us into a delicious state of relaxation. And when we are relaxed, we are open. When we are open yet focused, as in candle gazing, we are available to feed our intentions and magic.

. . .

Take some time to read through this practice and its purpose before beginning.

Sit or stand comfortably.

Light a candle and place it approximately two arms' lengths away from you on a table at eye level so your posture can be upright. Center yourself by aligning your body along its center of gravity. Breathe from your center—from your diaphragm and belly. Feel energy flow up from the earth and into you. Simultaneously, be aware of your body and allow it to relax. Come fully present with yourself in this moment.

Close your eyes and allow yourself to breathe five to seven easy breaths. This will allow your breath to find its natural flow.

Then allow your eyes to settle on the flame. Keep your vision focused and steady on the flame without blinking for as long as it is comfortable for you. Only blink as necessary.

Take in the different textures and layers of the flame. This is a practice of focusing energy. Keep your gaze anchored on some part of the flame rather than the candle or wick. I like to gaze into the heart of the flame. Breathe evenly and deeply.

When you feel complete, close your eyes. You may be able to still see the flame in your mind's eye. Take this image into you, allowing the magic of the flame to ignite your intent.

When the image begins to fade out completely, bring your awareness back to your breath.

Open your eyes and either repeat this practice one or two more times or give thanks, extinguish the flame, and draw this session to a close.

Spell: Candle Spell
THIBAUT LAURE

Time: 30 minutes or the length of time it takes your
candle to burn through

You will need: a black candle for purification, a white
candle for blessings, a receptacle to put the candles
in, salt, lavender and rosemary oils, and a tool to
engrave the candle such as an athame, pin, or knife

• • •

Candle spells are old; we've been using them since we have had candles. They can be very simple or very elaborate, but in the end they are all rooted in the same principles. A candle is charged with an intention, anointed with oils and herbs that support this intention, and then lit as you visualize your spell coming true. Candle spells are a combination of desire, need, intention, and will.

This spell is made to remove obstacles and energies that prevent us from doing our work in the world and opening the way, and ourselves, for blessings and the right energy to come in. It is composed of two parts, a cleansing and a blessing. They can be done one after the other or separately, as the need arises.

In addition to the candle or candles, you will need rosemary and lavender oils. Rosemary has many uses in magic: healing, protection, purification, love, stress relief, and mental clarity. Lavender is similarly a very powerful herb with many magical properties: love, psychic knowledge, healing, purification, and facilitating dreams. Here we will be working with them for their powers of purification, protection, and healing. They complement each other, but the spell will work just as well if you only have one of them.

• • •

The first part of the spell is purification and cleansing. The goal is to gather the stuck negative energies, the things that stop us from being ourselves. A black candle is used, as black is the color of absorption. No light nor energy is reflected from a black surface, which instead absorbs light. The candle will be put in salt, another purifying element, to ensure whatever is left of the candle at the end of the spell will not interfere with anything else.

The first step is to anoint the candle with the rosemary and lavender oils. Rub the candle with the oil from the bottom to the top. Before anointing it, you may also engrave the candle with the names of the things you want to cleanse. Once the candle is ready, place it in the receptacle with the salt around its base.

Light the candle and concentrate on the flame with a soft gaze. Visualize the things you want cleansed, removed, and purified. Feel the energy gather as it becomes absorbed into the candle, transformed and purified by the flame. Let the candle burn through to its end and the spell run to completion. You will either need to have a very secure container to allow for this and not leave the house for several hours or it will need to be a quick-burning small candle. If there is any wax remaining, bury it in the earth or keep it for use in another spell. Please ensure, therefore, that you buy beeswax or soy-based candles, not paraffin wax.

The second part of the spell is the blessing to bring positive energy to take the place of what was removed. This also can be done on its own to bring a blessing or positive energy. A white candle is used, as white contains all colors and is considered the color of possibility, truth, and reflection.

The first step is the same: anoint the candle and charge it with your intention and the things you want to bring into your life. Engrave the candle if you wish to and rub the oil from top to bottom.

Light the candle and feel your intention being sent into the universe as the flame burns. Let yourself be open and invite these energies in; visualize them gathering in the flame and being reflected by the candle all around you and within you.

Let the candle burn completely.

Sharing Power

COPPER PERSEPHONE

* * *

Power. Just hearing the word can trigger a whole series of cascading feelings. I think of power as energy. With fire, for example, the energy is a neutral source that can be destructive or, properly channeled, a source of warmth and inspiration. Energy in witchcraft can be focused and built in many ways and with many outcomes. Energy and power are present in our rituals, in our relationships with each other and with the world, in our life force, our magic, and our sexuality. When examining power in Reclaiming, we often work with ecosystems, starting with the individual and then spiraling outwards. Every part of an ecosystem, as well as all of its interactions and impacts, are understood as a whole. Each individual connects to other individuals, other animals, plants, and Mysterious Ones. Each group is impacted by many dynamics. These include each person's power and connections with other individuals, as well as leadership practices within groups, community, and larger ecosystems.

One way to frame thoughts on power and power balances is to think of different sorts of power that we experience. We adopt the model of examining three types of power: power-from-within, power-over, and power-with. Power-from-within is the intrinsic, inborn power that each one of us has just by existing. It can become the grounded sense of our abilities to take action in the world. Focusing on power-from-within can assist us to hold power in a balanced way that recognizes our own needs and desires, as well as the needs and desires of others. In this state we are able to recognize individual differences and respect others' points of view, even when we disagree. We connect to energy sources and channel power in a way that works toward the well-being of ourselves and others. Ideally, this energy is not just our own but energy drawn from other sources; for example, grounding into the earth and becoming a conduit for that life force that comes up from the earth.

Power-over is imbedded in systems where specific people have the ability to make decisions that control others. Power-over can describe the misuse of power, channeling power for our own gain to manipulate or dominate others and to exploit resources in a way that harms other people and the environment and pulls systems out of balance. We see the impact of using power to dominate others in the state of our communities, in a patriarchal political system that favors the wealthy, and in the current exploitation of our environment. The Reclaiming Principles of Unity state: "We work for all forms of justice: environmental, social, political, racial, gender, and economic. Our feminism includes a radical analysis of power, seeing all systems of oppression as interrelated, rooted in structures of domination and control." We are called on to change these systems by changing the way we hold power in the world.

One option is to begin to reframe how we connect to others. *Power-with* is a concept that holds shared power as a goal and ideal. We look to power-with to help us find common ground between different points of view and build collective strength. Based on mutual support, solidarity, and collaboration, power-with expands the skills and knowledge of individuals to form a collective skill base that is bigger than the sum of its parts. Power-with values the wisdom of the group while still honoring individual gifts, skills, and experience.

To support our work within the community and with others, it is important to participate in our own personal work. Engaging power-from-within, the essential power each of us is born with, we do the hard work of personal healing and development. One aspect of healing is addressing the wounding many of us have around our bodies and sexuality. The dominant culture is committed to controlling our connection to sensuality and sex through shame and commodification. But sex is one of our birthrights. It is a call to life-affirming growth and to conscious connection with the life force.

Pleasures of the body and in the body are one of the ways we experience ecstatic connection to spirit. We have been told that only people who look a certain way, are a certain age, or who are in certain kinds of relationships have the right to sexual pleasure and power. We are discouraged from talking frankly about sex, the emotional and spiritual aspects of sexuality, and the impact of working with sexual energy. It is critical to our personal growth and to developing our skills as witches that we reclaim our own connection to life force and find balance and connection to power-from-within. In addition, sex can be a powerful source of energy for spellwork and ecstatic connection with spirit.

This work is one of my passions, in part because it saved my life. Following the suicide of my brother, I went through a deep depression and spiritual fragmentation. I felt as though my connection to sex and life force had been cut off. I went from having a strong sex drive, which was sometimes challenging to manage ethically and appropriately, to feeling almost no sexual or sensual pleasure. I walked through the world in a fog, feeling an invisible boundary cutting me off from any sensual pleasure or hope, and I struggled with thoughts of suicide myself, feeling the pull to join my brother. It was through connecting with Reclaiming and reconnecting with my own sexual power and life force that I was able to emerge from that descent, not in spite of but because of my experience. As I opened to spirit, I felt my whole self come alive again. Thoughts of my death fell away. Like a dampened fire that had been fed fuel, sensuality and sexual energy began moving through my body. Flames of ecstatic life force rose up, overwhelming and all consuming. Learning to honor and channel that magic ethically and with joy has been one of my primary spiritual practices and the foundation of my work as a priestess.

One aspect of engaging sacred sexuality is claiming our ability to experience desire, sensual and sexual pleasure. When we do this, we connect to our life force and learn to make nuanced distinctions between those experiences. We can be so touch starved that a sensual experience, as simple as having someone touch our arm or hug us, can elicit deep feelings that are actually full-body sensual pleasure that doesn't have to build to sexual response. Cultivating a connection to sensual experience is core to resisting the dulling of our lives that our industrialized world seems intent on. Good, compliant workers are not distracted by the scent of jasmine on the wind, the feeling of rain against our skin, or the cascading series of flavors and textures as we slowly chew a dripping slice of mango. Connecting to sensual energy is an act of rebellion. To come alive and aware—to come awake—is a radical act in this culture.

Central to increasing our sense of aliveness is connecting to desire. Desire is a powerful and mysterious force, often aroused by a mixture of multisensory triggers including smell, taste, touch, and images. Desire is the honoring of beauty and the strong impulse or longing to connect more deeply with the person, place, or entity that is inspiring us. One core practice is to connect to ourselves; to honor our own beauty as we would that of any other beloved. We can become familiar with desire as an energy source in and of itself, even if the desire is not fulfilled. The welling up of desire can be a powerful energy that can be channeled into specific intentions in spellwork and magical activism.

Simply holding an ecstatic state is a magical act that changes everything around us. What we say and how we feel can profoundly impact the world. Ecstasy works its way through us, setting aside ego and moving us toward wild union in which the paradox of connection to self and loss of awareness of self as separate is resolved and celebrated. Dancing with this paradox, spirit takes us toward wild mystery, which heals, changes, and transforms.

Dancing with mystery is an excellent definition for sex. Although many books and classes teach sex magic and Western versions of Tantra, that body of work has often been challenging for me. Much of what has been expressed has been rooted in assumptions that sex means heterosexual sex and that there are only two genders, fixed from birth. In many modern Pagan and occult sex magic practices, there is an emphasis on fertility and polarity-based rituals with male and female constructs and the symbols of the chalice and the blade. As a queer polyamorous witch I have moved away from the concepts of male and female and work more with active and receptive energies. These can shift and change at any moment and are not tied to the body those energies are flowing through. It has been my experience that sexual energy is much wilder than generally assumed, as are gender and desire, which live on a complex multifaceted continuum. In Reclaiming there is a focus on ecstatic witchcraft, with an attendant expansion of possibilities. Lesbian, gay, bisexual and all sexualities, including asexuality, are acknowledged and honored as inherently sacred. We move beyond male and female as a necessary binary into gender continuums. We hold space for loving more than one person at a time—polyamory. The sex energy moves out of polarity and into a multi-strand network web, building many energy currents of different voltages.

In Reclaiming we often quote Dion Fortune's definition of magic: "Magic is the art of changing consciousness at will." I would add that magic is also being able to change energetic flow at will. Being able to refine and focus that wild sex energy takes practice; fortunately the homework is pleasurable. Some of that practice includes taking time in raising sexual energy. We are conditioned to move quickly toward orgasm as the conclusion of sexual acts. Working with slowing down our process, of coming close and then backing off the peak, slowing and then quickening, extends our ability to stay aware in the moment and allows us to have a more deliberate focus on a specific intention. It also makes the final raising of power in orgasm more powerful, pleasurable, and long lasting.

Channeling life force as part of a spell can include charging symbols and charms, holding an intention, and focusing that intention as the energy builds. This can be done alone or with other humans, deities, or other entities such as plant spirits. As with any magic, it is essential to do this work ethically and with the consent of all involved. It can be helpful to work with someone trained in sex magic, working collaboratively on the same intention. Communication skills become essential as we dance with these fires. Desire and sensuality can easily be confused by power dynamics that mirror the dominant paradigm. One person can have more power in the relationship and become coercive, manipulative, or abusive. Focusing on or playing with power consciously and consensually to heighten the sexual experience is a different matter and can be a powerful source of ecstatic energy. Balancing our power-from-within with awareness of other people's needs and desires being equally important to our own is critical to becoming empowered beings and witches.

Engaging awareness of our relationship to power is directly supported by another tool in Reclaiming, the Iron Pentacle. In the Iron Pentacle we find balance, calling back lost parts of ourselves including sex. Doing this practice means becoming aware of our own internal states in relation to others. Do we see ourselves as "less than" and feel shame and an inability to take action in the world? Do we see ourselves as the most important person in the room, with others there only to serve our needs and desires? In Reclaiming we sometimes refer to these states as *deflation* and *inflation* and work with identifying and coming back into our grounded and right-sized selves.

Developing as empowered beings, building our own internal balance of power, we find we do not exist in a vacuum; power is relational. One of the fallacies perpetuated by the dominant culture is the cult of individualism. We are told that we have to stand on our own two feet, take care of ourselves, and live in small nuclear families. Meanwhile, deep within us is a longing for community, for a feeling of belonging and a place where our contributions are valued. Living in community creates a system of checks and balances around our use of power. We are social animals, pulled to forming packs, connecting with others, and living within larger ecosystems of other beings, all of us in a dance of impact.

Reclaiming places a strong value on collaborative and co-created groups. In *The Empowerment Manual* Starhawk describes collaborative groups as having shared power and valuing the contributions and inherent worth of each member. Finding other witches and creating spiritual community can feel essential. Despite this longing, connection to a solid community is elusive for many people. Often we find ourselves searching for hearth clans and chosen family, covens, community ritual, activist and community groups and never quite finding our way. In addition to shared spiritual values, creating and sustaining community takes many other skills and qualities. Diana Leafe Christian in her work *Creating a Life Together* writes that forming community requires a community glue created not just from meetings or rituals but also from cooking and eating meals together, going on fun excursions, and having long, intimate conversations. So where do we begin? How do we connect or start a group that meets all these needs?

I have been part of starting Reclaiming communities in two different locations as well as being connected into many other communities. Over the years, I have found some key components that are helpful to supporting the sustainability of a community. Members who have diverse skills and complimentary abilities bring a vibrancy and growth. This works especially well when there are shared values around communication, personal growth, and love and support for each other. Clear and transparent organizational policies ideally outline how people become a part of and leave the group, how decisions are made, and how community input and feedback are incorporated. This helps build a foundation based on clarity and trust.

So how do we connect and begin to find community? Many people have attended a class in person or online and successfully created a coven out of that initial group. If there are no classes in your area, there are a number of Reclaiming teachers who travel to different communities to teach and help mentor fledgling communities. Others have attended a retreat or a WitchCamp and found their home group that way. Maybe we are inspired to start a regular ritual group, such as a full moon group, and see who comes. Many have said that they could not have dreamed of where they would end up when they started searching for what has become their community.

Starting community can be as simple as forming a circle or coven— a group that meets to make magic together. A useful structure to consider is to set systems in place that support shared power, with rotation of leadership. Having a system where people take turns, possibly in pairs, to lead or plan rituals can help everybody strengthen skills, and it also creates a non-hierarchical group with shared power. Or you might choose to create a group that offers seasonal sabbat rituals to the general public, composed of volunteers who make multi-year commitments, cycle off in rotation, and mentor new people. Generally there is a consensus process to have people become part of a group, and there may be requirements, such as having taken certain classes. Groups usually meet regularly, once a month or so; engage in other activities like potluck shared meals, social action, or service; and sometimes have retreats that help strengthen the intimacy and depth of the group and the work.

Power. Energy. Ecstasy of spirit in a supportive community. When we are self-examining and actively working with our own power, we become able to engage with community from our right-sized selves. As we reclaim the wild, ecstatic parts of ourselves that have been suppressed by the dominant culture, we can bring our whole authentic, joyful self to the community, enriching and fertilizing it. Those communities connect to other communities, challenging the existing structures of power-over. The fires burn bright, lighting flares of hope— one individual to another and one community to another—becoming beacons of connection.

Ritual: Creating a Wand with the Spark of Life
Preston Coyote Vargas

Time: 1 hour or more; choose a time when the
correspondences—lunar, day, or astrological—align
with your intention for this wand

You will need: wand materials; candles—one each of
black, white, and red; sage, cedar, and dragon's
blood resin, which you can obtain at occult or
metaphysical stores; censer or plate with charcoal
briquette; a lighter or matches

* * *

This ritual is about magically and energetically preparing the different
pieces that will become part of your wand prior to the physical making of the wand. If you also plan to construct the wand during the ritual, allow more time and ensure you have the necessary tools and
materials to do this.

A wand is meant to conduct power, energy, and magic via the precision of one's will. Yet some wands are more an aesthetically pleasing
ornament and less a magical tool. This happens when a wand is not
attuned to itself, when it has no spark of life. Most wand makers use
their intuition to collect an assortment of relics—wood, crystals, horns,
feathers, and metals that will work together as a power conductor.
Some wand makers go into meditation or trance to ask the assortment
of relics if they are in consensus about working with each other. This is
a wonderful beginning. However, it is just the beginning.

It is the witch's role to explain to the assortment of relics that they
will be doing more than just working with each other. They will be
fusing with one another, relinquishing their old existences so that
together they become more than the sum of their parts. It is the
witch's role to facilitate this alchemical process.

Sometimes the simple tree branch wand is so powerful because it knows who it is and what it is meant to do. The lifeless ornate wand is discombobulated and cannot reconcile its often conflicting energy patterns. Wands have a systemic intelligence. Every particle of matter is intelligent. All systems are intelligent. The tree is a complex intelligence that takes in the photons of the sun, the carbon dioxide of air, the water, and the nutrients of earth and moves those through its body as the spark of life. The simple tree branch wand still retains the energetic imprint, the intelligence, of the tree's spark of life. Each part of the would-be wand retains the spark of its existence.

Stone and metal retain their imprints of forming and existing under immense heat and pressure. A shell retains imprints of its existence as a mollusk on the sea floor. The impala horn carries its existence in the savanna as a prolific herding mammal. The molted feathers carry their existence of being a clowning and problem-solving parrot of the jungle. Each of these intelligences is a spark of life. They are the deep-running fires. As such, each is an energetic matrix eons old, residing in the relics at hand. Yet these matrices are flexible and readily malleable to the will of the witch. The witch can bend and weave together the fires within the stone, branch, and bone so that a new matrix evolves. *Thou creature of art.*

• • •

Perform this ritual in consecrated space, be that your circle, a crossroads, or a temple.

Place a black candle to the left of your workspace. Light this candle and invoke the below spirit world of fauna, flora, minerals, elementals, and the deep realms in the earth.

Place a white candle to the right of your workspace. Light this candle and invoke the above spirit world of ancestors, deities, guides, devas, and the high celestial realms.

Place a red candle far in front of you to create the apex of a triangle. Light this candle and invoke the middle plane of physical manifestation, the conscious, everyday world where you will be fire-weaving the evolution of this wand into being.

Burn a mixture of sage, cedar, and dragon's blood in your plate or censer in the center of the triangle. Sage will open the way, cedar will clear away energy patterns no longer needed, and dragon's blood will empower the energetic patterns you create.

Visualize this triangle of flame as a volcano rising and erupting from the ground. It is an alchemical crucible. Physically scoop up the light of the candles and bathe your arms and hands. Sense them dripping with magma and wreathed in flames. Swirl your hands through the smoke of the volcano.

Start with one of the pieces of the would-be wand you feel to be consenting. To find out if the piece consents might look like picking up the piece and breathing or sensing into it and asking whether or not it would like to be a part of the wand. You will likely feel an agreement or disagreement response. If something does not respond or disagrees, do not work with it. Place it to one side.

Place the consenting piece in the center of the triangle. Thank and honor the plant, animal, or mineral that has offered this piece. Let it show you how it was born, lived, and died. As it does so, use your flaming hands to untie, unbraid, and unweave the ends of its energetic matrix. Explain to the piece its new role as part of a greater whole. Listen to what this piece tells you of its own abilities and powers.

When this process feels complete, place the second piece into the center to join the first piece and repeat this process. Remember to weave some of the now-loose strands of these energy matrices together. Continue to do this with all of the consenting pieces of the would-be wand. Allow any messages to come forth, and remain open to the creativity of this newly woven intelligence.

When you feel this process is complete, visualize the volcano going dormant and sinking back into the ground. Thank the beings invoked at the red, white, and black candles and extinguish them respectively.

At this point, you might choose to complete the construction of your wand by physically affixing these relics together, or else you might leave that until another time. Jewelry adhesives and waterproof epoxies work well. However, if you decide to use leather or metal wire to affix your wand, remember to incorporate these materials into the energetic matrix of your wand.

Wrap the wand and allow it to rest.

Release the circle or sacred space if you cast it.

Practice: Expanding Your Senses
JENNIFER BYERS

Time: 1 hour or more

You will need: fire as a candle flame or sunlight

• • •

The elements are powerful allies in reminding us that we are not separate from nature. This magical exercise seeks to deepen our honoring and understanding of fire, asking it to help open our animal senses. As an ally, fire can enhance our perception with its unique flavors, including inspiration, creativity, passion, anger, and lust. These are powerful attributes for artists, lovers, warriors, organizers, and witches. It is important to set boundaries with this magic so that we do no harm to ourselves or others while in altered states. Part of being in right relationship with fire is practicing fire safety and using adequate sun protection.

• • •

Prepare an area for your experience so that you can be physically comfortable and uninterrupted.

To feed this fire working, you may choose to face south if you are in the northern hemisphere or north if you are in the southern hemisphere. You might wear fiery colors or jewelry; you might include fire-related tools in your working or build a fire altar. Note that working with fire can impact your sense of temperature, so drinking water and wearing layers can be helpful.

First, ground yourself. Remembering safety and sun smartness, light your candle or other fire source or position yourself in sunlight.

Begin by offering gratitude to fire for its sustaining gifts, perhaps offering a gift in return. With humility, invite the element of fire to be your ally. Let your invitation be heartfelt, and ask that fire hear and hold your boundaries. Be clear and specific.

Attend with your whole being, making space for a response.

If fire consents to join you, you can:

- Focus on the smell of burning or sunlight warming. Let your other senses fall away for now. Smell this moment and its heat. Draw air in through your nose, and invite the fragrance of your fire memories. Begin to breathe light out of your nose.

- Now breathe that light out of your mouth. What is its flavor? Focus on the taste of fire. Let your taste buds blossom in response, opening like cups to allow you to drink more fully. Taste your lips with fire on them.

- Feel your lips against your tongue as you taste them. Notice the warmth of your own mouth. Expand that noticing to all of your skin. Slowly breathe your pores open, like blossoms responding to a gentle sun. Listen to your body's needs as you explore levels of touch and feeling.

- Now move that listening outside of yourself. Hear with more than your ears and sense into what is beyond physical sounds. Catch the songs of color or temperature. Let messages come without judgment.

- Close your eyes and relax them. Behind your closed lids, imagine a gentle light dialing open photoreceptor cells. Feel it coaxing open your mind's eye. Invite the illumination of truth into your vision, and spend time seeing with your eyes closed.

Allow yourself time to be in this state, with all of your senses expanded. You may choose to let your senses play, experiencing food, music, art, or self-pleasuring. If you choose to open your eyes, do so slowly and carefully as you return to your usual state of awareness.

Whatever time you spend with fire, be sure to practice good magical hygiene to close. Finish by giving gratitude to fire for its support. Go through your senses one by one, thanking fire for its connection to that sense. Reground yourself and quench any physical fire or get out of the sun.

If you still feel ungrounded, drink water, eat grounding foods, or take a cool shower or bath.

WATER

. . .

Water is life. Life on this planet formed in water and is sustained by water. So much of life is made up of water. Water is used in blessings, cleansings, and rituals across religions and cultures. Although so essential to every moment of life, water is not always free and not always clean and safe to drink. Water pollution, both on land and at sea, is a major ecological issue. Access to clean drinking water is something that divides the rich from the poor in this world.

Water covers much of our planet's surface. Water is an everyday part of life—we turn a tap and water gushes out, or we walk miles to a well, or we harvest it from our roofs and gutters, or in a dam or reservoir, we build aqueducts or pipelines to transport it from one place to another, we pray for rain, we dance for it, we cup it in our hands, we drink it, bathe in it, play in it.

Water as an element can be hard to pin down, and this is its very nature. Lower the temperature enough and the liquid becomes a solid, ice. Heat it enough and the liquid becomes a gas, water vapor. Magically, water is associated with similarly amorphous shifting things—the emotions, dreams, trance. Water is understood as being in flow, a flux, in transition, emergent; not fixed, definite, or exact. We often work with containers for water, with chalices, cups, cauldrons, seeking some way to contain the wateriness. These watery realms intrigue us and send us searching for structures and processes to contain and navigate them—ways to understand ourselves and our emotions, to find meaning in our dreams, and to create ways to enter, be within, and leave trance states.

When we work with water, shadow begins to stir itself. There is a surface to water and then there are the depths. Within each one of us we find previously undiscovered realms, capacities, and powers: to create magic, to heal and know ourselves, and to meet parts of our lives and personality we may usually ignore and deny. Within our culture, our political, education, and other social systems, there may be the bright surface of democracy and egalitarianism, but looking deeper we discover the inequities, the flaws, the assumptions, the unjust designs. The Iron Pentacle, worked with in both Feri and Reclaiming traditions, seeks to take on some of these challenges, both personal and cultural, and transform them into medicine.

Just as water has such permeable and changeable boundaries, in water magic we find the flux and flow between things. Seeking to heal others, we must first heal ourselves; we cannot hold ourselves separate from the process, be it healing or any other magic. Our commitment to changing and being changed—to being in the crucible or cauldron of magic—is highlighted in elemental water work. When the elements are worked in the order of earth, air, fire, and water, water becomes the preparation for spirit, the fifth element. We have become progressively more mutable, moving from body to breath to spark to the subtle changing body of water into spirit. Our magic has had to shift and change with the elements, and here we meet the power *to dare*. We dare to dive deep into the wells of our souls, of who we are, of where we have come from, and—perhaps—of why we are here.

The elements are sacred. Water is sacred.

Water Is Sacred

Rose May Dance

• • •

This is an interview between Gede and Rose conducted over several months in 2017.

GP: In Reclaiming we make a link between water and our emotions. How do you personally relate to the element of water?

RMD: I'm a double Pisces and I'm very watery. I feel I'm really changeable, very emotional; I can tighten up and turn it off, but I have control over my feelings after all these years. I find water sensually so wonderful, down my throat, when looking at it, or when my feet are in it, or in the bath or shower. I really love the element of water. Easeful. Very intuitive.

GP: What does control over one's feelings mean to you?

RMD: When I said control emotions, that was a misspeak. I don't know how to control my emotions. I don't want to get so mad that I can't act or communicate. I don't want to fall so in love that I go down the drain. I don't want to get so frightened or jealous that I am immobilized. I want to work with my emotions and not get overwhelmed by them or lose my path to them. I want them to move through me appropriately. I want to be able to wield my emotions and use them to my advantage. I'm a writer; I want that to come through in my writing. I'm a healer; when I am doing healing, I don't want to think about me or somebody else who is sick, I want to think about you. When I talk about control, I mean facility.

GP: *How does facing your emotions make you a more skilled witch?*

RMD: Awareness is key to witchcraft. Having those emotions in your magical backpack gives you the material to raise the energy for what you need to do. Unless you have some real access to an emotional outflow, there is nothing of substance fueling the magic. The kind of witch I am is not a ceremonial who draws lots of little drawings on the floor and closes myself in them; I raise the magic through my emotions. The way this comes out is singing, dancing, chanting, drumming, or any of the ecstatic arts.

GP: *How do you feel this work makes a ritual deeper?*

RMD: It makes the ritual flow. It allows you to be cleansed if you are using a watery cleanser. It really lets you sing.

GP: *How does daring or to dare—as in "to know, to will, to dare, to keep silent"—relate to water?*

RMD: I asked this question of one of my teachers a long time ago. We were listing the emotions. I was not relating water with "to dare" at all. It's to dare because we are accessing the courage to face our emotions; we are daring to work with our emotions as the liquid of magic, the medium. When we can face each of the emotions—I mean the real emotions, not a false emotion like guilt—when we can truly face a real emotion and go down a list and face them, work on them, then we've found the daring to participate in the power of water.

GP: *What are some of your favorite stories and goddesses related to daring, emotions, and water?*

RMD: I love Venus rising in her half shell, so beautiful with her animals; I can see her being born from the ocean. That's love that's born from water, as we all are born from water. Selkie myths. Skeleton Woman. Fern Feldman, who I taught with for many years, who is now a rabbi, told us a Seattle-area story of a woman who fell into water and drowned. The nature of the water was such that she did not rot away, animals did not eat her, and she became the consistency of soap. She was soap woman. She surfaced from time to time, one would think bubbling from her mouth.

I very much like the rites we do in Reclaiming when we go into the ocean to bathe. At the Winter Solstice we go to renew our virginity. In the ancient sense this means that the woman belonged to no man, the woman belongs only to herself. This is something to renew. Love is a dance, if it's not a dance it doesn't work. If it doesn't go in and out and back and forth, it's no longer interesting. You don't just want to give yourself hook, line, and sinker to a lover, you want to do the back and forth dance. This is renewing.

GP: I know that in the early days of San Francisco Reclaiming, saltwater purification was a staple before almost every ritual. It seems a lot like the Feri practice of kala (see page 184).

RMD: I do feel that the saltwater meditation is a form of kala. Victor (Victor Anderson, a grandmaster of Feri tradition) taught everybody differently; Feri is an oral tradition like our own. I think that's how Starhawk received the kala information, or she may have juiced it up herself and added salt. I feel like kala, when it doesn't involve salt, is very similar to salt water and the great benefit is you can drink it on down, different to salt water because you can make yourself sick. The salt is interesting because it has a pumping action, it has its own magical chemistry, it separates the molecules and creates them…

I believe there are several different ways of doing kala. I like to fill as much as I can drink into a glass of water. Then I'm purifying myself with this water, perhaps by casting or draining or sending into it something that I wish to be transformed.

That doesn't necessarily mean something bad. I've seen you do kala when you are walking into a new house; what I imagine you are doing is you are putting away being a stranger and welcoming yourself into the space.

The reason for doing kala could also be tiredness or if you really want to concentrate on something, we could make kala with everything else. And so then you've got this water and you are doing the action instead of the salt, you are doing the transforming with your mind, your voice, your eyes, and then when it's good medicine for you, you drink it down. And then you feel the way that water is inside you and you feel it begin its journey through your body—usually about a twenty minute journey. And then you say a blessing when you pee it out, and you say a blessing when you flush the toilet.

GP: *In general, how important to you are cleansing and purification?*
RMD: Very important. One of the problems with our big public rituals is cleansing and purification get short-shrifted sometimes. But in a class when I am going to be in a room with seven to twelve other people, I want to make sure that something is not going to jump out at me from another person. It's a community commitment that we will not step into circle together with each other unless we are cleansed… that it will be a safe place for us all to be. How do we make it safe? By cleansing, by boundaries, and keeping those boundaries, and earthing the power, and enlivening with our breath, but cleansing, cleansing first.

GP: *What do you mean by safe space?*
RMD: There's no such thing, but there is safer space, like safer sex. Sometimes it fails because you've got the wild-card person who's not doing what you have asked them to do or who has so much going on that they can't. You are trying to eliminate as much trouble as you can. You are doing a working or a class

and you want to not be harmed by doing that work with other people. An important cleansing thing to do is the weather report or check-in—everyone does a check-in so you know what you are dealing with this week, and then you do the saltwater purification so you know what you are purifying.

GP: *When we teach Elements of Magic, we always teach trance in water. What is trance?*

RMD: Trance, or, as some of us call it, going forth by night—though it often happens during the day—is a mixture of many things. Trance, self-hypnosis, meditation, and dreams occupy similar landscapes, utilize similar techniques. Active imagination is an essential technique. I choose this term over visualization. We do not all visualize. We may be more skilled at obtaining information in our bodies—kinesthetically—we may be clairaudient, we may have a highly developed sense of knowing, which is also called claircognizance. I say active imagination and encourage students to *pretend* that they see or hear in trance. Trance gives us that delicious experience of synesthesia, where we see with our hands and hear with our eyes. When we say *visualization* we mean being able to actively imagine, to the point of belief or knowing, that a story we perceive magically becomes real.

GP: *Why do we trance in Reclaiming?*

RMD: As a magician or a witch, why do I trance…to travel to or occupy additional realms; realms that are extra-earthly. The body is not doing much; the mind is doing a great deal. We send part of ourselves into what is known as the trance world in order to have access that is extraordinary. For example, I could have access to all my Reclaiming witch friends that had agreed to focus on a certain thing at a certain time, even though we are far apart geographically. We trance to have access to extraordinary abilities that partake of magic.

I trance to travel to, inhabit, and act in other realms. We trance to get information that we are simply not receiving by reading a book, listening to the radio, or people talking to us. There are other kinds of information that we seek where we use our psychic abilities: to change ourselves. Almost always, magic is a kind of shortcut; trance is a shortcut. We are trying to change ourselves or change something in the outside world. We will be changed by what we change; by the act of changing something else, we will change ourselves because everything is connected.

And we also trance to communicate with spirit and spirits. Not only to communicate, but to do all sorts of things.

GP: *Where does trance come from?*

RMD: In terms of trance in Reclaiming, it is greatly influenced by Starhawk's chapter on trance in *The Spiral Dance.* I practically memorized it. My training as a hypnotherapist expanded the ways I thought about trance and deeply influences how I teach trance.

Among the four pillars of Reclaiming are the human potential movement and psychology. A lot of psychologists work with hypnosis. It was very important to Freud and other fathers of psychology. It was a way to have access to very deep parts of the patient or client. Perhaps because of Starhawk studying psychology at the same time as writing *The Spiral Dance*, it was very well lined out. Trance has also always been a tool of witches and spirit workers all over this earth. Trance is popular. It's something you can do in your living room.

I was taught to always leave the same way I went in, though for those who are more advanced in the ways and worlds of trance, one can take a priestess step—a term attributed to Pomegranate Doyle—out of the labyrinth. The priestess step out of the labyrinth is moving directly out from the center in a single step or stride rather than winding back the way we came in. We can do this with trance and trance realms as well.

We slip into trance because somebody is drumming or because the evening sky is colored in a very magical and translucent way. We slip into trance when we hear someone tell us a story, but to purposely go into trance is a wonderful thing and a skill that we nurture. Sometimes it doesn't work. In trance we may work on a problem and may not solve it, but we get further along. Mary Greer, one of my first teachers, says we cycle and cycle around the same thing.

GP: Starhawk once told me that she learned a lot about what she knows of trance through training in Balinese dance. That warmed my half-Balinese heart. How do you prepare for trance?

RMD: I purify and ground and cast a circle. I call in the four elements to protect us; it helps to ease us into trance. When we purify, we can put the big things on our mind aside and trance together easefully, skillfully. It's important to clear the ground before we trance, in more ways than one.

Before trance, be well-hydrated and nourished but not sleepy from a meal. Have your journal and a pen and a snack and drink nearby. Then you may make inductions into trance. There are many ways to go into trance, and as beginners you should use a formal setup with suggestions or cautions. *The Spiral Dance* gives us rainbow inductions, floating down into trance on successive clouds colored like a rainbow, descending from red down to violet. Or we may fly to an imaginary or familiar favorite place. Always ground first and maintain a partial awareness of your grounded body.

The trance circle is called a safe space. This is true so long as you follow the protocols. If in a group or leading another person, make sure beforehand that there is adequate trust in the circle. If everyone becomes safe within her own body, that is a good beginning. Then you have power-with anyone or anything you meet in trance. When you meet a being in trance, always ask them for a name. Because you have power down here, and your magical tools, they must answer you. We shape and name things so that we may work with them in trance.

GP: *What forms of trance are traditional in Reclaiming?*

RMD: In Reclaiming we work a lot with group trance. Everybody goes to the same place and speaks aloud together what we are seeing and sensing. In this way we create or make accessible an inner landscape through evolving consensus. This is very Reclaiming. We enjoy trancing to music, and we have among our people many talented musicians who are able to create complex and simple soundscapes that aid us in our magical work.

We also like to move through real landscapes with different stations—places to pause along our way—perhaps with different tasks and happenings following a storyline. This is done while in trance. We might begin this with the drum, walking in the twilight. A priestess might tell us that every step takes us deeper. And it usually does.

GP: *I want to ask you about the roly-poly trance...*

RMD: Starhawk invited these shamans home, they were Russian. They seemed to relate to us—Reclaiming—they said they were just like us. We made a really beautiful circle. The Reclaimers did lots of wards, lots of protection, lots of ease; the shamans led us in trance.

What we understood is if we are in a star shape, with our limbs extended out, and we do a cartwheel or a roll, we are able to move through time and space. Left hand on the sky moves down to where the left foot had been, like a wheel. I have spoken to others who interpreted it differently and did barrel rolls or two-handed cartwheels, but it doesn't seem to matter. You think which way to go and you do something with your body, or you think you are doing something with your body…go into the past, back to center, and then into the future.

It works for me if there is something I am really frightened of in the future. I start and meditate a little bit, and I ask to go find some of the roots of that in the past. When I am there in the past and this is group trance, we are communicating about what we see and what we might want to change, we make a group decision, which helps us to make a wise decision because there are more heads on it. We make the changes, we come to the present and breathe, gather an insight, we go into the future to see how it played out. If there's something that was a little extreme, we fix that, and then we roll back into the present, breathe, back into the past, and adjust—and so on. When we are done, we come back into the center and integrate. That's the roly-poly trance.

GP: Wow. I remember doing that with you at the 2012 Dandelion in Oregon outside of Portland. It had a deep impact on me. What about the famous barrier trance? The well trance? (You can find this trance on page 181.)

RMD: This is something I learned in my first Elements class and I continue to teach on water day. It's a teaching tool—it teaches you how to go down into trance, and usually this is on the rainbow alternating-colored clouds. Really, you can do any induction that works, just come back the same way. After the induction you land at a place that I like to call Reclaiming Academy. You turn and face the east, and you imagine what that is through all your five senses and more, and then you turn down to the south and repeat and you get what is in the south for you personally, then to the west, then to the north.

It's a toss-up if you start in the east or the north, but if you start there, you finish there.

Then you are led to go in a direction. You are asked a question by the trance leader: *Are you going this way because it is the most beautiful, the easiest? Which is the most challenging or more challenging? I sense that there is a barrier in one of these directions you need to seek out.* You go down the path and you are noticing everything. You are led to believe that there is a barrier coming up, I don't know what that's going to be. Maybe it's a ring of briars, a cliff, a huge bear. Then you must sit and figure out how to get past this barrier. This could be harder for some than others. It's hinted to you that you might want to use your tools or call to a guide. Some people just slash the head off the bear and go ahead. Some people get stuck, and the trance leaders help them to get unstuck, putting their hands on them, asking them to breathe, asking a question that needs no answer.

After passing, you rest, and after you have rested, you sense that there is something ahead of you that is nice. You follow the trail down. I was always told you are looking for a spring, but the first spring you pass on your left, do not stop there because that's forbidden. Later I found out what this spring is.

GP: Yeah, it's the Well of Forgetfulness under the white cypress on the left after you have descended into the underworld. It comes from Orphic tradition and is recorded on tablets that were meant to aid initiates after they had died to this world.

RMD: Don't go there! Bypass that and go down to the well, the spring. You do some searching in the spring; look at what's on the surface, reach your hands in and feel inside the water—you can stick a hand or a foot down to the bottom and explore that—and from one of these areas, there's a gift for you. You ask what this is…it has to answer you. Say it's a cup: *What are you, what are you for?* The cup tells you. You find a way to take the gift in, you go back up out of the well, pass the barrier again. We are learning magical skills rapidly in this trance. We go back up and back to the circle cast in the trance. Go the other way with the directions. Come back up on the clouds.

This trance teaches about elemental power. When we come to the barrier, there might be a lot of ice in front of you; well, you call on the sun to melt it or wield fire. This might be the first time you are using your tools like this in the otherworlds, between the worlds. When you come to the well or spring, there are three levels: what is reflected on the surface, what is inside the water, what's on the bottom—deeper. This indicates different ways to analyze, helping with self-reflection. When we are given a gift from the water, we ask, *What is this? What is it for?* We are learning how to talk to spirit, how to interact with spirit. And then we are learning how to return and re-emerge the way that we came in. And this is the Reclaiming barrier trance.

GP: *What are some of the ways that water and healing link up for you?*

RMD: Drinking water is important for healing almost anything. Most medicine is made with or taken with water. When we think of someone who is really stiff, we might massage them; to me this is water, water in the body flowing the right way. Cleansing is an important part of healing; we want to cleanse out what is causing imbalance. We want to take in healing, we can take it by drinking water. There's no practitioner that will say don't drink water.

GP: *I always get people to drink a lot of water when we are doing magic and trance. I think you have to have more water in you.*

RMD: Bathing, swimming, showering are really important. And cleaning your surfaces, cleaning the table before you start making food. Your household and gardening tasks can all be made sacred with this wonderful element of water and your energy. What am I doing, what is it made of, how can I bless it? Am I doing something that has to do with earth when I am cooking, gardening? Am I doing something that has to do with air when I am breathing or I require deep breathing? Fire...am I warming something, am I energetically releasing? If you start to think about your activities to do with elements, you bless and use the elements.

Bless the elements of life. Bless them with enthusiastic good feeling. Bless the positive qualities of each element. *Oh, water, you reflect all this light, you give a home to the creatures within this gorgeous bay.* The more often we do this, the more we experience the benefits of the blessings of the elements. My teacher Uma taught me the elements love to be blessed, they respond to love. They will ally quickly with us. The more often we bless an element, the more help for our personalities and bodies. This prayerful act integrates parts of ourselves with corresponding parts of the world, the universe.

GP: Thank you so much, Rose. You are an inspiration in my life, and your contributions to our tradition are beyond detailing. Blessed be, water witch.

Trance: Place of Power
Thibaut Laure

Time: 30 minutes

You will need: a comfortable place to lie or sit while you
trance, a journal and pen, coloring things (optional);
you may choose to record the trance and play it back
to yourself

. . .

This ritual will help you find your place of power, the safe place within
you from where your magic emerges or is anchored to.

The place of power has many uses. This is a place of strength,
where you can be truly yourself. It can be a space to make magic and a
starting point for trance; a known location to start from and return to
when exploring spiritual realms. It may even be a place to retreat to in
a time of need.

. . .

Find a comfortable place where you can sit or lie down.

Set up your ritual space and create sacred space.

Ground yourself. Let your body settle and be comfortable.

Breathe slowly, relax, and start to let go of the busy mind. With
each out-breath, let go of the annoyance and worries of the day. Let
go of all the things you should do. Let the mind quieten, knowing you
will be able to pick all these things back up if you need to. Breathing in
and out, feel yourself at the center of heaven and earth, connected to
the mother below and the stars above.

On your next breath, knowing that you are safe in this space and
time, start to gather your consciousness. With each breath gather
more and more threads, letting your consciousness become a ball. Let
this ball of attention move freely and effortlessly to the center of your
being. The center may be your heart or your solar plexus, or it may be
in a completely different area. Wherever that center is, let yourself settle into it.

Once you are in this center, look around and pay attention. What do you see, hear, and smell? How does that center look? It may be a well-tended garden or it may be wild and untamed. How does this place feel to you? How do you connect to it? (If you are recording these instructions, leave a pause of three to six breaths between each question.)

Explore your place of power. Find its edges, find its center. Is there a place that attracts you especially? Take some time to really be in the space. You might find your tools, an altar, or a familiar place to do magic. You may find your place of power already has a permanent circle around it that you can just activate when you need it. If not, you may want to build one as a way to support your magic. Play with the space; explore some of its many secrets. (If you are recording these instructions, leave thirteen breaths here.)

When you are ready, take one last good look at your place of power. Remember how it feels, how it looks; remember your connection to it. This is your place for you to visit whenever you want, and you can use this memory to will yourself back at any time.

Taking a final breath in your place of power, gather your consciousness back into the ball of attention and transition back to where you concentrated it—that is, your heart, solar plexus, or other location. Feel free to gather any or all the things you left behind on your way in. Bring yourself fully back into your body; feel your muscles, your bone, your skin.

Write or draw in your journal. You may want to describe your place of power, draw a map, and record any strong feelings and thoughts. This place belongs to you, and it will evolve with you as you use it. You can also add to it. For example, I built an altar in the center and created a cave underneath for a magical working I needed to do. Feel free to experiment and play with it.

Trance: The Barrier and the Well
HEIDI MARIAN

Time: 30–45 minutes

You will need: a quiet room, a journal, a pen

• • •

In this trance we explore and overcome barriers by working with the elements. Perhaps your intention is working to better speak your truth, open your heart, or establish a relationship with a specific element or tool. This barrier trance will allow you to enlist your own power and ability to overcome obstacles and find new strength. You will need a quiet room. This trance is best done in a seated position. Make sure to ground before beginning this journey.

• • •

Take a breath and set your intention for this journey.

Breathe again and open to your heart. Feel your life force.

As you take a third breath, notice a red cloud slowly forming around your feet. The red cloud fills the space around your feet and ankles and begins to make its way up your body slowly, rising until your whole body is enveloped in this red cloud. Bring your awareness to how it feels to be in red. What does it bring up for you, and how does your body feel? This is the beginning of what we call the rainbow induction in Reclaiming.

Slowly the cloud transitions from red to orange. The orange cloud begins to take shape around your whole body, melding with the red until you are surrounded by orange. Notice what the orange brings up for you. Take a moment in orange and shift into yellow. Do this through every color of the rainbow: red, orange, yellow, green, blue, indigo, and finally violet. Make sure to take a moment in each color to observe your responses to the colors.

From violet, you find the colors have taken you into a place of power. Here you can access all of your tools of magic. Open the cross-roads in all directions—from east to west, south to north, above and below. This is akin to casting a circle, but we don't focus on the circumference so much as concentrate on the center and its relationship to directions and orientation. If the ritual and poetry of casting a circle does not work for you, perhaps opening the crossroads will. From the center we reach out into the east and feel that direction's presence and powers; we anchor them into our center. We go across the compass to the west. We repeat the process. We do this with the south and the north, and then above and below. And after all this, we hold the six directions simultaneously in the center and breathe with the power that gathers there.

In this place of power, you will explore a deeper relationship with one element. Think back to your intention and ask yourself what your greatest challenge is right now. Assign an element to this challenge. Perhaps you feel the need to work with fire to feed your work for justice in the world. Perhaps you feel challenges in accessing your emotions and you wish to work with water. Follow your intuition rather than trying to choose what might be the correct element to work with. It is important to remember that you have tools you can access in order to overcome your challenges.

Face the element you are called to work with and, in your mind's eye, walk toward it. Open to the realms of this element. Name your challenge; speak it out loud. A barrier appears before you, and you will use your tools to overcome it. Spend as much time here as you need. Once you have overcome your barrier, thank the element and move back into your place of power. If you do not overcome or remove the obstacle in this trance, you can return another time, grounded and with renewed energy to do so.

In your mind's eye, you will see a fresh water spring or well off in the distance. Walk toward it slowly, noticing what else you see along the way. There will be a first spring, but continue to walk toward the second one. Face this spring; move toward it. Look upon the surface of the spring or well; what do you see or feel there? Then delve deeper. You may even decide to plunge an arm or leg into the water. Find a gift waiting there. Ask the gift what it is for. Thank the spring, and, if it is right to do so, take your gift with you.

Return to your place of power and notice if things look different now. Does the obstacle look different? Does the path look different? Do you feel different?

Back in the center of the circle, thank the directions. As you thank the directions, notice if your relationship to any of them has shifted.

When you are ready, take one step back into violet. Let violet surround you and notice how violet may feel different. Slowly move through each of the colors again, from violet through indigo, blue, green, yellow, orange, and back to red. As the red disperses completely, find yourself back in your room.

Arrive back to your body. Thank yourself for this work and give yourself a hug. Say your name three times and reground.

Take some time to journal your experience. It is done.

Practice: In-Drinking

IRISANYA MOON

You will need: a cup of water and a copy of *The Charge of the Goddess* or some other spell, chant, or poem

• • •

Water transforms. Water shapes. Water restores. You already experience this through baths and showers and visits to local bodies of water. This exercise is designed to help you connect with the healing and cleansing powers of water, no matter where you are and no matter what aid you need in your life at this moment.

You might notice there are parts of your life that need healing, blessing, or reshaping, and in-drinking is a practice that can support you to receive what you need. With just a cup of water you can bring your entire body and spirit back into a place of restoration. Just as water can quench your dry mouth when you're thirsty, in-drinking can help you enliven your tired heart.

In-drinking is a term we use in Reclaiming to signify any magical act in which we are drinking a liquid to transform consciousness. This specific practice outlined below is equivalent to kala, which is a core practice within the Feri tradition.

• • •

Start by creating or acknowledging sacred space in the way that suits you best. Or you can choose not to create sacred space; for example, if you need to perform this rite in a public place. You might decide that a certain phase of the moon is the best time for this working, or you might choose to use in-drinking at a time when it just feels right.

Remember, this is a working that is about you and your needs, so what feels right is right.

Whether you've created sacred space or not, take the cup of water in your hands. Look deeply into the water and begin to pour into that water anything that might not be helpful in your life right now. You can do this by visualizing the ickyness as a dark mist or liquid that drips into the water. Or you might gather up the energies you don't want in your body and breathe them into the cup of water. Or you might choose to yell into the water and release what needs to be changed into that cup.

Even the smallest cups can hold all that needs to be held.

Once the cup is full of what you are pouring into it, look at the water. Look at the way it holds what you need it to hold. You might take a moment to thank the water and ask it for help in shifting these energies.

This is the place to recite a chant or a poem, if you wish, that speaks to you of healing and growth. *The Charge of the Goddess* is a lovely choice if you're not sure what to use. Read or sing or dance whatever sacred words work for you. Let the words, the energies, the shifting begin. Push the poetry and the beauty into the water with your heart and with your sincere attention.

You might see a new light coming from your hands or from the world around you moving into the water, filling it, changing it, shifting the molecules around into a new pattern, a new story. Let that light become brighter and brighter until it fills the cup to its very edges.

When you feel the time is right and the water has shifted, put the cup to your lips and drink it in. Take it all in. Feel yourself take in the blessing of the water. Drink in the healing, the ability to change, and the power of this element.

Repeat as needed and desired.

Open the sacred space if you created it.

Ocean of Emotion

JANE MEREDITH

* * *

Know thyself.

It's so easy to say, yet almost impossible to do.

After all, who am I?

Am I a four-year-old girl sobbing silently in her bed? Am I a fifteen-year-old desperately wondering how to be myself? Perhaps I am in my twenties, learning how to put words together the way I've always longed to, seeing myself made manifest on the page? Maybe I am a young mother meeting my child with all the conflict and delight that brings. Or a struggling, heartbroken woman being left by her lover in her early thirties. Perhaps I am fifty, surrounded by friends and community in an extraordinary ritual under the night sky, or that same fifty-year-old alone in Paris learning that her mother has died on the other side of the world.

No—and yet, yes. I still carry those selves within me. Am I an author and teacher with half a century of history, learning, and growth, beloved friends, and a grown, happy child? Yes—and yet…I am still untangling issues from my childhood. I deeply long for sensual and sexual love. I am terrified by the state of the world. I realize now I am my mother's daughter, something I fought my whole life against, but now that she's dead I see that is who I am, or more accurately, I am who she is now, the living one of us and carrying all the women of our line within me. Yet I am still that baby, her first, born by caesarian section half an hour into Gemini. All these layers fold into the learning of who I am.

Knowing myself is not something I have got to the end of yet. My interest in the topic comes and goes. Sometimes it's fascinating as I uncover yet another layer of ingrained personality, as I try to understand why I am the way I am, and therefore seek explanation of why anyone—or everyone—is the way they are. I used to be an introvert. In the last few years—since my mother died—I seem to have lost that social anxiety, the debilitating shyness, and while I'm not exactly an extrovert, when I'm having a good day I can look like one. I gained confidence, I got to the right age for myself, I released the story about how I wasn't like my mother—who knows? But I feel ever-changing, enough to say that I think this journey of discovering who I am won't be over anytime soon. Not as long as I'm alive.

Learning about oneself, one's own emotional and psychological makeup, can seem terribly self-indulgent. Aren't there more useful things to be getting on with—saving the planet, work, raising children, caring for others, creative pursuits, pure spiritual devotion? After we arrive at the point where we are functional as independent adults, isn't it okay to leave that stuff behind and concentrate on being a productive member of society? What priority can personal work really have while icecaps are melting, country after country falls to right-wing governments, refugee crises rise and rise, and species become extinct at a terrifying rate?

Here's the thing: it seems we probably have more chance of saving the planet if we're clearer, stronger individuals who can make choices with integrity and form functional and effective collectives. People submerged in their own stories, shadows, and unresolved past traumas don't do too well in groups or often in any sort of relationships, and while it might sometimes seem as if we need to heal the planet before we can afford to spend time or resources healing ourselves, actually we have to do both at the same time. One way to think of healing is that it happens on three levels: the personal, the social, and the planetary. They don't work in isolation. Planetary and social issues impact enormously and irrevocably upon the individual. Because those same individuals make up society, enough individuals working on a particular issue can change the whole social realm. Witness recent historic changes due to feminism and gay rights, the social condemnation of domestic violence and child abuse, awareness of racial issues, and the reexamination of binary gender.

Many mainstream and some alternative spiritual practices or religious beliefs teach that focusing on oneself—or even focusing on this world at all—is a false direction. Believers are encouraged toward separation of body and spirit, with the spirit holding all that is of value and the body merely seeking to distract and disempower the seeker. These religions teach that the earth is fallen or is where we are tested, a place we must transcend. In these paradigms emotions can become inconvenient, seeming like backward steps to achieving happiness, detachment, and inner peace.

Reclaiming, Paganism, and earth-based spiritualities teach almost the opposite: that the sacred is not separate from the mundane. Spiritual development lies not in the denial of our experiences, emotions, and relationships, but within them; they are the immediate teachers that we meet every day. Similarly, the earth, nature, and all the elements are our fundamental teachers, the context within which we live each moment of our lives. We find ourselves here, in a dynamic web of life. We belong to and are part of this planet. Everything we learn, we learn within a body and through the body. The sacred is inseparable from everything else, thus our bodies are sacred, their experiences and emotions part of the spiritual teaching we receive.

The personal work we do, the transformations we undergo, and the self-knowledge we acquire has a direct impact on the social groups we belong to. Noble, beautiful, commendable goals and visions are frequently undermined, destroyed, or derailed by personality or personal issues that—instead of being understood and healed by those individuals—are played out in the context of a group to its detriment. Considering how to make environmental, political, or social action effective, we can easily see that if the individuals involved are mature, self-responsible, and self-aware, they will be able to work with each other and toward their goals much more effectively and powerfully. If we wish to have an impact—or even simply be fully present—in our magical, political, and social lives, for each of us to do our personal work is a necessity.

Personal work is a broad term intended to cover the set of issues we each carry with us. For some of us these will be unresolved childhood issues. For others it might be our physical or mental health, or both. It may be our addictions, anxiety, low self-esteem. It might be abuse—current, past, or both—and for a frighteningly high percentage of people, mainly women, it is incest. Personal work can take the form of meeting with our grief, anger, disconnection, self-harm, depression, and stress, resolving issues, healing, and transforming. Personal work is not something that is addressed once and then completed, although parts of it may be completed. If we are on the path of self-awareness, there will be another part, another issue that becomes available for us to work on once we have resolved one issue, or it may be that we are confronting several different issues at one time.

Many, even most people have a dominating theme that recurs again and again, progressively at different levels, as we transform and grow. So we resolve it at one level, go on with our lives, and meet it again a little further down the track. Sometimes this makes it seem as if we've achieved nothing, but, looking closer, we can probably see how this is a another layer of that issue, wound, or pattern we continue to work on, continue to see the world through, and return to for ever-deeper levels of healing, understanding, and integration. Doing personal work might feel as if we are unpicking every thread of ourselves to arrive back at the beginning, that pure self we were at birth or pre-birth, as a soul or a speck of stardust. That might be the case. Each piece of personal work that we do brings us closer to healing, to being whole.

There are possibly thousands of modalities of personal work. They include and are not limited to meditation; reflective journaling; shamanic or trance-style journeying, which is sometimes called soul retrieval; breathwork, also known as rebirthing; body work; support groups; twelve-step programs; men's, women's, or queer work; family constellation work; counselling and psychotherapy; dream work; shadow work...the list goes on.

When and where would we begin such work? The answer is pretty much always, right in front of us, right away. The next step. Now. Perhaps our next step is to deal with a long-unresolved issue concerning work, relationship, or living arrangements. Perhaps it is to dare to reach out for what we truly want or begin to take steps into the future: moving to an unknown city, enrolling in a course we've always longed to do, starting to see a therapist, taking a week out of our lives to find stillness or any one of a thousand other things. Getting to know our own emotions, accepting that they are what they are and that our lives will be enriched and deepened as we understand them, is a crucial piece of this work. Perhaps our emotions are all over the place or we can't really connect to them or they seem uncontrollable so we mainly ignore them or they are disproportionate to what is actually going on. Each one of these things can be a gateway into the inner realm, the beginning or the continuation of a life-long journey of discovery and the deepening work of knowing our selves.

An "ocean of emotion" is what a friend called me once, but just as when we are out on an ocean we can watch the wind and waves and work out where we are from the stars, so too in emotional work we can study the signs, the emotions—recording them, maybe in our journals, and working to understand them. Following the ocean metaphor, doing this work will enable us to learn about where we are, the general conditions surrounding us, and how they affect us. When we wish to plot a journey—to head in a particular direction or end up at a destination—understanding all the factors that contribute to that course are vital information. Perhaps the waves—of grief, maybe, or doubt or anxiety or self-blame—are threatening to swamp you. Or perhaps you're stranded in a flat calm, unable to steer or move at all? Possibly you're in the grip of a powerful current, being pulled in a direction you haven't entirely chosen.

Right now my ocean of emotion includes deep rifts of grief over the deaths of my mother and one of my closest friends. Closer to the surface are some driving winds, quite often ruffling the waves, of overwhelm and tiredness. There are tides or currents that rock me and draw me slowly toward what I want, of longing and vulnerability and hope and desire. This ocean of myself includes sudden bursts of sunlight in the form of joys of intimacy as well as patches of weed that threaten to tangle or disorient me: impatience, hurt feelings, loneliness. But the stars are up above, orienting me with visions of how it is possible to live my creativity as I continue this dance with words on the page and the joy I have in ritual and connection with others and nature. The sun and moon still rise and move overhead as I, the ocean of emotion, continue to seek to know myself.

All of us can do the step-by-step work of getting to know ourselves and learning compassion and understanding as skills applied to our own lives, past and present. All of us can begin to know what our wishes are, who we aim to become, what we hope to do with our lives, how we wish to relate to others, and what values and actions are most important to us. In this ocean of emotion, we do not have to do it all by ourselves. We can ask for help. Not just from navigation maps we happen to have with us—whatever our parents taught us or didn't teach us, or however we have done things in the past—but also by reaching out. Most of us have friends or family members we hesitate to tell what is truly going on, not because they are untrustworthy or uncaring but because we don't let ourselves. Almost all of us have access to teachers, books, and discussion or support groups. Or we can find some way to journal, to meditate, to let our creativity flow or to take time out in nature. Many tools of personal growth are available.

In Reclaiming we work extensively with a construct called the Iron Pentacle. There's a whole class devoted to it, but just like Elements of Magic, we would never say that once you've done the class, you're finished with Elements or finished with Iron. Often it is said that the Iron Pentacle is the work of a lifetime, and here's why: the Iron Pentacle has five points, and their names are Sex, Pride, Self, Power, and Passion. If your main language is not English, I recommend working with the translations of those terms because the Iron Pentacle is not just personal, it's cultural. Understanding, clearing, and healing where we are at with issues of sex, pride, self, power, and passion is deeply fascinating and often excruciating—a fiery purge and remarkably liberating. These points don't go away or get resolved forever. After months of intensive work with pride, I can still be affected by an unkind comment, a rejection slip, a falling out with a friend. Back I go to pride with another piece of myself revealed to myself and more work to do. It's not starting from nothing—my previous work gives me somewhere to stand, some confidence and comprehension of the process—but we don't get to the end of it.

Small groups are amazing containers for deep personal work. It might be a group of two people or four people. Two of the strongest small groups I have ever been part of had these numbers—one of them was literally me and a friend. We committed to spending one night a week together, exploring magic, personal work, and interconnection. It might be a larger group, maybe even an open group whose membership is flexible. In any kind of a small group—including covens, men's groups, women's groups, support groups—there is an opportunity to connect deeply with others over time, sharing and listening to each other's experiences and understandings as each one of us navigates through our own oceans. If you aren't currently part of a small group that meets regularly and holds space for personal work, creating or finding such a group can be one of the most powerful and effective things you can do toward your emotional learning.

Perhaps you know people who claim their personal work is finished; they are essentially enlightened and have no issues anymore. It almost seems as if humans were designed to rub up against each other in difficult ways, to provoke and question each other, to offer moments of challenge, conflict, and healing on a more or less continual basis. Someone who's not engaged with that—who views it all as external and nothing to do with them—are counting themselves out of the communal human realm of relating, change, and growth. The teachers I've admired most have been open about their personal challenges and the work they do to try to meet them. The friends I'm closest to are those who reveal their depths to me, not those who show the shiny surfaces. These friends know me in my strengths and vulnerabilities, and the connection we forge is based in trust, intimacy, and truth.

However happy, strong, and successful we may be in one part of our lives, nothing is more inevitable than that we will continue to have times when this is not the case. A loved one dies. We have our health challenged or compromised. We lose a job or a relationship. We make a mistake that really counts. Something awful happens to one of our family. These things occur—often randomly but to everyone. Some people may believe that it is enough to face the difficult things when there's no avoiding them, when they've already happened. I'm suggesting the opposite, that the time to cultivate patience, understanding, self-knowledge, compassion, and inner resources is exactly the time when the challenges are not all screaming at us, when we are relatively stable and collected.

One of the truly amazing benefits of doing deep personal work is not just that it helps us develop as human beings, and not just that when difficult or devastating things happen to us, we have the resources to begin to cope, but that it frees us up to be available to others in ways that would never be possible if we didn't do this work. Qualities of clarity, courage, and compassion that we can bring to someone else's process are usually only available to us to the degree with which we have been able to hold those things for ourselves, travelling through our own challenges and dark nights and despairs.

All rivers run to the sea...following our own rivers, our own emotional responses to whatever it is that's happening around us this week...today we arrive at the ocean of ourselves. My son, in Paris to meet me for my birthday, doesn't bring me an actual present, and I am taken off-guard by the surge of emotion I experience, feeling distressed out of all proportion to the event. Eventually I trace it back to loneliness, having so few people to depend upon, the unsettling nature of travelling for months, away from my friends and home, and then underneath that I find my grief over my mother's death, three years ago now but still underlying so many of my responses to the living people around me.

My mother gave me presents, and their absence indicates her absence. When I let myself feel that, my frustration, confusion, and hurt make sense, begin to dissolve somewhat and take me back into this deep tide of the loss of my mother. Perhaps I will find some way to tell my son how I feel. Perhaps I will go out and buy myself a present, one she might have given me. I realize that I am in Paris, which is where I was when I learned my mother had died, so no wonder it is strong for me. Perhaps those waves are backwashing into me so I am experiencing a fresh level of that world-changing knowledge of her death. So I will take some more time to ponder my mother's life and death in this place that seems so woven into that grief.

Who am I now? In Paris, fifty-three years old, I let emotion take me on its tide all the way back to the four-year-old Jane crying in her bed for her mother. Another round of deepening begins.

Process: Deep Check-In

JANE MEREDITH

Time: 30 minutes

You will need: a journal and a pen;
coloring things (optional)

. . .

The deep check-in can be spoken, written, or drawn, but it is never only felt, it is always expressed in some way. It is both an inner reflection and also a recognition of what may not have been fully conscious until now. A deep check-in has three purposes. Firstly, to still and center oneself, dropping through different levels of awareness into the depths. Secondly, to recognize and speak aloud, write, or draw what one finds in those depths. Thirdly, to reflect on what one has found.

If you are doing this process with others, the answers to the third and final question are spoken aloud in a round, with each person speaking in turn within a strong agreement of confidentiality.

. . .

In a quiet and comfortable space, spend some time physically relaxing your body. For this exercise, sitting up is better than lying down. Ground and center. Cast a circle if you wish.

Focus on your breath. Follow it in and down, allowing the breath to continue relaxing you and using this time to let go of whatever external thoughts you might have. When you feel still and centered, begin.

Allow yourself to think of a body of water. It might be a lake, a river, or an ocean. Imagine the top layer of this water; what is it like? Probably it is affected by currents of air; perhaps there are waves or eddies. You might visualize this or imagine yourself within the water. You might feel the water as part of your body.

After a minute or two, address these questions: *How are you? What is going on for you in your life?* You might imagine these questions as cast across the surface of your water. Imagine that someone you know reasonably well has asked you this, perhaps a friend, a caring relative, a coworker, or a professional with an interest in your well-being. What would you answer? You might like to note down what your answer would encompass, speak it briefly aloud, or just acknowledge it in your mind. Then take a breath or two, let it go, and take yourself deeper.

Drop down further into the water, into a middle layer. At the same time, allow yourself to drop down through your emotional layers into a deeper level of truth with yourself.

What is it like in your ocean, river, or lake at this middle level? You might meet currents here and the water might change color, temperature, or motion. Spend a moment thinking or feeling into this middle level of your body of water and your emotional self, and then ask yourself: *How are you? What is going on for you in your life?* Let that question resonate through this middle layer of the water of yourself. Imagine that someone you trust completely has asked you this, someone you would be able to give a full reply to. Perhaps it is your best friend, your partner, your high priestess. What is your answer? Once again you can briefly speak this aloud, write down the main couple of points, or simply acknowledge what your reply would contain. Take a breath, release it, and let yourself sink further down.

Travel down into the depths, the river bed, the deep water at the bottom of the lake, the depths of the sea. At the same time, allow yourself to drop into the depths of your truth, of your own reality, of your emotional being.

Feel how it is down here; feel the qualities of the water. Perhaps you become aware of deep tides or still depths or smooth flow. Breathe with this. Wait. Then ask, at the deepest level of yourself, to your own watery depths: *How are you? What is going on for you in your life?* Let your deep self answer. What comes through you may be information you didn't consciously know, never chose to or never found a way to articulate before, or issues that run beneath everything that you think and do. This is the deep check-in.

Let yourself answer this third question fully. Take your time to acknowledge what you find in these depths. Speak aloud, maybe for four or five minutes, about what you find here or record it in your journal over a page or two. Maybe you prefer to draw it, having understood what is there. If you are doing this process with another person or a group, this third level of check-in is spoken aloud in a round where only one person speaks at a time and the check-ins are not discussed or commented on.

Having spoken or written your deep check-in, take some further time to integrate what you found and what it means to you. You might like to journal or draw or spend some time meditating or simply breathing. If you did the exercise alone, you might choose—now or later—to share with someone else what you discovered.

Trance: Water Cycles

PHOENIX LEFAE

Time: 30 minutes

You will need: space to lie down undisturbed

• • •

One of the most impactful ways to connect to the element of water is to allow yourself to encounter water in all its forms by experiencing yourself as water.

This trance can be done sitting or lying down. Allow yourself to be comfortable.

Focus on your breath, the easy inhalation and exhalation. Don't try to control the breath, just notice what it wants to do and allow it to flow. As you breathe, allow your edges to soften. Allow the boundaries of you to widen, smooth out, and spread, making yourself more fluid and boundaryless.

As the boundaries of you spread and soften, you begin to sink. You sink into the ground below you, shifting into droplets of water that are then drunk up by the earth. How is it to be droplets of water absorbed by the land?

There is a shift in the landscape, and the drops of water that are you begin to move, to flow, and before you know it you find yourself flowing as a creek or stream, flowing, flowing, flowing. The droplets of you begin to combine with other droplets, spreading out and shifting. You feel the ebbs and flows of being the creek.

Again, you notice a subtle shift in yourself as you, the creek, flows, expands, and grows. You become wider, deeper, more powerful as many creeks flow together and you become a river. You can expand to the wide width, touching each bank. You can sink into the deepest depths, feeling the rocks worn smooth at your bottom. The pools, the eddies, the rapids—all of these pieces of the river are pieces of you. How is it to flow like the river?

There is another shift: you as the river meet up with the ocean. You shift from freshwater to saltwater. For a moment, you are both fresh and salt as you move, pulled by the tides. As part of the sea, sink down into the deep, dark, cold ocean floor. The water that is you shifts slowly down here in the darkness. You can feel the kelp beds and the odd creatures of the deep. What does it feel like to be in the deep, cold ocean?

The tide turns, and you as the sea are pulled upwards. You rise up through the dark waters toward the light of the surface. As the ocean you rise, feeling the warmth of the sun shine down on you. You as the sea float on the foam surface, feeling the bends and bobs of the waves. The sun begins to warm you, hotter and hotter; you feel the pull of the heat, and you as water begin to rise from the ocean. You rise as water vapor moving faster and faster into the sky.

You rise and gather, coming closer together with other molecules, forming a big bright cloud in the sky. More and more molecules gather. You as the cloud become heavier and heavier until it is too much to hold. You as the cloud fly, float, shift toward the land, and begin to fall. You are big drops of rain falling from the sky and landing softly on the ground around the very spot where you left your human body.

The droplets of rain that are you begin to gather and to pool. Swiftly and easily, you flow back into your human body. Your edges firm up, becoming solid. Notice your breathing, and feel the edges of you.

Slowly connect to your body. Open your eyes, pat your edges, and say your name out loud three times. Welcome back.

Personal Healing
WILLOW FIREFLY KELLY

• • •

My first experience of the Reclaiming community was at a Witch-Camp in 1996. It changed my life. I finally found what I had hoped existed: a group of witches doing powerful, ecstatic, world-renewing, life-changing magic, not just partying together in cool ritual garb. The collective spellwork and rituals we did together were like nothing I had ever experienced, especially the healing ritual midweek. This gorgeous, flowing ritual was a practical manifestation of healing as well as a metaphor for my philosophy of the watery nature of healing.

Elemental stations in the four directions marked the outer edges of the space, designed for people to come to for restoration and nourishment as needed throughout the ritual. Participants held hands in a circle, dancing and singing to create a flow of energy that was focused into the center. There a fire burned, encircled by mattresses covered in beautiful fabrics, serving as platforms for healers and recipients to engage in consensual healing practices. People moved in and out of roles as healer and recipient throughout the hours-long ritual, sometimes singing and dancing to raise energy, sometimes seeking respite and restoration at one of the elemental stations on the edge. The movement between self-care and community care in the context of a powerful healing rite was beautiful and reminded me of how my path of healing is indeed a watery one of interconnection, ebb and flow, action and rest, giving and receiving, intuition and movement. Sometimes I seek and receive, sometimes I give, sometimes I step outside of my circles for respite and self-care, sometimes I work tirelessly for my community and our healing, sometimes I tend the fire of hearth and home at my center.

As witches, we acknowledge, celebrate, and create rites of passage for the cycles of life, death, decomposition, regeneration, and rebirth.

We do not try to step outside of nature's laws; instead, we work to understand them and apply our energy, will, and intentions in alignment with these forces. We do not see death as a failure to heal. We understand it as part of this great cosmic dance of ineffable mysteries. So if healing isn't the resolution of symptoms, the expiration of a disease, or the avoidance of death, what is it? Is healing a state of being, acts of focusing, directing, and receiving energy, or some other mystery?

To shed some light on this question, I find the principles of homeopathy useful, which state that the difference between poison and medicine is the dosage. This provides a perfect understanding of what it means to balance health and be in a state of healing. What we take into our bodies can be medicine or poison based on the dosage, and even that is influenced by countless other factors to which we are exposed moment by moment. This also applies to what we take into our minds, by choice or happenstance. Sometimes we process poisons safely; sometimes too much at once or other complex contributing factors compromise our ability to do so, and we experience illness.

There are always pockets of disease, poison, and toxins within us and in the world around us. In a state of wellness, the body—or, in the larger context, the family, community, area, nation, maybe even species—works to remove or contain these life- and health-threatening forces. However, if these pockets continue to grow, especially if unseen or unnoticed, they may become powerful enough to overwhelm wellness, and the scales tip. We fall into an illness that dominates the landscape unless the wellness is able to reorganize, strengthen, grow, and shift the balance back. Healing practices help us achieve this delicate balance. The movement between illness and wellness, the swinging of the pendulum from one side to the other, is sometimes barely noticeable and other times radically impactful, but it is always in motion.

Those of us who are engaged in the magical arts and earth-based spirituality view healing as less about seeking specific results and more about a journey, a personal practice and an integrated way of life that engages us in the act of creating and continuing to balance an environment within and without that is life-sustaining. These acts of creating balance can be physical and ethereal and could include many possibilities. This may include cultivating a sense of connection to spirit and inner peace; shadow work; mending relationship to the earth, others, and self; taking in healthy, whole, and clean food and water; and getting proper exercise for our body and ability. We may seek help from others who are more knowledgeable, including therapists, doctors, and other medical practitioners as well as alternative healthcare providers such as acupuncturists and massage and energy therapists. We continue to apply proactive healing and health-maintenance practices, taking care of the body and the environment together, continuing to ask questions and seek answers or whatever else inspires healing within us.

During the summer of 1997, the year after the healing ritual, I contracted a debilitating disease that went undiagnosed for several years as my health plummeted. A bacterial infection spread throughout my body, crossing the blood-brain barrier and finally rendering me incapable of working and, at its worst, even of caring for myself. I was experiencing an astrological transit of Pluto conjunct my natal Sun, a time of great and intense transformation, the best and the worst of times. It was the beginning of an epic healing journey spanning two decades.

In my desperation I searched within myself for any subconscious information, patterns, or beliefs I might be holding that were contributing to my health struggles. Had I done something wrong? Was I not in right relationship to the Mysterious Ones? Had I brought this sickness upon myself? Was I being punished or cursed by some outside force for some supposed sin? Was I sabotaging myself? Was I manifesting my own self-loathing? Was I making myself sick by thinking the wrong thoughts or not thinking the right thoughts? Was I being forced by the Mysterious Ones to learn to establish boundaries with parasites in all forms for my best and highest good? Was any of this true? Was it all true? At first these questions fueled my anxiety and uncertainty as I grasped desperately for answers. My tendency to blame myself is usually my first response to any crisis, but over time I learned to explore my role in the illness I hosted with much more compassion, self-love, and curiosity.

Brain wrangling is a powerful component of healing. Our minds can be our greatest allies and worst enemies. When we practice a state of grounded mindfulness and awareness of the body, we begin to pick up more of the subtle and not-so-subtle messages our bodies are constantly sending to us, divulging an astounding amount of information that we can train our minds to understand. For example, if we are seeking to heal anxiety and pay close attention to the responses we have to stimulus received by our body, mind, and emotional being, we might discover certain foods, disrupted sleep patterns, mold, media consumption, or any number of things are contributing factors and potential sources of our symptoms, thereby empowering us to either change the stimulus or work to change the body's response to the stimulus. Cultivating a body-listening practice can help immeasurably when undertaking the task of restoring a state of wellness.

Exploring techniques for accessing the subconscious—or shadow stalking, as we often call it—serves us well in our endeavors. Careful to infuse this work with deep compassion, we seek potential underlying causes of illness and subconscious beliefs or wounds we might be harboring or perpetuating that impede our capacity to receive healing. We can also benefit greatly from cultivating a daily practice that includes grounding, mindfulness, and listening to our bodies, seeking how to best meet the challenges we face. We endeavor to find meaning in what is happening but know we must release attachment to attaining it. Understanding may remain a mystery of the watery depths.

Healing rituals can help us process our experiences and do the powerful magic of giving and receiving healing energy and support. In the water section of an Elements of Magic course, we often create a healing ritual following a trance journey. Each participant has the opportunity to come into the center of the circle, or not, and ask for what they want from the group to support their healing. Flowing between the roles of healer and recipient happens quickly in this ritual. We acknowledge that we are not really healing anyone, that they are healing themselves and we are providing a form of access for them to do so, and that we are healing ourselves by consciously becoming vessels of healing energy so that even the roles of healer and recipient are blurred, watery. We cultivate an environment of nonjudgment and relentless support as we affirm our ability to heal and be healed, encouraging us all to share these much-needed gifts with the world.

I worked a lot of magic to change my consciousness, and while that helped my mental, spiritual, and emotional states, it wasn't enough to physically fight the disease that had me in its grasp. I knew I couldn't accept my illness without investigating every possible avenue of healing available to me. Realistically, there is no end to that kind of searching, which, while giving me hope, also overwhelmed me by considering all the options: traditional Western medicine, homeopathic and naturopathic medicines, Eastern healing techniques, acupuncture, meditation, fringe alternative treatments and clinics, mainstream research studies...the possibilities were endless.

To help steady our balance in favor of wellness, we aim to satisfy the mind, be proactive for the body, nourish the spirit, and process the psychological impacts we experience. Only the individual can decide what path to take and which options to explore. There are usually plenty of advice and opinions available, sometimes overwhelmingly so. Active engagement in the healing process is important, along with feeling good about a chosen healing strategy. We persevere in our efforts to restore wellness and let go of the results, remembering we cannot know what is best.

Rooted in love and reverence for the earth, we also expand our awareness to hold a broader view of what restoring healing balance means. One profound aspect is encoded in this first line of our Principles of Unity, which states: "The values of the Reclaiming tradition stem from our understanding that the earth is alive and all of life is sacred and interconnected." We as individuals and as a species do not exist in a vacuum. The struggle for our own healing is the struggle for the earth's healing and each other's healing. The scales are always in motion and deeply interrelated. We are inextricably interconnected, and that is inherently one of our greatest gifts and greatest challenges. We cannot remove a single thread to examine it, for each one is connected to the pattern of the whole. What we do to the earth and ourselves sends vibrations through the entire web of life. We cannot understand the full ramifications of our choices and actions, which affirms that it is arrogant to think we know the best outcome in any given situation or for any one person, even ourselves.

This healing thing is a lot more complicated than it might initially look.

Because of this beautiful, challenging, complex interconnection and interdependence that is our birthright as living beings, we cannot help but deal with countless toxins—naturally occurring biotoxins; cleaning, beauty, and waste products; pollutants; viruses; infections; compromised water sources; soil and food toxicity. How we respond to the presence of those toxins in our bodies will fluctuate due to other contributing factors, some still largely unknown, but we do know that we cannot be separate from the illnesses of the earth. Our healing and the healing of the earth are inextricably tied to each other. Many threads of cause and effect pass between us.

The last line of our Principles of Unity states: "We work to create and sustain communities and cultures that embody our values, that can help to heal the wounds of the earth and her peoples, and that can sustain us and nurture future generations." When we lobby for earth, food, and environmental justice, we are lobbying for our own health and the health of our communities. When we increase our awareness of the deep mysteries of interconnection or begin to catch a glimpse into that ineffable mystery, it changes how we approach life, potentially turning each day into a healing ritual for our surroundings and ourselves.

As lovers of nature and the earth, we tend our health and the health of the planet together. If we are to be healers and to be healed, we must do this magic of reconnection that shifts the balance from illness to wellness inside ourselves and around us in the world as an ongoing practice of active attention, assessment, and correction. Balance. If we're paying attention to the world around us, we might feel we are facing impossible challenges. It isn't easy or pleasant to stay aware and engaged, but it is necessary a fair amount of the time in order to bring about wellness. In trying times this also means noticing if we need to step up our healing practices or develop better coping strategies and trauma resilience, and take the necessary measures to do so.

Three years after the onset of my illness, I was at another Reclaiming WitchCamp where a healing ritual was scheduled one afternoon. By this time I had been disabled for six months. I spent a fair amount of that camp lying or sitting down or in my tent, motionless in bed. I was ready to be healed!

During the instructions for the ritual, we were told not to use our own energy but instead to become a channel of a divine and holy healing energy that is limitless and intelligent. By doing this, the theory is that the healer doesn't become depleted from using their own energy; that the seeker receives exactly what they need, with no assumptions on our part about what is best; and that running this energy through our bodies simultaneously heals the healer. I love the poetry of this. We don't have to know what's best. We offer ourselves in service to this limitless healing presence. We heal ourselves when we heal each other, and when we ask for healing, we are creating a healing opportunity for the healer, too. This is such sweet community magic.

What does it mean to call oneself a healer, to be deeply engaged in the process of healing? Healing practices can focus on an energetic approach, such as Reiki or acupuncture, or on a more physical approach, such as herbalism or massage. Some healers apply science, folk medicine, or other tangible forms of healing, whereas others work intuitively and with the energetics of illness and wellness as they understand them.

Most will agree that the seeker takes an active role in the experience in one way or another.

At this WitchCamp healing ritual, I asked an elder in the tradition who I greatly respected if she would come into the center and channel healing energy for me. We met outside the dining hall under a canopy of redwoods to talk about it. She asked me if I resented the Goddess or nature for giving me my disease. I suddenly saw with crystalline clarity that the Mysterious Ones of nature were initiating me. I had been in the forge of transformation and would remain here a while, but I would emerge or at least reach another level in that endless spiral of evolution eventually, either by getting well, coping, or dying, and I would somehow come more wholly into my power and sense of self through the process regardless of the outcome. She smiled at my understanding and agreed to step into the center of the circle with me.

Within these two decades, my philosophy of healing has evolved, and so has my relationship to magic and my own healing gifts. If I had limited my magical intentions throughout the years to what I wanted specifically, I believe I would have sold myself short of the magical life I now live.

Illness, though a harsh initiator, can carry its own gifts. We do not know what fires or floods will destroy us or forge us into realizing our potential. We can only wonder what doors will open to us and who we will meet along our path of healing. We can imagine, but we simply do not know. This is where a spiritual practice becomes essential to help us find some way of having hope, agency, and trust during states of not knowing, to help keep us moving forward on our healing path as best we can with no idea where it will take us, to find some peace in that sacred nature of initiation and transformation.

We can move through our lives in the same way that the priestesses moved through that first WitchCamp healing ritual I witnessed. We can listen to our bodies and know when to actively seek, receive, and give healing, restore ourselves at the edges in the elements of nature, tend our energy management, hearth, and home, or work in service to community healing. And in this beautiful song of interconnection, by cleaning up our environment, air, food, water, and soil quality to support our health, we are extending the same healing energy and kindness to the earth and our neighbors of flesh, fin, and feather. We mirror each other's journey. As children of earth and starry heaven, how can we not? As the Principles of Unity claim, we work to create and sustain what can "heal the wounds of the earth and her peoples." It is work that we undertake joyfully and mindfully together as witches.

Ritual: Herbal Bath

RIYANA ROSE SANG AND CHUCK

Time: 1–2 hours

You will need: herbs of your choosing,
  sea salt, purification supplies, a bath;
  journal and pen (optional)

* * *

This is a devotional working of earth and water.

Water is powerful medicine, and ritual bathing has been a practice humans have engaged in since ancient times. From the baths in the temples of Aphrodite to ritual bathing in the Ganges in India to indigenous traditions at sacred hot springs around the world, humans have engaged in ritual to honor the waters and through bathing for millennia. Modern witches often work with water for cleansing, healing, and strengthening.

Rebecca Tidewalker, a Reclaiming ancestor, dedicated her life to the waters and taught of the importance of praying with water, making offerings to the water, and listening to the waters. It is in the spirit of her love and dedication to the waters that we share this ritual with you.

* * *

Take some time to cleanse the space, whether that's simply an energetic cleansing or an actual physical cleaning of the bathtub or the whole bathroom.

Begin your sacred bathing by grounding and connecting with the present moment, whether that's doing a grounding tree visualization, triple soul alignment, or mindful breathing.

Next, cast a circle and call in the elements as well as any allies you would like to invite into the working. These may be deities you work with; fae, animal, or ancestor spirits; spirits of the land; or spirits of a place. Invoking the plants that you will be using in the bath is a wonderful way to call in the blessings of the greenbloods.

With a breath and a prayer for the waters, fill your bath. As the tub is filling, breathe and connect with the spirit of these waters. Imagine the connection between the waters in the tub to all the healing waters of the world. Allow yourself to sink into your intention as you listen to the waters running into the tub.

When you feel ready, add the herbs or essential oils that you have chosen. As you add each new plant ally, open your heart to a deeper knowing of this plant's medicine and express your gratitude to it for its presence in your magic. Notice any shifts or changes in the energy as you add each plant to the bath, and listen for messages that may come through.

Remove your clothing slowly and with intention. Connect with your senses as you step into the bath and relax into the pool of magic that you have created. Take in the scents and sensations as your body drinks in the magic of this bath. Allow yourself to reflect and relax in the magic. Let whatever insights come to you unfold in these sacred waters, and intentionally release the blocks and energetic leaks that are holding you back. Listen for guidance and wisdom from the allies that you have called into this sacred circle.

When you are ready, step out of the bathtub and give thanks to the waters, the plants, and all the allies you called in. Then devoke, dry off, and rest, reflecting on the ritual in your journal or Book of Shadows, through artistic expression, or taking a walk in nature to deepen your connection to the plant world.

Trance: Meeting Our Ancestors Through Our DNA
LISA LIND

Time: 30 minutes

You will need: a quiet space, a journal and pen

• • •

Getting to know our ancestors not only helps us to understand our-selves more fully, but it is often a deeply rewarding experience. Our ancestors usually have a vested interest in our well-being—it is a bio-logical drive to maintain a healthy lineage, and therefore they can become strong allies in our magical work. They may or may not have raised us, but they certainly gave us their DNA, which affects not only the way we look but also how we behave. Our DNA is an information storehouse and is helical, like twisted string looped around many spools of protein known as histones. If you are unfamiliar with this imagery, the internet has many images to offer.

In this exercise we will travel in trance through our own blood and bones to read our DNA and see who we may meet there. If you already work with some ancestors, I invite you to keep an open mind—who knows who you may meet this time?

If you are doing this ritual in a group, someone often leads us on the journey; however, one can easily lead oneself. I suggest reading through the text below to get the gist of it and then putting the book down, resting assured that the details do not matter. Alternatively, you can record yourself speaking the instructions.

Sit or lie down where you will be comfortable but not fall asleep. Ground and center.

Gently close your eyes or create a soft focus, and begin to slow your breathing to help your body and mind relax. When you feel settled, let your awareness drift to your heart.

Perhaps you can hear it beat within your body or in your mind. Follow that sound of the beat in your chest into your heart. When you feel ready, you can go on an adventure through the blood that is pushed around your body. Travel through your arteries, around your body, and into the core of your bones, where blood cells are made. This traveling can help you go deeper inside yourself and deeper into trance.

As you travel in your bloodstream, a particular cell may attract you or you may pick one at random. Travel into it to where your DNA strands are floating inside. Allow yourself to travel along a DNA strand and when you feel called to a certain spot, like passing your hand over tarot cards and choosing one, dive into that DNA and let that ancestor who gave it to you come to you.

You may meet them in a landscape or you may just observe them or hear them speak. You may feel their presence.

If you are meeting them for the first time, treat them as you would any other stranger. Introduce yourself and ask if they are interested in communicating with you. See where things go. If they are willing, continue your interaction. If you are recording this to make a guided trance, give yourself at least five to ten minutes here.

You can always continue traveling along your DNA strands to meet someone else.

When you feel ready, fly back into your cell, your blood, again traveling up and back into your heart. Let your heartbeat bring you back into the present. Slowly open your eyes and pat yourself down.

Record what you have experienced in your journal.

SPIRIT

. . .

Whichever element we begin with, usually spirit is the final one of the five that we study. Or else it's the first—Reclaiming is often said to be composed of a bunch of anarchists. Spirit is first and last, there before everything and there after everything. It's where we work most directly with the divine, with essence that goes beyond what we can put our hands on, with soul, with gods and goddesses and other spirits, including the ancestors and descendants to come. We can think of spirit as the coming together of all the other four elements, composed of them, containing them, giving birth to them. When we cast a circle, spirit is both the circumference and the center.

Some people work very directly with divinities—named or unnamed gods, goddesses, and other deities. Some don't. Some might only work with a few deities that they feel a personal or cultural relationship with. Some work with the spirit world but not with deities. In Reclaiming we are eclectic—if it resonates with the Principles of Unity and it works for you, probably it will fit into a Reclaiming ritual somewhere at some time. We regard each person as their own spiritual authority. Having said that, Reclaiming ritual structure and technology is relatively tight and high functioning. We tend not to invite strings of deities to any ritual or magic we're conducting; only those relevant to the work, celebration, or exploration we're undertaking. Perhaps only those we have been working with for months or years beforehand, with whom we have deepened our relationships.

We are eclectic because our witchcraft roots are in Feri, which doesn't drink from only one well or particular region of the world. We are also a political tradition, focusing our political critique not just on the outside world but upon ourselves and our processes, forms, and assumptions. Reclaiming is an avowedly inclusive tradition that aims—in right relationship and with justice—to hold space for all who turn up, decentralize social and political privilege, and listen to voices that are usually silenced.

We also take very seriously the issues of respect, cultural exchange, and cultural appropriation. In societies that have historically and institutionally marginalized and oppressed indigenous peoples and people of color—and continue to—appropriating or taking customs, traditions, or even deities or spirits from cultures outside our own may become equivalent to disrespect, denigration, and at its worst, continued exploitation and oppression.

We come together and share everything we are with each other, sometimes including our ancestors, cultures, and spirits. Although currently our communities, cells, camps, and covens are predominately white, we are an eclectic contemporary tradition of witchcraft situated in multicultural times and places: we are not only descended of European peoples, we are also of First Nations, Aboriginal, Middle Eastern, Asian, Latinx, Pacific, and African descent.

The difference between respectful engagement and cultural appropriation may lie in how we approach something if we are indeed called to it. Do we enquire with or encounter a lineage or a deity through a person or tradition who carries the authority, context, or relationship to share it? Or do we simply go ahead and take that custom or teach a workshop about that goddess without ever considering the social and political ramifications or the appropriate and original context? How do we learn to work in right relationship? These are questions spirit-in-action asks of us.

Reclaiming does not demand anyone leave their previous magical or spiritual work, dedications, or communities behind. Anyone can turn up to Reclaiming public rituals, core classes, and WitchCamps if they agree to abide by the Principles of Unity; you don't have to identify as a Reclaiming witch to gain admission. Reclaiming is one of the few modern witchcraft traditions that does not require a person to go through initiation to fully participate in the tradition. There is an initiation in Reclaiming, which concerns only the individual initiate and their own choice to enter into that mystery. Reclaiming initiation has been part of this tradition since the beginning, but it is not required of any participant.

In earth we practice the powers of *silence*, in air we wield *knowing*, fire ignites our sacred *will*, while journeying in the realms of water requires *daring*. These are known variously as the four powers of the sphinx, the magician, or the witch. Working with the fifth element of spirit we learn *to be, to love, to trust, to hold all*. And in this we surrender into the mystery of the elements all over again…and what dies away is reborn, in a new form, in a new way.

The elements are sacred. Spirit is sacred.

Spirit Is Sacred

Dawn Isidora

Alone, awesome, complete within Herself, the Goddess,
She whose name cannot be spoken, floated in the abyss
of the outer darkness, before the beginning of all things.
—A Feri Creation Myth, *The Spiral Dance*, Starhawk

• • •

Spirit, our fifth element—what we call center and circumference, betwixt and between, mystery and paradox—is at once the simplest and most complex element to grasp. When we talk about or invoke spirit in the Reclaiming tradition, we are generally referring to any number—or all—of the following: our souls, goddesses, gods, ancestors, the fae, and other beings of all sorts, as well as that invisible web that holds us all in connection with one another.

Discussing or defining spirit is as challenging and uncertain as the Indian parable in which a group of blind men encounter an elephant. Each of them reports an entirely different experience, but all are discussing the same thing. I consider it probable that we humans do not have the necessary senses to behold spirit in its entirety; however, we can listen to each other's perceptions and in that way we gain deeper understanding. Perhaps this cumulative process leads us toward wisdom.

Unlike the elements of air, fire, water, and earth, the element of spirit cannot be defined in scientific terms. We cannot break spirit down into its chemical components, nor measure it by volume, speed, heat, or weight, nor any other measure. Those of us who grew up with science as the One True God might struggle to describe just what, exactly, we mean when we say *spirit*. And I have struggled. I have spent the better part of the last fifty years tumbling the craggy question of spirit around in my head and heart until that question is as smooth and comforting as the touchstone in my pocket. I have come to understand spirit not as a *what* but as a *how*. The thread of understanding I have to share with you is that spirit is the sense of connection.

What evokes that sensation of connection? This is myriad and possibly unique to each of us. Some people may best find that sense of connection while walking in the forest or sitting silently beside the ocean. Some may experience it while playing music or creating art. Others access connection by being of service or through hearing inspirational words and music. Still others may kneel beside their bed at night and pray or burn incense while chanting the names of their gods. Many folks best access this connection through making love, sharing a meal with loved ones, or laughing with friends.

While we might find many of these activities pleasurable, it is the presence of this sensation of connection to your own core, or to something larger or beyond yourself, which differentiates a pleasurable experience from a spiritual experience. Only you can tell which things are simply, if delightfully, pleasurable and which things hold for you that unique sensation of connection. It is possible, through practice, to strengthen one's capacity for connection until every experience and action is imbued with this glorious sense of connection called spirit.

> *As She spun, She perceived her own reflection in the curved black mirror of space. In that moment of Self-awareness, Other was born. The Star Goddess gazed upon Other and named Her Miria.*

When we look within ourselves to seek the nature of spirit, we work with the concept of as above, so below; as within, so without; as the macro, so the micro. It is as relevant to turn one's attention to the mysteries within as the mysteries without. Victor Anderson, father of the Anderson Feri tradition, which Reclaiming draws extensively from, was known to say: "God is Self and Self is God and God is a person like my Self." This juxtaposition of God and Self invites us to contemplate the nature of our own self. We might begin wondering if the soul that is our self came into this lifetime for a specific purpose. Such have been the ponderings of seekers throughout time.

I have spent a lot of time with that question and others like it. I could have pondered and wondered for the rest of my life; however, my earthy nature won out and I just needed to get on with life. I have found that the most useful answer to this question of what the universe needs from me is for me to be the best human that I can be. Though I may never know if I choose with free will or if I am pulled onward by fate or some other invisible hand, I make my peace by dancing with Mystery while ever endeavoring to know myself and all of my parts.

To be the best human that I can be, I first turn my attention inward to my personal work. I take to heart the Dalai Lama's analogy of a pebble dropped in the middle of the pond, whose ripples flow outward all the way to the edges of the water. I know that who I am and what I do ripples outward, having impact I may never know. In addition, when I am grounded and centered, my energy seems to positively affect those around me—which in turn supports those others in being the best humans that they can be. The ripples carry on.

Self-awareness enables me to have realistic expectations of myself and better notice when I'm having expectations of others. It helps me make commitments that I can keep, and it allows me to learn from past experiences so I can make appropriate adjustments in the future. The Iron Pentacle, which comes to Reclaiming through the Anderson Feri tradition, is a tremendously useful tool for self-awareness. In working its five points of Sex, Pride, Self, Power, and Passion, we are able to reconnect with these integral aspects of our humanity in healthful and life-affirming ways. Working with the Iron Pentacle encourages us to be right-sized, so that we become neither paralyzed nor grandiose, and it helps us to realign the ways in which we run our life force.

Drop your roots down deep into the earth and feel that energetic pulse of life force at her center. Let that energy rise up those roots and fill your being. Gaze into the mirror, into your own eyes, your own pupils, and see yourself reflected, as the Star Goddess sees herself reflected in that curved black mirror of space. Fall deeply in love with your own soul. Self-love is the deep, strong root system that supports the wide-branched canopy of compassion that is necessary for each of us to be our best possible self.

Being a good human involves outer work as well as inner, and our external good works build upon our internal good works. Activism has been a part of the Reclaiming tradition from the very beginning. Our Principles of Unity state: "We work for all forms of justice: environmental, social, political, racial, gender, and economic." How this looks can vastly vary from one to another of us. All of our activism and good works are needed, whether we are impacting one person at a time as we move through our days or leading large, global movements —as well as everything in between.

Good works and activism strengthen our souls just as exercise strengthens muscles, and it is imperative that we balance the outer with the inner lest we cause harm to ourselves or others. Too often I have seen beloveds who identified strongly as warriors for a cause turn their fierce aspect toward their own loved ones and community members, lashing out and isolating themselves. I have witnessed beloveds dive so deeply into service that they cannot spare a moment for their own care and become desperately sick. Let us be strong and compassionate in our actions with ourselves and others, and exercise our soul's purpose in this way. Knowing your self, your gifts, and your resources, take the steps that are available to you and remember that you are one of legion working to make this beautiful blue planet a better place for all beings.

> *In love, the two danced together—drawing ever closer, ever tighter, swirling inward and inward until this great contraction could contract no more. In orgasmic release, in this first exhale of energy, the lovers were thrown open and apart; in this rush of power, all of creation was born.*

We can know and practice all these things and still be left wondering about how to truly connect with the mystical and divine. The Anderson Feri tradition is one of the roots of Reclaiming, and some Reclaiming witches choose to work with the Feri concept of the triple soul. Many mystical traditions hold similar notions of a tripartite soul—it is found, for example, in some ancient Egyptian texts and in Hawaiian mystic practices. In the Jewish mystical tradition of Kabbalah there are three aspects of the soul with which we interact in this lifetime, as well as others beyond this lifetime.

The first aspect of the Feri triple soul is the primal soul, also referred to as younger self, fetch, or sticky one. This is the most ancient aspect of our humanity, the facet of our soul that is engaged with needs and desires and is best reached through the senses, dreams, images, and symbols. The second aspect is the communicative soul, also known as ego or talking self. This aspect moderates all the messages that come in and go out—in all the many ways we communicate—and governs our conscious self. The third aspect of the triple soul is the meta-soul, also called higher self, god soul, or sacred dove. The function of this aspect of our soul is to connect to our past and also potential future lifetimes, the meta-souls of others, and the gods. To align these three souls is to endeavor to know ourselves and all our parts—and in knowing, to connect more deeply with the mysteries within and the mysteries beyond.

I did not grow up in a religious household, and belief in anything other than Santa Claus and the Tooth Fairy was initially difficult for me and left me unsure as to how to approach Goddess, gods, and spirit in general. Luckily for me, participation in Reclaiming does not ask any specific belief of us beyond the awareness that the earth is alive, which has always seemed to me to be self-evident. Reclaiming does not work specifically or exclusively with any particular pantheon. Each person is encouraged to listen to their own soul to learn which goddesses, gods, and Mysterious Ones love them beyond all reason. Ancestors, too, can be of aid in connecting us with the deities of our bloodlines.

In my early years in Reclaiming, I worked nearly exclusively with spirit as an elemental force—more akin to gravity or magnetism than anything else. I did come to realize that there were several goddesses, gods, ancestors, and other entities with whom I was in relationship— and perhaps had been for my entire life. In one ritual we were singing a chant by Ravyn Stanfield adapted from a line toward the end of Doreen Valiente's *The Charge of the Goddess*: "I have been with you from the beginning, from the beginning I have been with you." The lines fold into and onto each other, layering until my throat is tired and the words are no longer words but a melody of connection. Images from half-remembered dreams, childhood fantasies, and vague imaginings superimpose themselves one atop another, montage-style, until suddenly Isis is standing there before me and a shiver of recognition runs through me. She reminds me of all the times she had been there with me, though I did not then know or realize her name. She shows me the hawks who are sacred to her, ever circling my childhood home and who loudly guarded the altar I had felt called to make of the burned-out oak tree on our back hill.

Yes, some gods may be with you from the beginning. Wherever that is for you. Whatever that means to you.

> First to take form: the androgynous laughing Blue God, orbiting close to the twin Mothers of Creation. The pulse of the first orgasmic contraction and expansion pattern expressing Their very being. Then arises the Green God, god of all growing things and seasons, of life, death, and rebirth. And finally, thrown furthest from the matrix is the Red God, He of circumference. He holds the edge and knows the shape of all things, walking the boundaries yet ever yearning to return to Center. Love is the beginning and the end, the apex and the nadir, the center and the circumference.

In this way, we also endlessly desire to return to her, to feel again that holy union. It is this desire that drives us to seek, to try, to practice, to come again and again into that sensation of connection. We are all born with the capacity to connect with and experience spirit. For some of us it comes easily; while for others it may feel more difficult. However, with regular engagement this can come to feel more natural. I have found that the best practice is to practice. Each of us can devise a plan to intentionally engage with our sensation of connection through our own curated daily spiritual practice.

For me, a five-point approach to daily spiritual practice is effective to clear and strengthen my receptors for the sensation of connection. The five points I work with are Gratitude, Energetic, Inward Gazing, Active, and Stillness.

Gratitude practice can be any practice acknowledging your many blessings. It can be a devotional practice where you offer gifts of thanks to your deities; some people may use prayer beads or mala, meditational beads used in Hindu and Buddhist traditions. In this practice we write down, name aloud, or think silently to ourselves the things for which we are grateful. Some people begin with the micro and move outwards, thanking the microorganisms in their body that are fighting off a cold, pollinating insects in the fields and gardens, the food in the cupboard, the tree that shades the house from the summer heat, and onward to the oceans, mountains, moon, and sun.

Energetic practices are those practices that address the energetic aspect of your being. Grounding and centering, chakra work, running the Iron Pentacle, the triple soul alignment, making kala, and purification with water, smoke, or sound are all examples of energetic practices used by many Reclaiming witches.

Inward Gazing is the practice of taking stock of your emotional, mental, and physical state. Journaling, checking in with another person, self-reflection, mirror work, painting, and drawing are all ways of connecting with oneself.

Active practices offer a multitude of options. This can be any practice of moving your physical body and can be adapted to whatever level of mobility is available to you. For some, a few minutes of deep breaths and gentle head rolls might be right. For others, walking, tai chi, swimming, dancing, yoga postures, martial arts, running, or going to the gym are all possibilities.

While there are many ways to be active, there's really only one way to be Still. It has been well-documented that meditation provides a host of benefits for mind, mood, body, and spirit. Sit, stand, or lie comfortably, unmoving save for full breathing, and allow your mind to come to a point of stillness. This is called sitting practice. I recommend using the focus of counting your breath—I use the four-square breath: four counts inhale, four counts hold, four counts exhale, four counts hold, repeat. Some use a candle flame or bowl of water as a focus point. I've also had excellent results with gong meditation; it washes my mind clear of everything. When you find your mind wandering, simply note it without judgment and return to your breath or focal point.

My own practice includes ten to fifteen minutes of sitting practice upon waking. I either sit up in bed and do my four-square breathing or go downstairs, put the kettle on, and then do my sitting practice. When I have time, I add in a session in the sauna with a gong meditation tape. My Active practice is to walk for half an hour. When I have time, I add in a yoga kriya, a series of postures, breath, and sound. My Inward Gazing practice is a simple inward scan in the shower or bath, but sometimes also while walking or doing the dishes. For Energetic Practice I run the Iron Pentacle before I sit down to work, make kala between clients or phone calls, and ground at the beginning and end of my workday. I will often do the triple soul alignment at the end of my shower. As Gratitude practice, I thank and praise Ganesha, the elephant-headed Hindu god, whenever I leave or enter my home or whenever a loved one leaves or enters my home. I name to myself all the things I am grateful for as I prepare food, garden, or clean my home.

Ideally, time would be spent every day with each of these five aspects. Begin gently, with just a few minutes for each practice. You may want to experiment with different practices until you land on the ones that feel most effective for you. Pay attention to your own nature as well as the externally imposed rhythms of your day, noticing which practices come easily for you and which stretch you. A degree of stretch is beneficial; overstretching is not. There is great value in doing the same practice every day. In part, this is so that when crisis occurs, as it inevitably does, you will have a base practice to turn to and won't have to decide, in that stressful moment, which practice might be best. Think of this daily practice as a necessary self-care ritual; just as we have self-care rituals around our physical nourishment and hygiene, we can develop rituals around our spiritual nourishment and hygiene.

Your practices do not need to be done in a single chunk of time; they can be broken up and worked into your day as appropriate. Gratitude practice can happen while preparing a meal or in the last part of the day, as you go to sleep. Energetic practice can happen while you shower or in a few minutes' break between meetings. Inward Gazing can happen while washing dishes or waiting for the bus. Active practice can be worked into a busy schedule by walking to work or getting off the bus at an earlier stop and walking the rest of the way. Stillness practice can happen in the moments just after waking or before going to sleep, although it is important not to actually be asleep for this practice. Begin and end each practice with intention. Endeavor to bring your intention to the various aspects of your practice and stay in the moment. Focus on being present in your daily spiritual practice.

All began in love; all seeks to return to love. Love is the law,
the teacher of wisdom, and the great revealer of mysteries.
—Starhawk

Our English word *spirit* comes from the Latin *spiritus*, meaning "breath." When we are born into this world and take that first breath, we begin our journey with spirit. At the end of life, we release that last breath, then move on to whatever mystery lies beyond. Every breath in between is an opportunity to connect: to oneself, to one another, to this beautiful planet, and to whatever piece of the mystery is there for you to touch. We awaken ourselves to this sense of connection every day through our good works, both inner and outer, and through our daily spiritual practices. We grow our capacity to know this mystery by practice and by listening, stretching our senses with every breath. For me, spirit remains that ineffable stuff of betwixt and between, center and circumference—the gravity that keeps us all from flying out into the far reaches of the multiverse. And this has been enough for me. More than enough—it is everything.

Ritual: Creating an Altar for Spirit

SusanneRae

Time: 30 minutes to an hour

You will need: objects for your altar, detailed below

• • •

Spirit is what holds all together; it is the thread of connection, the weave. Spirit is the center and the circle; it is everything and nothing—the void.

As a place of focus, your spirit altar should be connected to you. What you have on your spirit altar will be a reflection of your relationship with spirit. The altar may change as this relationship changes.

An altar for spirit can be as elaborate or as simple as you like. It can take you five minutes or weeks to create. Whether it is permanent in your home, garden, or workplace, or temporary, as part of a ritual, the principles are the same.

Spirit altars can be tricky because of the amorphous nature of spirit. Sometimes less is more, so maybe your altar for spirit is just a space marked by a cloth or a single object.

• • •

Before creating your altar, spend some time in contemplation or meditation with spirit.

Ask yourself:

- How is spirit for me now?
- Is the purpose of the altar to hold energy during a ritual, a place of offering, or to just hold space for spirit?
- What objects, colors, or ideas symbolize spirit for me?
- Will the altar be on the ground, a small table, or a shelf?

Choose a Space for Your Altar That Fulfils Its Intention

If your altar is going to be permanent, it should be somewhere it won't be disturbed by the movements of daily living. If it is for a ritual and in the center of the circle, make sure to leave plenty of room for movement around it. If you intend to make offerings here, make sure there is space to do so.

Gather the Objects That Embody Spirit to You

Examples include:

- Candles
- A beautiful or raw image of nature
- Crystals
- A mirror
- A cauldron
- Cloth of white / silver / purple or patterned with stars
- Musical instrument
- Images or symbols of deity
- Small table or box if height off the floor is wanted
- Incense
- Something to represent each of the elements (a stone, a feather, a shell, a candle)
- Objects that relate specifically to your intention
- If you are in a natural setting, you may just gather objects from nature. Be mindful not to deplete plants of their flowers and leaves. Often we leave something in return, such as fresh water, honey, or even your own nail clippings or hair.

Include Objects That Relate to the Intention of the Altar

If your altar is for honoring the ancestors, images of ancestors may be added. If the intention is to send healing to the environment, you may include a potted plant or soft toy animal. Make your altar relevant and meaningful to the task.

How To Set Up the Altar

Prepare the space both physically (by sweeping and clearing) and energetically (by purifying with burning herbs or clearing with water or words or toning).

Mark the space by laying your cloth on a small table, box, or shelf, or place it directly on the floor or ground.

Arrange your objects, perhaps around a central item that expresses the intention. This can help focus the altar. Make it beautiful and meaningful for you.

When you are done, sit or stand before your altar. Ground and call the energy of spirit into the altar. Speak or sing or read a poem—whatever seems right. Light the candle and incense. Say, "Welcome, spirit."

Enjoy your altar.

Practice: Aligning the Three Souls
FORTUNA SAWAHATA

Time: 20 minutes initially, then 5 minutes for
subsequent practice

You will need: a place where you can practice
undisturbed; journal and art supplies (optional)

• • •

Soul alignment is a practice that brings all of our three souls together—
animal, human, and divine—anchored in the glorious vehicle that is
our body. And it is through our body and the energetic power of our
breath that we create this alignment, connecting all three souls as one.

The concept of three souls comes through such diverse religious,
philosophical, and psychological traditions as Kabbalah, Freudian and
Jungian psychology, Hawaiian spirituality, Reclaiming witchcraft and
Anderson Feri tradition, amongst others. Plato examined the nature of
the soul and also found it to be tripartite.

It's helpful to understand the anatomy of our soul parts for the purpose of soul alignment.

The Animal Soul: Aligned with Emotion and Instinct

This part of the soul is also known as the etheric body, fetch,
younger self, animal self, sticky one, *nephesh* in Kabbalah, lower self,
child self, and *unihipili* in Hawaiian. It extends about one inch or three
centimeters from our dense physical body and is a sheath of energy
that can be charged up with breath or sex or exercise. The wordless
wisdom of the animal soul is felt in our bodies, where it is charged
with feeding, healing, and protecting us. From the terror of snakes to
the pull of desire, from the awareness that a place is haunted to the
instantaneous understanding that a person doesn't feel right to us, animal soul is instinctual and just knows things.

Our animal soul is the gateway from the physical realm to our god soul. Bypassing the logical and time-based talking soul, animal soul takes the intent of our magic and ritual, the energy and ecstasy of our sex and our dance and our breath, and carries it directly to the highest, or deepest, part of our selves, our god soul. The animal soul has needs—and when we dampen our instincts and ignore animal soul's desires for privacy or company, nature or more time spent dancing, for the variety of sexy play that melts us, for a color or scent or a song that gives delight, it may result in addiction, compulsion, rage, or exhaustion.

When we align our souls, it helps our animal soul to behave in service to our greater purpose.

The Talking Soul: Aligned with Intellect

This part of the soul is also known as the ego, the conscious, talking self, middle self, shining body, *uhane* in Hawaiian, and *ruach* in Kabbalah. It extends out about twelve inches or thirty centimeters or more around the physical body, an inverted egg of brilliance that is the seat of our rational, analytical, left-brained, word-oriented, logical, dualistic mental energy.

The talking soul is likely what we think of as "me." This is the soul part that makes plans and makes myths and stories about its own—and others'—lives. But talker is also the skeptic that fills us with doubt, often about our magic or activism or sexuality or dreams or other heartfelt desires, like a cruel parent who asks us, "What makes you think you deserve that? What a ridiculous idea!" That's why it's a good thing that talker can't speak directly to our god soul. It can, however, plan a fine ritual, and be inspired to compose a chant or poem by the wordless perceptions of animal soul, like the feeling of sun on the skin, the taste of chocolate on the tongue, the wonder of a season. It also remembers that we have to do the dishes after ritual or a meal.

When we align our souls, it helps talking soul to support us with its genius ability to think, plan, communicate, and help us practically in manifesting our goals and desires.

The God Soul: Aligned with Divine Connection

This part of the soul is also known as the deep self, higher self, divine self, personal god, *aumakua* in Hawaiian, *neshemah* in Kabbalah, or holy guardian angel.

The god soul is most frequently seen as a ball of light that is colored cobalt blue, brilliant gold, or white and rests a few inches above the crown of our head. This is the halo or mandorla seen in medieval or Renaissance representations of angels and saints. This is our perfect, whole, immortal soul that is beyond considerations of personality (talking soul) or physical need (animal soul).

The god soul is our personal god, our connection to all that is, was, or will be. This is why our true heart's desire, often expressed spontaneously by animal soul, when sent directly to god soul can result in miracles on every level, from instantaneous healing to love at first sight. When we align our souls, it allows our god soul to add its eternal, loving power to our lives, lifting the perspectives of animal and talking self. Our task as spiritual practitioners is to have knowledge of and conversation with our god soul and bring its love to all the worlds.

How To Align Your Souls

Stand or sit comfortably. Breathe in a way that fills your physical body with energy. This is known as pranayama in yoga or the collection of mana in Huna.

A fourfold breath is a good way to begin:

- inhale to the count of four
- hold to the count of four
- exhale to the count of four
- hold to the count of four
- take one fourfold breath for the body
- take one fourfold breath for the animal soul
- take one fourfold breath for the talking soul
- take one fourfold breath for the god soul

Do you feel the buildup of energy? Do you sense it in your chest or your sex or up your spine? If not, do another cycle of four fourfold breaths. Then gather that energy into a final full breath: tilt your head back and fiercely breathe your life energy up to god soul on a fast exclamation of *ha!*

State: "May all three souls be in alignment."

Feel the blessing of the breath you sent up to god soul showering down around you. You may feel your souls snap together or get a chill down your spine or spontaneously feel your pubococcygeus muscle contract or feel a lot of sexual energy.

This is the time to journal or draw what you may have seen, felt, or sensed.

As a daily practice, the soul alignment exercise can bring new awareness of your soul parts and their connection and interaction with each other. Most importantly, you build relationship with the highest and most sound part of you: god soul. Our ultimate goal is to bring the eternal wisdom of god soul into our embodied lives, informing and integrating this with our physical, emotional, mental, and magical work.

For more information on the three souls, you may want to read *The Spiral Dance* by Starhawk, *Evolutionary Witchcraft* by T. Thorn Coyle, or *Etheric Anatomy* by Victor Anderson.

Practice: Dropped and Open Through Ritual Space

LISA LIND

Time: 45 minutes

You will need: a journal and pen or a voice recorder; a space where you will not be disturbed that has enough room to cast a circle

• • •

When we create sacred space, we are often concentrating on the main body of the ritual ahead of us instead of being fully present. In this exercise creating sacred space will be our primary focus. We will deeply feel into the changes each step creates. For those who have cast circles many times before, this is a chance to excite your fetch, or younger self, while casting and calling the elements, which may have become routine. For those who are just starting out, this exercise can help to deepen your understanding of why we prepare for ritual by casting a circle.

• • •

Begin by clearing a space to work and setting a recording device (either pen and paper or a voice recorder) close by. I prefer a voice recorder, as I do not have to step out of process to take notes.

Enter a dropped and open state in this way: collect your thoughts into a ball about the size of an apple inside your head. When your focus is centered on that ball, slowly let that ball drop through your throat, past your rib cage, and come to rest in your belly. This brings your attention to the place in your body we associate with our intuitive fetch, the sensing and instinctual part of ourself. Allow the ball to flatten out parallel to the ground. Let it expand as a disc or as tendrils about a meter or a few feet outside your body. This technique was developed from martial arts practices. It allows us to stay present and grounded while increasing our intuitive energy-sensing abilities because our focus is in our lower body, not in our head.

While maintaining this dropped and open state, send roots down into the earth. Do this slowly—our brains need time to compute all the data our senses can give. Pay particular attention to how this feels in your body. Because people experience energy changes in very diverse ways—such as color, taste, sound, knowing—take the time to explore all your senses, even those you may feel are not your strengths. Before you go on, jot down some notes or speak what you are sensing in real time if you are using a voice recorder. If you feel you have slipped out of dropped and open, reenter that state before you go on.

Next, slowly cast a circle. How is the space changing? How are you changing? Does your state of mind or emotional landscape change? Does anything look or feel different? Do things smell and taste the same or different than before? Can you sense the border of the circle you cast? Take your time. Record your findings.

Repeat this process after the calling in of the elements and again after any deities you may want to invoke. Record your experiences at each step. As you go through devoking and releasing the circle, again notice what changes for you, both within and without. When you are finished, return your focus into a ball in your belly and let it slowly rise back up into your head. Let the ball dissolve. You may wish to flesh out your notes after you are finished.

If you have the opportunity to work with someone else, the exercise can be modified so one person creates sacred space while the other sits in dropped and open. Swap roles and share your experiences.

Divination
FLAME

• • •

When I need information and guidance, as a witch I seek insight from the divine, that part of ourselves in touch with goddesses, gods, nature, the elements, ancestors, and other spirits. For all these things I use divination. This helps me to feel more empowered to address difficult questions and to change things that may be blocking me from achieving balance and harmony in my daily life. I also use divination to seek answers and ask for clarity about my place in the universe.

When we work with divination, we access a deep, developed intuition. We often work with divination practices, systems, and tools to discover information not available by other means. Intuition is the ability to understand something internally, without the need for conscious reasoning. Often people use the phrase *I feel it in my gut* to describe intuition. Divination is most effective and easily practiced when we are empathic, compassionate, psychic, intuitive, and imaginative. One of the exercises that can assist in developing these traits is the triple soul alignment. Other practices I find important are cleansing, purification, and communing with my ancestors. These exercises are explained in other parts of this book and are extremely useful. They are used to ready oneself for magical work.

Divination also can be used to increase and hone our intuition. It is a practice that arouses the inner senses, opens the way to deep wisdom within ourselves, and connects us to the wisdom of other beings in the cosmos. Through the integration of divinatory skill sets, we learn to better see the patterns underlying circumstances in our lives; we become enchanted by our own knowing, learning to become confident in accessing what is already there within us.

Other ways that Reclaiming witches get information is to practice self-reflection and seek feedback from peers and mentors. Self-reflection is the ability to exercise introspection, which is the examination of one's own thoughts and feelings. Both self-reflection and introspection require the willingness to learn more about one's fundamental nature, purpose, and essence. This assists in achieving a balanced life and being an ethical witch. Divination can also be a creative, fun, and informative practice.

There are many different forms of divination. These vary from the simpler, quickly picked up techniques to complex techniques that may take more direct experience to become confident with. When I took my first Reclaiming Elements of Magic class, I was exposed to many divination practices and taught how to use some of them. When I teach Elements of Magic, I try to teach those same divination types, as well as some others that are not so common. We often teach the uses of tarot cards, the pendulum, scrying with various tools, and runes.

Tarot

Tarot cards are often the first form of divination we meet. The tarot is the most used and practiced divinatory tool among Reclaiming witches I know. Tarot is also fairly easy to find, to learn, and to use. I have been using tarot cards for over twenty-five years, and I still find them one of my most useful and fulfilling sources for communing with the spirits (or Goddess, gods, God Herself, ancestors) to guide me.

The tarot is a deck of playing cards that was originally used in mid-fifteenth-century Europe as a game. In the eighteenth century it began to be used for occult divination and other mystic purposes. This includes the practice of using cards to seek answers to questions from the past, present, or future.

Like our common playing cards, the tarot has four suits. There are fourteen cards in each suit, numbered one (ace) to ten, and the face or court cards of king, queen, knight, and page (or, in many contemporary decks, king, queen, prince, and princess). There are also other variations on these court cards, always denoting a group of four related characters. The number and court cards together are called the minor arcana. The tarot also contains the twenty-one major arcana cards and a single card, the Fool, which is often marked as zero and usually counted as a major card.

I use tarot cards almost daily and often draw one card for the week. I often trance as a way to open my mind, heart, and spirit as I begin this practice. I shuffle the deck while holding the question "What gifts and challenges will there be for me during the next week?" I then pull one card from the deck and observe the emotions, thoughts, or guidance that arise in answer to my question. When we pick out a card like this, we do it with the deck facedown so that we cannot see which card we have chosen until we turn it over.

In reading tarot we might use a spread, which refers to how the cards are laid out in a pattern. Each placement or position of a card within the pattern is ascribed certain meaning. For quick answers I use the three-card spread, where the three cards represent the past, present, and future of my question. There are many other spreads, which can be found in books, on the internet, or you can make up your own. The major arcana contains the more esoteric cards, and it is from these cards that much of the divination might be received. These cards usually have beautiful drawings, paintings, collage, or photos on them. The major arcana cards are named things such as Justice, the Moon, the High Priestess, the Chariot, and the Devil.

The Rider-Waite-Smith Tarot deck is one of the most commonly used and referred-to decks. This deck is often erroneously only referred to by the publisher, Rider, and A. E. Waite, the male director of the project. Pamela Colman Smith was the artist and is therefore responsible for some of the most memorable tarot scenes in history. This was also the first commercially released deck to create pictorial narrative through the minor arcana cards, those listed one to ten and the court cards. One of the main reasons for using this particular deck

is that it has been used by people for over a century. The same meaning has been attributed to the same cards over and over for many years.
Every tarot deck comes with a beginner's booklet that explains the
divinatory meanings of each card.

There are now many different decks with various pictures and
meanings. Some of the other popular tarot decks are Motherpeace,
Wildwood, and Aleister Crowley and Lady Frieda Harris's Thoth deck.
Many of the available decks are relatively new, and some people appreciate that there are not centuries of use in them, freeing them from
meanings that are traditional in the older decks.

Although the tarot is often used by oneself alone or in reading for
beloveds or clients, it can also be used in groups and communities.
One example of this is using tarot cards when planning ritual in a
group. Tarot can be used to get ideas for what the ritual will be, or
how to bring the intent through into the ritual. The group lays out a
spread and everyone suggests meanings gleaned from the cards. They
then use these meanings to find an intention for the ritual or to suggest parts of the ritual.

In choosing the tarot cards as a divination method, you will find
yourself in good company. This creates a community of diviners that
can share their experiences with this form of divination. Tarot might
help you with a variety of everyday situations, including at work,
home, and in relationship. I invite you to begin this practice. It will
most likely deepen and clarify the questions you have about different
things in your life and thus make you a wiser witch.

Pendulum

The pendulum is perhaps one of the quickest and easiest divination
tools to teach and learn. The pendulum is a string, jewelry chain, or
piece of twine tied to a heavier object like a rock, a weighty silver coin,
an old key, or any heavy object that is also fairly small. The two major
things pendulums are used for are sensing energies or receiving
answers to questions. The use of the pendulum was taught in every

Elements of Magic class from the earliest days of San Francisco Bay Reclaiming.

My own pendulum is made of a light silver chain that has a small silver T-bar where I hold it, and at the bottom is a snowflake obsidian stone. One way to begin using a pendulum requires a piece of printer-sized paper. Draw a circle big enough to fill the page and a line down the center, making two halves; write yes on one side and no on the other. The person asking the question grounds, focuses, and prepares. Then, holding the pendulum in one's hand as still as is possible (probably with your elbow resting on the surface of a table) and thinking only of the question one is seeking an answer to, the pendulum will usually start to move. It may either move back and forth or in a circular pattern. Eventually it will stop on one side of the paper or the other, or it may swing directly to the answer. This is a great exercise for skeptics, as it is they themselves who hold the pendulum and notice the response.

The pendulum as a divination tool has been used to explore the bigger questions of life. Answers to questions about one's place in the universe and how to find a path in it are some of these questions. Sensing energy or life force and its flow is one of its other uses, which both beginners and those more experienced may find useful in the practice of witchcraft.

Scrying Tools

The scrying tools of both the mirror and the crystal ball are wonderful forms of divination. They are vital aids to my own abilities in sensing energies and in answering questions I might have, including questions about my own personal path, influences from my past, present, and future, and questions of a larger nature concerning my place in the universe and how I relate to it.

Scrying mirrors are both a powerful divinatory tool and a common household item. This makes it useful for those witches in the closet.

Conversely, the crystal ball has no ordinary uses and is seen as a divination tool immediately. I suggest a handheld mirror for beginners' use. Any handheld mirror is fine, from a dollar item to a silver Victorian vanity mirror. As mirror work became more a part of my daily practice, I obtained and now use a more ornate handheld mirror.

When looking into the mirror, I let my eyes go soft and continue gazing straight ahead, trying not to have left-to-right or up-and-down eye movement, although I do continue to blink. I begin to notice more and more—perhaps shadows or images appear in my features in the mirror that shiver and glisten. There may be other senses involved too, such as sounds, changes in temperature, or smells. I introduce myself to myself in the mirror.

In working with scrying mirrors, blockages might be sensed. Initially, I just take mental notes that I write down after finishing. As we become more experienced, we learn to interact, change, and grow with insights gained in mirror work. The mirror may expose both past and future visions. A black mirror is used for scrying by many of my witch friends. Instead of a mirror, try using a smooth water surface or any reflective surface. Flames are also sometimes used in this way. The experience of using different reflective surfaces may assist your ability to use scrying successfully as a divination method.

Crystal balls are another scrying tool. They have been used traditionally to see the past, present, and future in the cloudy depths of their crystal nature. There is a sense of timelessness in my experiences of using crystal balls, as if past, present, and future are all mixed together, so while I love exploring with this divination tool, it's not one I feel confident with.

Runes

Runes are a method of divination used by many people in Reclaiming. Initially the Nordic runes were a writing system, although historically they were also used for magical purposes. I choose the runes to work with when I seek to understand my higher self, as opposed to seeking answers about the past, present, and future.

The runes are considered a type of oracle. The Elder Futhark, the traditional Nordic set of runes, comprises twenty-four runes. Modern runes also sometimes include an extra blank rune known as the Wyrd rune. This is the set I use. The runes are divided into three groups, or families, of eight runes, known as an Aett. They were named after the Norse gods Freyr, Hagal, and Tyr, respectively.

I consider the casting of runes as sacred play. When I have limited information or wisdom about things, I like to consult the oracle of the runes. When I reach into the bag to pull a rune, it is as if the right rune always seems to jump dramatically into my fingers. There are many books to assist in the interpretation of the runes. The one I always return to is Ralph Blum's *The Book of Runes*. Runes are a special type of divination tool that might aid us to understand more about our higher self and the blockages that may be stopping our full potential.

Other Tools

There are a few other divinatory tools I'd like to briefly discuss that are not as common in Reclaiming practice. Reclaiming boldly states in our Principles of Unity that "Our ultimate spiritual authority is within, and we need no other person to interpret the sacred to us." It is with this in mind that I invite all to choose whichever divination tool works best, even if it might be considered outside of common Reclaiming practices.

Tea leaf divination is known as tasseomancy. It is a divination or fortunetelling method that interprets patterns perceived in tea leaves. The method of this form of divination is fairly simple. A cup of tea is poured, then drunk or poured out. The diviner finds patterns in the tea leaves in the cup and uses their imagination to find shapes suggested by the tea leaves. They might look like a face, a heart, or a tower, for example. These shapes are then interpreted intuitively or by means of a fairly standard system of symbolism, like most types of divination. Another divination method is the I Ching, which is an ancient Chinese divination text using a type of divination called cleromancy, which produces seemingly random numbers to determine divine intent.

· · · ·

Divination can be used for oneself, others, and communities as a whole. I currently mostly practice divination for myself. I use it to glean knowledge about myself and my current situation and how things will be if I continue along the path revealed in the divination.

Divination for the purpose of helping others is probably its most universal application. Divination for others is a great way to develop friendships and to assist people in finding ways to improve their lives, while serving oneself and one's community. It can be especially helpful in groups to address issues of power, inclusivity, and diversity. Divination for groups or in a community setting allows for a greater presence to be known than just those of individual people in the meeting. It gives the group a chance to listen to everyone's input. This is helpful for those people who have a hard time speaking up in groups or don't feel included. It could also be that their demographic has traditionally been excluded or they are one of the only people of their race, gender, sexuality, or other identifying group there.

Divination can also be used as a filter for your magical practice. It can help to reveal things that no longer serve you and offer advice on how to create change. It takes one out of ordinary consciousness and reveals the shadows and lights within. One is then able to address unhealthy practices, behaviors, or styles of communication. It offers the diviner an ability to achieve distance from their own preconceived notions. My magical practices are acts of service, and divination can be an act of service, both to individuals and communities.

Divination may also employ the use of a powerful intuitive gift known as second sight, or what Starhawk calls acrostic vision. Second sight is the power to perceive things that are not present to the senses;

this information usually is received in the form of a vision or a knowing. It may contain information about future events before they happen or about events in remote locations. Acrostic vision uses the technique of softening the gaze so that the eyes are able to include a wider field of vision. It works very well for helping to plan direct political actions where dangerous and noncontrollable elements may be involved. Divination increases our abilities in intuition, empathy, imagination, and sensitivity to energies. This will all help us develop deeper connections with ourselves, each other, and spirit.

For those of you seeking to connect with spirit, divination is one of the best ways to do so. I hope it brings enlightenment into your lives, as it has to mine.

Exercise: Elemental Pentacle
Rae Eden

Time: 30–40 minutes

You will need: tape or string to create a
large pentacle on the ground

• • •

This exercise can be done individually or in a group.

To prepare for this exercise, use the tape or string to make a pentacle about three feet long on each side. If you are doing this outside in soft dirt or sand, you can draw the pentacle on the ground. Label each point, starting with spirit at the top point. Going around clockwise as you look upon the pentagram, label the next point air, then water, then fire, and then earth.

• • •

Stand on the point of spirit. Ground and center.

Walk directly from the point of spirit, along the tape, to the point of fire in the direction that we draw an invoking pentagram. This will be the bottom left-hand point if you are looking at the pentagram from above. Breathe in and out. Feel the qualities of fire, of passion, of vitality, of energy. Feel your heart pumping life force. Visualize the fire in the earth and the fire in your body. Spend a few minutes meditating on the qualities of fire. When you are ready, take a breath and say out loud, "Blessed be fire."

Walk from the point of fire directly to the upper right point of air. Stand on the point and breathe in. Feel the qualities of air, of breath, of communication, of the intellect. Fill your lungs with air. Inhale and exhale slowly, feeling the oxygen in your blood running through your body. Spend a few minutes meditating on the qualities of air. When you are ready, take another breath in and say out loud, "Blessed be air."

Walk from the point of air directly to the upper left point of earth. Breathe in the qualities of earth, of the trees rooted in the ground, of foundations and stability. Feel the earth under your feet and the earth that is your body. Spend a few minutes meditating on the qualities of earth. When you are ready, say out loud, "Blessed be earth."

Walk from the point of earth directly to the lower right point of water. Breathe in and feel the qualities of water, of emotion, of change, of intuition. Connect with the waters of the world and the water making up your body. Spend a few minutes meditating on the qualities of water. When you are ready, take a breath and say out loud, "Blessed be water."

Walk from the point of water back to the top point of spirit. Breathe in. Feel the qualities of spirit, of centeredness, of immanence, the joining of the directions, connection to all. Spend a few minutes meditating on the qualities of spirit. When you are ready, say out loud, "Blessed be spirit."

Now walk in a circle along the outside of the pentacle (you might choose to move clockwise in the northern hemisphere and counter-clockwise in the southern hemisphere) to seal the energy. From spirit to air, to water, to fire, to earth, and back to spirit, or from spirit to earth, to fire, to water, to air, and back to spirit. At each point name the element aloud or internally and feel its qualities. As you walk around the circle, notice how the energy shifts between the points. Walk around three times.

Blessed be the elemental pentacle.

A more advanced version of this is to run the energy of the elements through the body. This is done with spirit in the head, fire in the right foot, air in the left hand, earth in the right hand and water in the left foot. These elemental associations are drawn from the way elements are worked within the Iron Pentacle.

Spell: Creating a Sigil

PHOENIX LEFAE

Time: 15–30 minutes

You will need: pen and paper

• • •

A sigil is a magical symbol. Sigils can be used for creating a spell, as a representation of your magical name, to keep something secret, or for a myriad of other purposes.

Words are powerful. They carry meaning and intention, but they are also understandable by others, and we might not always want others to know about the magical words that we are using. With a sigil we are able to take the power, intent, and energy of many words and condense them down into one symbol, keeping the original meaning secret. This symbol retains the power of the many words, but another person looking at it would be unable to ascertain what that original meaning might be. A sigil is the potent, crystallized concentration of something—whether an intention or a name—and because of that profound synthesis it becomes even more powerful, greater than the sum of its parts.

• • •

The first step in creating a sigil for spellwork is to craft your intention.

When you are working a spell, it's important that your intention be clear, concise, and specific. However, don't write out an intention so specific that you limit possibility. This process can be tricky, and it may take some practice. You need to be clear about what you want to manifest, but not so narrow in focus that you cut off potential that you may not be aware of. Some examples of effective intentions are *I make the choices necessary to create love in my life* and *Let me find ways to be of service to my community.*

If you are creating a sigil for another reason, such as to represent your magical name, the name of your coven, or for anything else, the process is a lot easier since you don't have to write out a whole intention. You already know the words that you want to incorporate; the time it takes will be less because crafting an intention can take a lot of time.

Steps in Creating a Sigil

- What is your goal, the reason you want to do spellwork? Write out your goal, your intention. For example: *I call in prosperity.*
- Now strike through all the vowels and rewrite your intention. Our example intention would now look like this: CLLNPRSPRTY
- Strike through any duplicate letters, so you are left with one of each consonant from your original intention. Our sample intention would look like this: CLNPRSTY
- Take the remaining consonants and create one symbol using them all. You can layer them on top of each other, flip them upside down, or put them backwards. There isn't one correct way to do this; rather, you have the opportunity to create something that appeals to you and contains the power of your original goal. You can see many examples of this on the internet.

Once you have your sigil, you can activate it by grounding, centering, aligning your souls, and bringing all your attention to your breath.

You might enter a fourfold breath cycle as mentioned on page 231 or you might start to lightly tap a rhythm on your thighs or belly or on a drum. Raise the power while focusing entirely on beholding your intention as being fulfilled. Surrender into possibility and mystery as you carve out how it could be with your magical will.

When the power peaks, release it all into the sigil. See the sigil glowing fiercely with that power, or just know firmly that it is now activated and alive.

You may now draw this sigil repeatedly in various places or just keep it on a single piece of paper on your altar or in a special place.

Working with the Spirits
GEDE PARMA

* * *

Witches and spirits go hand in hand. There is a history to this—vast tracts of historical record, scholarly research, folk legend and lore, and even, within orders of witches, hidden legends we tell each other around fires and curled up together, remembering and seeing into what might still come to pass. In all of this we journey with the spirits, with deities, with powerful allies, guides, initiators, guardians, and watchers—familiar spirits—and we deepen into the heart of the Star Goddess Herself, who is all things. Reclaiming is a tradition of witches who invoke, connect, and commune with the Goddess and her infinite rain of bright spirits.

If you grew up with stories from the Old Testament, you might remember the Witch of Endor who conjured up the prophet Samuel at King Saul's command. You might remember that the witch was scared, resentful of this summons because she and people like her had been banished and reviled by the Hebrew tribes. Some of you might recall what happened in Scotland, England, Iceland, Germany, France, and Salem…tens of thousands of accused witches were killed at the pyre or by noose or by drowning after enduring starvation and torture. It's still happening: in Papua New Guinea, in India, in various countries in Africa.

The European persecution of witches happened for many reasons and is a whole study in itself. A fundamental accusation was that the witch had engaged with familiar spirits or the devil himself, who seemed to manifest in multiple guises: angelic, faerie, ancestral, animal, plant, planetary, and even as Christ or Mary. Via these pacts, the witch was said to be able to blight someone's crops, spoil the milk, kill livestock, harm people, and generally bring disease and poverty. All of this same behavior was assigned to the faerie folk as well. Witches and the fae have been kin for millennia. All witchcraft today arises out of this quagmired and complex history. We still work with spirits because we are heirs to the folkloric, shamanic, oracular, and sorcerous practices indigenous to various parts of what we now call Europe, North Africa, and the Middle East.

The terrors of the slave trade, of invasion and colonization of lands to which other people belonged—the traditional owners and custodians—has meant that both our and their traditions and spirits have met and been changed. Witches are spirit workers; we ally with, conjure, and invoke—even make love with—various spirit-beings, including deities, because we know we are peers in the infinite web of relationships of which we are all part. The Star Goddess, by all her many names, is all things. Every being we meet inside her is another embodiment of the Goddess, and thus in connecting through meditation, prayer, trance, spellwork, ritual, initiation, dreams, and daily life, we deepen our intimacy with She Who Is All.

The Reclaiming tradition has been called an invocatory tradition. I first heard that statement from Rose May Dance, an elder and one of the founders of Reclaiming, sitting outside the ritual room in her home in San Francisco. I interpreted it to mean that our ritual style performs various functions in and between the worlds. First, to become grounded in place and sensitive to the powers in our bodies and the powers in the land so that we may connect and commune with them. Second, to create a strong and secure magical container that will act as a compass to orient our journeys between the worlds and as a cauldron in which to brew our spells or to scry for wisdom. Third, to invoke and call or conjure into that container various spirits and often deities who will aid in fulfilling the magical intention we have crafted for the purpose of the ritual. We conjure and invoke these spirits to ally with us in our work. We also sometimes call them because we are curious, because we're beginning to feel seduced, or because we are completely, emphatically in love.

Reclaiming is an eclectically available tradition in that we have no single pantheon, or family of spirits, we are bound to—other than the Star Goddess—although there are beings and pantheons that have become enmeshed in the magical work of Reclaiming. Reclaiming is rooted and grows wild from a group of witches who invoked and worked intimately with beings known throughout Celtic, Greek, Sumerian, Yoruban, Hindu, Egyptian, and Nordic pantheons. Inanna, Persephone, Demeter, Brighid, Yemaya, Kali, Isis, and Freyja are familiar presences in Reclaiming communities and WitchCamps. However, a Reclaiming witch may form relationships with whomever or whatever in their own time and in their own way.

Reclaiming draws upon Feri cosmologies and practices as part of its spiritual inheritance. Our understanding of and poetry relating to the Goddess is connected to this. Whereas in some forms of modern Wicca the Goddess is one of two beings in active sexual or magical polarity with each other (the other being the male Horned God), in Reclaiming it is more common to wield the word Goddess to refer to everything in existence, and especially as a naming of the cycles of birth, growth, death, decay, and regeneration. In 1979 Starhawk wrote that the Great Star Goddess birthed a rain of bright spirits; so instead of active gender-polarity creating all, it is holy lust and desire between the Goddess and her own reflection that births infinite beings with whom we are in relationship.

A spirit, in animistic cultures, is any person or being who is not a living human being, even those we consider to be non-living by the dictates of modern science. Human beings are, of course, spirits, but when witches and Pagans say "the spirits" it is simply a poetic and all-encompassing way of saying "all other-than-human beings." Some people believe that spirits are discarnate, that they are not fleshy or sensual, but in my experience the duality between what is considered to be material or physical and what is considered to be ethereal or spiritual is a false and often debilitating one. Spirits certainly have bodies, all centers of awareness have bodies; we just might not always be sensitive to them. An oak tree is a spirit, a river is a spirit, a mountain, a crossroads, a knife, a cloud...all spirits. We could say a spirit is a being of nature, a being belonging to God Herself, who is whole and complete unto herself. The world is filled with spirits.

In Reclaiming we often call and invoke deities, a special kind of spirit: gods, goddesses, and non-gendered or other-gendered deities. Deities are complex beings, and what they are in the scheme of things is truly for each of us to discover. There are many perspectives and opinions based on noticeable patterns within direct experience and lore. In my experience deities exist, and I conjecture there is a reason we use that word to designate them within the infinity of spirits and beings. An important caveat in the Craft is that the spirits and gods don't necessarily require my belief for me to encounter them. I consider this to be one of the most remarkable precepts of witchcraft and Paganism; these traditions and systems of practice do not require belief and certainly not blind faith!

One way to regard the origins and natures of deities is that a deity may be born of three rivers, or roads. One river is the indwelling nativity of a place, the intrinsic numinous aliveness of the land. One river or road comprises the great and volatile forces that fill the raging cosmos or void. Another river is a potent and mighty act of sacrifice, exchange, or initiation. So three rivers converge and catalyze the genesis of a god or goddess.

Let us imagine that at a particular place, on a particular land, someone travels to an old ash tree. Here they are haunted with visions of wolves and ravens. They have been called to go to that particular tree in that particular place because of fate, because there is a needful desire swelling in the cosmos for a god to be born and a people to become initiated into wisdom. They hang themselves on the tree for nine nights, or perhaps one night that feels like nine nights, and two ravens come to the tree to witness what is becoming. Perhaps Odin, the All-Father, Norse god of runes and magic, existed before this one went to this tree. Perhaps this act raised enough power to open a door for great force, powerful land, and the consciousness of people to converge and catalyze the genesis of a being who is greater than the sum of these parts. Then as those people who are filled with the power of that land and its legends travel, their ancestral deities wander and voyage with them. Now the whole world is filled with gods and people and spirits in every place.

A deity seems to be a great and noble spirit. Those who are assigning these qualities of great and noble are humans and our communities. Great and noble when it comes to what they have gifted humanity with: their own sacrifices and initiations that have empowered and aided us in our actual lives and our deaths, one of the few things we can be sure of. Auset, Isis. Nebt-het. Hermes. Llew. Rhiannon. Arthur. Oshun. Durga. Ganesha. Thor. Tonantzin. This mixed list might seem sacrilegious or disrespectful to some Pagans and witches today, but Reclaiming is filled with many people with various ethnicities, ancestries, and relationships. How could we not make room for all our spirit-beloveds in our tradition where community is the capstone?

There are multiple entries into working with spirit-beings. Before working with a spirit, we need to introduce ourselves and then begin to cultivate a respectful and conscious relationship. It makes no sense to call Aphrodite to aid you in a love spell if you have never felt her presence, aspected her in ritual, or heard stories of her from friends who honor her, or at least made a purposeful introduction. Aphrodite is a goddess; she is a big being. She is likely to hear a genuine call full of yearning and the tender aches of desire and need. You may have researched in various ways what foods, smells, colors, and plants she likes and made a charm bag, or found a dove feather and tied it to red thread with bells to play with as you chant and sing to her. If one is earnest, if one is opening their heart, if one is risking connection, when we are willing to meet the reality and power of magic, then the spirits and gods come.

Reclaiming invocations are often beautiful and startlingly clear. Some options for invoking a spirit or deity to come into presence include silent or verbal invocation, gestures and movement, incense, scents and oils, drama or mummery, song or chant, or instrumental music. A powerful and effective invocation is one that will seduce the senses of the spirit and those gathered, give them a reason or purpose to attend, and raise enough power so that the space is vibrating with life force and intensity. The invocation may seem small and silent or loud and colorful; just as often it could be wordless and yet expansive and rushing, or boisterous yet concentrated to a needle's point. What could you imagine would capture the attention of this Mysterious One, of this ancestor, of this deity?

In order to deepen connection with a spirit or deity, research is a good idea, and it gathers up and focuses energy toward your relationship with this being. Examine books, both primary and secondary sources. Go to a museum and gaze at ancient art. You could even Google modern devotional art to particular deities or spirits. Trance into the edges of their stories and myths. If this is an ancestor, try to find their birthday and death day; if they are familial to you, ask your family for something that links to them directly—a letter, a piece of clothing, a recipe for food or drink that they loved in life. If you can afford it, travelling to the lands of that spirit or deity will offer many portals of depth and insight into who they are.

The witch is in her circle, the directions and elements are honored, she is grounded and aligned within her being. He has invoked the spirits and they have come. We can feel it, our hair has stood on end, our minds are filled with flashes of color or clear visions. The wind has rushed in or died down in answer; the chimes sound. Maybe you just know that they have come. Utilizing the skills of trance and journeying, of raising power, of scrying, divination, aura sensing, deep listening, meditation, and open-heartedness, you will engage in the encounter with the spirit. Use the skills you have learned and sharpened in the course of working through the elements to practice presence with this being.

A significant part of cultivating and deepening relationship with the spirits is presence. For me this manifests in many ways. I have a daily practice of soul alignment, grounding, centering, cleansing, clearing, divination, and discernment. You can find examples of these processes throughout this book. This all helps to wake up my presence by honing my awareness. I am loosened and elucidated by these practices. I must come to the spirit as clearly and consciously as possible if I am hoping for the same quality from them.

At this point I might begin to rock or sway, or get up and dance and play my drum or clap a rhythm with my hands or on my thighs and chest. I sing and chant, usually words that honor and praise this particular being. There are countless chants out there in the world. Look them up, ask after them. The internet is a boon in this regard. There is an exercise in writing and singing chants on page 98 if you feel your creativity emerging. Reclaiming is rich in its chants.

We can build shrines or make tools, power objects, or fetishes while we are communing. These are great ways to anchor the essence of your connection with a spirit into something tangible, which you can go to or pick up again at another time and reinvigorate with a breath or two. These shrines, tools, or fetishes are now imbued with the power of this spirit. They may be worked with in other rituals, spells, or exercises in order to bring the power via memory and life-force connection (sometimes we just call this energy) into the experience. An example of this could be a mask for Pan that is created in a devotional or magical working with Pan. That mask will therefore hold the spirit of that experience and be able to be worn or used to invoke Pan again in a later ritual or working. These touchstones or anchors make things more easeful over time; they also gather potency with regular use and therefore open doorways to the mystery more efficiently.

We can invoke and call the spirits to come to us in order to ask questions, or to find a solution that we might not be able to come to on our own. Along our paths we will discover certain spirits have knowledge, areas of expertise, and skills or gifts and challenges. I often invoke or lean into my connection with Aphrodite when I am feeling lost, stuck, confused, or disoriented concerning love, sexuality, sensuality, or pride in self and beauty. When I am wondering about my travel plans or money, I work with Hermes and meditate on my connection with him, making more room for it in my consciousness and stepping through those portals to greet him and strategize together.

Maybe an ancestor of yours was of the same or similar profession as the one you have. You might consider contacting this ancestor or beloved dead to enquire about how their experience was, what they learned, and what insights they possess. Perhaps there's someone in your lineage who was considered especially wise, gifted, intelligent, humble, or proactive; is this someone you could forge a magical connection with to gain more insight or empower your life in this world?

Particular plant, animal, fungi, and mineral spirits also have knowledge, experience, and wisdom that humans just don't possess. These sovereign spirits can also be contacted through trance or called into ritually cast circles to magnify the connection, like a lens. The best option is to harvest, find, or collect the physical body of such a spirit (that is, a plant or stone person) and wear, burn (if it's dried), sleep with, or carry it as a charm.

Witches are spirit workers. This is one of the reasons our kind have been sought after, valued, feared, ridiculed, and killed for millennia. We have always existed under various names wherever humans have been, in whichever time, society, or place. Our covenant with the spirit peoples is an important source of our power, and in Reclaiming we aim to act from power-from-within and power-with. The deities and spirits I am most intimate with have consistently helped me to access my own power-from-within and thereby necessitate power-with in deepening relationship. They have often given me insights or responses that have surprised or chilled me. Aphrodite once told me to return to my primary lover rather than find other lovers. I realized how wise this was. Persephone once asked me to *Stop!* and I bound myself into a vow in which the only alcohol I could drink was wine, and that vow was kept for ten full years. My fetch-mate, Felix, who lived several human lives in the seventeenth and eighteenth centuries, has helped me to retrieve lost or stolen knowledge and lore that has been foundational and inspirational to my practice in the Wildwood tradition. This information was later meticulously and specifically verified by multiple external sources.

I have witnessed the gods as they appeared to me corporeally, heard their voices clearly and profoundly, seen their faces flash through humans in the street or on the train, and bumped into them in both ancient temples and clubs. I have met them at crossroads in every land I have stepped into. All the world is full of spirits. A witch is one who pays attention, consecrates relationships, cultivates connections, draws life force, power, and wisdom from these connections, and brings the magic through. In the Reclaiming tradition, we enshrine, adore, and respect the magic of relationships, and we invoke the spirits in the circle and out.

How do the spirits move you into deeper relationship, into intimacy, with God Herself? How are they in you, of you, through you? Do you dare to invite the risk of connection with the Mysterious Ones into your life?

More questions fill my mind and heart…because I am related, I am in relationship. This is inescapable fact. It is often said the witch is never alone, even when she is in solitude. We dance with the Mysterious Ones. We live, breathe, celebrate, cry, love, break open, and triumph with them. Will I turn up; how will I know when to draw a boundary or to open my arms wide to the rush of love and desire that comes with being alive and with the work of magic? And when it is all too much—when I am anxious at even the thought of having to engage with another being, another person in my life—I will remember that I can lay down, curl up, ground, and let the earth hold me…

simply breathe, chant, pray, and praise the air...lay in the sun, drum, make love, and praise the fire...shower, bathe, swim, and drink water. In everything we do, we are in relationship with the spirits, and the elements of life support us all.

Ritual: Calling an Ally

GEDE PARMA

Time: 10 minutes to an hour

• • •

This technique and exercise are key to Reclaiming cultures of relating to the Mysterious Ones. I never learned it in a specific way from any Reclaiming teacher or witch, but we all do it in some form or another. This works especially in times of deep need and feeling. It also works extremely successfully if you already know the ally you are reaching out to.

• • •

Ground and center. Align your three souls.

Begin to contemplate the expanse, the depth, the distilled essence of your aligned souls, and notice how you are feeling. Draw upon the emotional currents in your being. With your breath, will, vision, and sensing, call the raw power out of those emotions. Begin to collect that raw power into one of your hands, the hand you feel most drawn to in that moment.

There is a reason here, it doesn't have to be immediately clear or make too much sense, but there is something behind why you need the presence of this ally. Open yourself to curiosity, compassion, and kindness for self, as well as the courage and daring inside that allows you to ask and open.

When you are in the state described above, and the power is palpable or available to you in your hand, send it out as a song, vibration, cord of light, fragrance, or messenger to the ally, known or unknown. Do not be afraid to feel your need, your longing, your desire to connect; this is the fuel of this magic. We all need connection. This is holy; this is the stuff we are made of.

Soon or quickly or gradually, you may begin to notice the ally draw near. If this is one of your beloved deities, perhaps you hear their voice or feel the way you do when they arrive. Perhaps this is an ancestor of some kind and you smell a familiar scent or hear your name being called in a voice unmistakably their own. This could be a plant, animal, or even the god soul, the deep self, of a friend that lives outside of your city or in another state or in another country.

As you begin to notice and perceive the presence of your ally, surrender into the connection a little. Breathe through your alignment, your grounded and centered state, your roots, your core worth, and feel with all your capacity into what is happening…You could be silent during this connection, you could hum, sing, rock, sway, dance, laugh, play, or make love to yourself or with this spirit who comes to you if it feels appropriate.

If you are noticing that you cannot perceive an ally coming, you may choose to meditate or move life force instead; return to this exercise at another time.

You might have called the ally because you need help with a spell or a ritual you are planning. Primarily this exercise is for pure connection and whatever communion arises out of that.

When the intensity and the presence of the ally connecting with you begins to lessen, fade, or draw away, allow yourself a few breaths, and let go. You may feel that this is all anchored in the hand you originally held out, or perhaps it expanded, grew from that hand-holding, and became something else, something different, during the experience. Now is the time to let go and re-center and ground again.

Trance: Divine Purpose
JANE MEREDITH

Time: 30 minutes

You will need: journal and pen; drawing things (optional);
divination tools such as tarot cards (optional)

• • •

Why were we born? What is our life purpose? What is the best, most perfect use of our time and resources? Are we unique? These are questions we do not ask only once and then never consider again. Each time we are drawn back to them, we can spend some time investigating, perhaps using divination, talking it over with others, and free writing or meditating on them. Trance is another technique we can work with to explore these vast questions.

This is an inner trance, designed so that we can meet or touch our divine purpose. Other ways to think of divine purpose might be to discover what the Goddess or our god soul asks of us, how to live our truth or follow our path, or how we can live this life to the fullest.

The trance can be done more than once, as we continue to learn and grow and seek further refinement to these questions and answers. It can be incorporated into a ritual or done on its own; it can be done alone or with others. Afterwards you might choose to journal, draw, or practice divination.

• • •

Ground and center. You might also like to align your three souls and cast a circle.

Begin by focusing on your breath and allowing yourself to drop into a light trance. As you breathe, spend some time allowing the trance state to deepen until you can feel the multiplicity of worlds and times around you.

Speak your intention aloud or internally: "I seek my soul purpose" or similar words.

Let yourself relax more deeply. Then imagine stepping into the time stream of your life and beginning to travel backwards through it. For you this might be very visual, seeing yourself at progressively younger ages, or it might feel somatic, in the body; you might hear the rush of time flowing backwards or it may be some other way. Travel back to your birth, and then back even beyond that to your time in your mother's womb.

Take some conscious breaths, slowing your breath deliberately. Now let yourself travel even further back along your own timeline to the point where you were one with the divine, perhaps just beginning to separate from it. For you this might be the moment of your conception. Or you might travel back before that, to being a thought, a possibility, a piece of stardust, a child of the Goddess, or another concept. It might not be as concrete as that for you.

Breathe into this thought, this place, this idea. You might feel rocked by tides of the universe, you might be aware of the connection between your parents, you might feel a draw or a pull to incarnation or embodiment, or you might experience an emotion such as doubt, reluctance, yearning, joy, or fear. See, feel, or know yourself as a soul or as the possibility of a soul. Perhaps you feel identical to all the other souls or potential souls; perhaps you feel particular.

At some point, when it feels right, ask yourself or the stars from which we are formed or the Goddess or this soul-in-becoming these questions or questions similar to these: Who are you? What is your purpose? What piece of divine will, or divine action, do you express? How can I, this human self, serve you and fulfil your purpose?

Perhaps the answers will come to you very simply and immediately in words, images, or felt understandings. Perhaps they will be complex, slow, or unclear. Whatever answers you receive, even if they don't at this moment appear to be actual answers, accept them and thank whatever source they came from. You might wait and breathe for a moment to see if anything further comes.

Then, holding tight to your answer—even if that was only a fragment, maybe a color or a brief flash of feeling—locate and travel back along your timeline through conception, pregnancy, birth, and all the years of your life up to the current time.

After any trance experience, it is always recommended to re-ground. Some ways of doing this include stretching, walking around, drinking water, and patting one's body down.

If you wish to try divination, you can do that either before or after you record your experience, whatever it was. Often something that seems unclear at the time will be more obvious later, when we look back over it.

Release the circle if you cast one.

CREATING A RITUAL

. . .

We are standing together in a field on the slopes of the caldera—everything is verdant, alive, wet. We have journeyed with the elements over four days and nights together. We are aware of the vivid green of the thick and luxurious grasses, the warm autumnal day; we can hear the ducks near the stream and the parrots in the hinterland trees; we crane our necks toward the stunning arc of the sun as it gradually sets into the west over the rise and into a valley of clouds...

We are gathered under a tree in a summer garden, a group of twenty adults and children after a weekend spent immersed in an all-ages, skills-based Elements of Magic class. We have traveled the paths of spirit, earth, air, fire, and water, returning to spirit, and we delight in the power and magic of this group as we come together, irrespective of age, and put on a ritual created by the class that celebrates the unique magic of each one of us.

Sitting in our bedrooms, living rooms, kitchens, and verandas, by the magic of the world wide web we hear each other clearly. We remind each other to ground and honor the spirits of the land that we are in; we are weaving this magical circle with threads of many sacred places. We recite our joint intention. Elements are named, honored, exalted; we begin to tap rhythms on our computers, we sway back and forth, and we begin to tone...from each direction and toward each direction, from multiple centers across the planet, we raise a cone of power between the worlds, and the web vibrates...

In a meditation center we come together for the sixth Wednesday night in a row, a combination of meditators, spiritual seekers, and witches, to create a ritual. We have spent one week dedicated to each of the elements, huddling together under blankets as if around a campfire to tell our stories in fire; working with mirrors and altars, seeking our life purpose, in spirit; and learning how to breathe, sound, and speak our truth in air. The ritual arises organically.

• • •

At the end of every Elements of Magic course—during a WitchCamp, over a weekend, over six months via distance, over six weeks or worked through this book, alone or with others, over whatever time period—a ritual is created, bringing together all the elements and what we have learned.

Earth...We have learned to ground and center, to become the world tree, to come alive to our senses and deepen into them. We have listened to the land and the spirits of place, and we are still listening. We have anchored to our core worth, casting magical circles and learning about silence.

Air...We have opened our mouths and bodies to verbalize invocations and to acknowledge and honor the elements and the Mysterious Ones. We have practiced crafting and setting our intentions, exploring the power of words and how to wield them well, seeking to understand something of our verbal magic and of spells and invocations. We have studied our breath, the rise and fall, the cycle of it. We met the challenge to know as we read the histories of our tradition's foundations and beginnings, where we have come from, where we are, and the principles that unite us.

Fire...We have learned about life force and how to sense and work with it, directing our focus, our intentions, into building spells and cones of power. We have reflected on the intricacies of power and transformation and on the sweeping changes a fire transformation can bring. Gazing into flames, whether candles, campfires, or another source, we have found ways to relate intimately with this changeable element.

Water…We have let ourselves be touched and begin to be shaped by water. We have drunk it and bathed in it as magical spells; we have tranced into its cycles and felt ourselves to be part of those cycles. We have entered the realms of trance and begun to know ourselves there, and perhaps we have searched deeply for healing or understanding our emotions or seeking the truth of who we are.

Spirit…We have declared, by every step of this work, that we believe in magic. We have opened ourselves to learning, to experience, and to the numinous; we have trusted in spirit. We have called to gods, to the Goddess, to ancestors and other deities and spirits; we have reflected on our own understandings of the unseen worlds. Reading and working with the elements of magic, we have sought to tread the path of our soul.

Earth is sacred. Air is sacred. Fire is sacred. Water is sacred. Spirit is sacred.

We are ready.

How to Create Your Ritual

At the culmination of every Elements of Magic class is a ritual. The purpose of the ritual is to consolidate and integrate what we have learned—how we have grown and been challenged during our journey with the elements of life and the practice of Reclaiming witchcraft and magic. All of the tools and learnings of Elements of Magic are drawn together in this final ritual, which marks the completion of the course. The ritual has all of the elements present in some way and is created completely by the participants, the students of the course; in this case, it will be created by you, the reader, or readers if you are working through this book as a group.

One of the purposes of the ritual is as a symbolic act, setting those who have been students free from that role and transforming us into co-creators. However wonderful our teachers may have been, the real learning is in how to take this material and these experiences into our own lives and let them find their place in our own paths. In this ritual the teachers do not participate in the planning other than to give basic instructions at the beginning. The teachers are usually guests in the ritual itself, participating but not leading any of the pieces. Through this process we learn that ritual and magic intrinsically belong to each of us and can be an expression of our spirit, our enquiry, our knowledge, and our power.

The ritual usually has a celebratory focus, although it also may include gratitude, enquiry, blessings, healing, divination, trance, play, and strategies for taking ritual and magic home into our lives.

When we participate in a live, in-person Elements of Magic class, we are immersed in ritual each session, sometimes for day after day or for one evening a week. Each time we ground, we honor the spirits of the place and the land, we cast the circle, we acknowledge and adore the elements and ancestors, we might even invoke deities or other Mysterious Ones, and then we focus on earth or water or spirit and the skills and practices we associate with those elements.

Reading this book, we might not have practiced ritual in this way each time we engaged with an exercise, technique, or practice—or maybe we have. Ideally, we have learned and practiced these skills along the way. If you have read as far as this without yet engaging with the practices, exercises, spells, and processes in the previous sections of this book, we encourage you to go back now, before doing this ritual, and try them out. Experiment, find what works for you, and bring your previous experience and knowledge to the work. If you have been working through this book with a group or partner, ideally you will create this culminating ritual together.

Throughout the elemental sections of earth, air, fire, water, and spirit, this book, or the teachers of any Elements of Magic course, will have largely guided the work for the participants or readers, offering processes, facilitating discussions (replaced, in this book, with the three essays in each section), and following an organized plan. In this final piece, those who have been students step into their power to work together and create a ritual, the intention, form, and content of which is decided by them. Working solo, we advise a time of reflection and gathering up the pieces of what you would like a ritual to contain and the circumstances of where, when, and how the ritual will occur before moving into the planning and enactment stages.

. . .

The ritual as the final section of Elements of Magic is a spell that helps open the space and time for reflection, immersion, integration, and celebration.

Reflection allows us to cast our minds back over the preceding days, nights, weeks, or months as we worked with each of the elements, and we drop into understanding how this learning and these experiences have been for us. We consider our emerging or deepening relationship with the elements, and we begin to wonder, and then to focus, and then to design the completion ritual.

Immersion occurs because in this process of reflection and design we become aware or can conjure the feeling that we are held within a cauldron, a container, perhaps even an alchemical crucible, and we are in some way being initiated into a mystery. The way into that mystery is to immerse ourselves within this cauldron, to cast the circle and step between the worlds, to lean into curiosity, to invoke with the full strength of our hearts and the full knowing of our bodies, to be truly human and animal and divine all at once, and to surrender into the flow of the real ritual, which, after all the careful or strategic planning, is the one that actually happens.

Integration. In this ritual a magic spell is cast. It is part of every Elements of Magic ritual at the close. It is a natural culmination, a magical sealing, and therefore a promise of all kinds of possible beginnings. We won't know, however, where these beginnings might take us. At this liminal time, in this threshold place—this ritual—we gift ourselves the generous blessing of integration. We integrate not just all we have learned and experienced, and possibly with others who are involved in the ritual and learning, but also our ritual joins us to every Elements of Magic class that has ever been. They all did this thing, the same as us. In their own ways and circumstances and times and places, each person who has followed an Elements of Magic course has helped create, and been a part of, the final ritual. As we continue in our lives and magic beyond this ritual and this course, the art and practice of ritual, over time, helps us allow and integrate these learnings more and more.

And celebration. No matter what, we have passed through the gates of power. We have honored earth, air, fire, water, and spirit as sacred; we have awakened our deep selves to the divinity immanent in everything we can taste, touch, perceive, feel, smell, and hear, and we embrace knowing. In this ritual we celebrate the reflection, the immersion, and the integration, and we celebrate ourselves as made up of these elements. We celebrate our bones, our breath, our beat, our blood, and our bonds. We celebrate life. We celebrate the Goddess in her infinite forms and expressions and, most significantly perhaps, we celebrate and praise ourselves.

Reflect, immerse, integrate, celebrate. These, too, are gifts of the elements and of the Elements of Magic course.

Planning the Ritual

Below are the steps in planning and designing a ritual at the conclusion of Elements of Magic. If you worked through this book with a partner or group, plan your ritual together. If you worked solo, then your ritual to complete the course probably also will be solo.

1: Gather Information

Do this before the ritual itself, perhaps a week before or a day before or a month before. When we are in a live class, this usually occurs only one or two hours before the ritual itself. Ground and center. Perhaps align your souls. Purify or cleanse in some way. You might do an in-drinking or you might build a spirit altar and reflect on your entire experience. You might hold your hand out to an ally and ask for guidance. It might be a good idea to look through your journal to see how the entire process has been for you. You might even like to do some divination.

Ask yourself some questions: What have you learned that is important to you? What is your relationship to each element, and how might you like to foster it? What mood would you like your ritual to convey? What pieces of ritual work are you confident with, and what pieces might you like to include that you are less confident in?

2: Weave an Intention

Taking the raw information previously gathered in the step above, you might like to take a pen and paper—perhaps your journal, which some witches call their Book of Shadows—and begin to take down notes. Why are you doing this ritual? You might even like to think and feel about it this way:

Earth: What are my physical/environmental needs and desires?

Air: What are my intellectual/communication needs and desires?

Fire: What are my creative/energetic needs and desires?

Water: What are my emotional/intuitive needs and desires?

Spirit: What are my mystical/political needs and desires?

Perhaps if you look at it through those filters, an intention that encompasses all of these needs and desires might begin to form. Write some words down toward your intention. It could start off looking as long and unwieldy as this: *Through the power of all the elements, I seek restoration of my authentic self, deep communion with my ancestors, a radical embracing of my magical identity, and a dedication to my path.*

At this point we might do more divination, more free writing; we might do a dropped and open, meditate, align our souls, ground again, draw from an anchor…or we might leave it for a time and return to it if we have a larger time container. The next draft of our intention might be: *I seek deep communion with my ancestors, I embrace my authentic self and dedicate to my magical path.*

We might decide this is a workable and specific-enough intention. We might not yet know what is in the ritual, how it will look, or how we will feel when we are in it, but we at least know why we are turning up to the ritual and what we are hoping to gain from it.

3: Work from the Intention

Once we have the intention, we can start addressing the content of the ritual. What pieces would you like to have in your ritual? Each piece should address the intention. Possible pieces include (and are not limited to) trance, energy raising, dancing, singing or playing music, divination, spellwork, and honoring each element.

Choose the pieces you wish to work with. Three different activities, or chunks of a ritual, build a satisfying form. For example, the pieces of a ritual designed for the intention above might be to create an ancestor altar, meditating with it and journaling; to do mirror work seeking one's authentic self; and lastly to perform a ritual dedication with tools or symbols from each element, raising energy to empower and consecrate them.

We can order these pieces the way that seems best to us. Sometimes this will echo the progression of the intention, other times we might mix it up. Raising energy usually comes toward or at the end of a ritual, once we have done all the preliminary work and have had time to sink deeply into the flow of what we are doing.

4: Create the Outline of the Ritual

At this point we list, in order, everything we plan to do in the ritual, from the acknowledgment of indigenous land followed by grounding, casting, and calling to elements all the way through to the end, finishing with the release of the ritual space. Some people also like to have a meal or snack at the end of the ritual.

5: Assign Times and Parts

Working alone, the time difference that sections of the ritual might take may become less important, and obviously if we are by ourselves, we will take all the roles. However, if we are working with others, it's good to plan these things before we are actually in the ritual.

Having an understanding of how much time to assign each part of a ritual means that we can make sure our ritual doesn't go on for three hours (unless that was our desire) or, conversely, that it is disappointingly finished within twenty minutes. For a ritual of this type, anywhere between thirty and ninety minutes is probably good to aim for.

If you are with a group, sharing roles fairly equally is ideal. Some people may choose to take smaller roles or roles they are already familiar or comfortable with, but one of the guidelines always offered at an Elements of Magic class is that everyone must take an active part in the ritual. Encouraging those with less confidence or experience to try out roles or to take on a role supported by others is very much part of the Reclaiming ethos, and this is a perfect opportunity for stretching into areas that we often name our growing edges.

6: Check Over the Whole Ritual

Once you have planned your ritual, take a few moments to check back with the intention. Does that still express what you want the work of this ritual to be? Then check all your activities against that intention; does each one of them help to express it or a part of it? Perhaps you will even adjust the manner of casting a circle or calling to the elements or other small pieces of the ritual so that they align with the intention. With the example intention above, we might decide to call to the lands our ancestors came from as we cast the circle, and when we call to spirit, we might state clearly our request to understand our spiritual path.

Also take a moment to check through what supplies you will need for the ritual, and perhaps write these down in a list.

Structure of Ritual

In Reclaiming we have a ritual form that is common to most practitioners, camps, classes, and communities.

1. First we acknowledge where we are and pay our respects to the peoples whose traditional lands we are working our magic on. These peoples may, in fact, be your ancestors.

2. We state our intention aloud. We often do this three times because, as we like to say, "three times makes a spell."

3. We ground and we center.

4. We purify if the grounding and centering did not do that for us.

5. We cast the circle or, if not a circle, we somehow acknowledge the inherent sanctity of the space, of the place we are in, in a conscious manner.

6. We acknowledge and honor the powers of the elements within our circle or sacred space.

7. We invoke, invite, or conjure any other allies, deities, or Mysterious Ones we would like to be present with us in our ritual space.

8. We begin the work of the ritual. We refer to this as the body of the ritual, or the meat or tofu of the ritual.

    There may be a trance component in which we travel to another realm or go within or simply deepen or shift our awareness to be open to more information than usual.

    There may be other work, possibly crafting a spell with materials such as candles, thread, colors, stones, or plants; there may be meditation, sacred drama, aspecting, divination, stillness, listening, or discussion.

    There often will be some type of energy-raising to charge something or to send healing into the land or into ourselves.

9. We thank all the beings and elements we called into our circle and devoke, or release, the circle or once again affirm and honor the sacred space.

10. We may ground again. Afterwards we often like to journal, to record the ritual and what we learned or how we felt during it.

Sample Rituals

1. A Simple Ritual Outside in a Garden or Park

A small altar with found objects is created. A circle is cast, and elements are recognized in the forms that they are present: the living things in the park for earth, the fresh air, the heat of the sun, and the moisture in the ground. The main body of the ritual is a dedication to one's own magic and sense of the sacred, beginning with a meditation on connection to all, the dedication, and followed by journaling and feasting.

2. An Inside Ritual with Altars to the Five Elements

There are colored candles on the different altars, as well as magical tools, symbols of the elements, and other special or sacred things. A circle is cast, and then each altar is visited in turn. At the earth altar a Tree of Life grounding occurs and an intention is set, at the water altar a cleansing is done with a bowl of water, at the air altar cycles of breath work lead into the creation of a song, at the fire altar an energy raising happens, and finally at the spirit altar tarot cards or runes are used for divination to commune with the divine within and without.

3. A Journey Through the Elements Ritual

A circle is cast. For earth, dancing energetically until physically tired, followed by consciously resting one's body on the floor. For air, writing and singing a song about one's path. For fire, making a candle spell. For water, bathing either inside or in the sea, lake, or river. For spirit, taking a trance journey to connect with the divine. The circle is released.

The Ritual

However carefully we have designed and planned any ritual, the real ritual is not the one in our heads or the one on the page, it's the one that happens when we do it. Things occur we never could have known about—changes in weather, we forget a piece, something unexpected happens in a trance or energy raising, we access a deep emotional place—but all these things are still held within the container of the intention and the ritual space itself.

The best we can do for any ritual is to have a plan and then show up to the ritual as prepared as we can be and willing to step into sacred space and let the ritual come to life. To do the ritual, a ritual entirely created by you, is the point of this sixth and final piece of Elements of Magic. Whether you are completely happy with every little bit of it may be interesting and useful to you as feedback and consideration for future rituals, but it is not essential or expected.

Like any other art or relationship, creating great ritual is something we work at piece by piece and ritual by ritual. If you have a moment where you feel the presence of the gods, your ancestors, the liminality of sacred space, or the power of your intention striking through you or sending out into the world, that is wonderful, but it is not required. Even if you sweat through the entire ritual, not especially enjoying any part of it, or you skip parts or mess them up, or the reality is nothing like what you thought it would be, still you have done it. And the point is to do it, to be your own active spiritual authority in a ritual space, and to learn from it.

Ritual enables us to connect and commune with what is most real to us, and often this means discovering that some things in our lives or the societies we live and work within are less sustainable or important to us than we may have previously thought. Or perhaps that is why we are doing this—because we know that the earth, air, fire, water, and spirit are sacred. We are seeking the sacred.

The elements are sacred. All is sacred. When we reclaim this awareness of the sacredness of everything, magic is renewed through us and within us. Being alive in our magic, it is possible to encounter mystery, to break old habits, to speak with the birds, to heal relationships, to remember and retrieve lost ancestral wisdom, to understand our dreams, and to fall in love—again—with this earth we are a part of and who we really are.

Blessings on your magic.

GLOSSARY

Anderson Faery or Feri—an American tradition of modern witch-craft dating back to the 1940s with earlier roots. It is a tradition that weaves together Appalachian folk magic, inspiration drawn from Hawaiian and West African cultures, Welsh and Gaelic folklore, Middle Eastern sorcery and legend, and Italian witchcrafts. It is one of the foundational roots of Reclaiming. The triple soul alignment, Iron and Pearl Pentacles, the theology of the Star Goddess who is all things, and an openness to all gods of all times and cultures are inherited by Reclaiming from Feri.

Archetype—a term used by the Swiss psychotherapist Carl G. Jung (1875–1961) to refer to original, great, and primeval patterns, images, and symbols that are stored in the human collective unconscious. Examples include the Great Mother, the Sage, and the Hero. Sometimes this term is used by occult practitioners and modern Pagans to refer to the nature or origins of deities. Another view is that deities are not archetypes, they are very real beings or persons; yet another is that deities are archetypal but still their own agents.

Aspect and Aspecting—is akin to possessory rites and practices of other magical, Pagan, or spirit-working cultures and traditions. In Reclaiming, aspecting refers to the broad range of inviting a deity to be present within one's body. Most often this refers to less than full possession, in which the aspector or priestess still retains awareness of their own behavior, choices, and needs. There are multiple levels of and ways into aspecting. In Reclaiming, any person—of any ethnicity, gender, and sometimes even age—is able, with training and context, to aspect a deity or spirit. If someone is to aspect, they will require a tender: a priestess or person who is trained to help protect, guide, and aid the person aspecting in both magical and logistical ways. The tender may invoke and devoke the deity or being into the person aspecting.

Athame—a knife or blade dedicated to magic. Traditionally this is a double-edged knife with a black hilt that is used for ritual and magical purposes, although it may also take the form of a pocket knife, a kitchen blade, or a letter opener. This is a Gardnerian Wiccan term derived from a corruption of the Latin *artavus* via the Key of Solomon grimoire, which Reclaiming has adopted. In Reclaiming, we associate the knife, which it is often called, with the element of air and the powers of discernment, delineation, and knowledge.

Beloved Dead—an all-encompassing term used to describe those of our beloveds—human and other-than-human—who have died. See *Mighty Dead*.

Book of Shadows—a term for a witch's or coven's private magical recipe book or journal, borrowed from the Gardnerian Wiccan tradition. Some Reclaiming witches might simply call this a journal or even grimoire. The latter term will be used more specifically if the book codifies particular magical methodologies and correspondences.

Casting the Circle—is the demarcation of ritual or working space, a magical container for the work we do in the ritual, and a way to step between the worlds so that we are both grounded in the place and also oriented to the various worlds we might move through in our magical work. The ritual and method of casting can look a thousand different ways.

Ceremonial Magic (also called High Magic)—refers to various systems and orders of magic which are highly ornate, formulaic, and structured in methodology and cosmology. Often ceremonial and high magic are related to notions of the universe with a single creator deity—whose many names or aspects may be invoked in order to control various sub-orders of beings, including angels and demons—and a oneness that is at the center of all magical and spiritual operations. This is a philosophy of magic that is known as theurgy, which translates as "god work" and aims to reveal and exalt the divine within. This contrasts with what might be called popular or low magic, which is usually more visceral, sensual, immediate, and folksy in aesthetic and feeling.

Chakra—meaning wheel or circle in Sanskrit. Chakra systems derive from tantric practices within Hinduism, Buddhism, and Jainism. In 1918 Sir John George Woodroffe (aka Arthur Avalon) published an English translation of traditional Hindu tantric texts and catalyzed a deep interest in Eastern philosophy in the West. The well-known seven chakra system is referenced and utilized by many Reclaiming teachers and witches, as it is the most popular in the West. Going from base to crown, these chakras are usually called the root, sacral, solar plexus, heart, throat, third eye, and crown. The Sanskrit names that correspond are muladhara, svadisthana, manipura, anahata, vishudda, ajna, and sahasrara. Colors, deities, mantras, sounds, scents, and more are associated with each chakra, or energy center, and many books in many languages have been written on these ideas.

Charge/Recharge—to fill up an object with magical power or to consecrate a magical item or tool to a purpose.

Charge of the Goddess—The *Charge of the Goddess* comes from the traditional Gardnerian Wiccan Book of Shadows (see *Wicca*). It was originally compiled by Gerald Gardner or his initiators as a declaration of witchcraft theology, ethics, and directives that would be spoken at someone's initiation into Wicca. Its sources are predominantly Charles Leland's *Aradia: Gospel of the Witches* (1899), Aleister Crowley's poetry, and the author's inspiration. Doreen Valiente rewrote the charge she received in the 1950s, and her prose version is beloved by modern witches and Pagans all over the world today. The charge was adapted by Starhawk in *The Spiral Dance* (1979) into contemporary American English and has been adopted by the Reclaiming tradition.

Cone of Power—a term originating from Gardnerian Wicca referring to a magical working that raises and directs power (see *Energy*) toward a predetermined goal or intention. Historically, the name "cone of power" is related to a renowned working in the New Forest during World War II aiming to dissuade Hitler and the Nazis from launching an invasion of England. In Reclaiming, a cone of power is an umbrella term for the way in which our energy-raising culminates in an ecstatic building and release of the collective power.

Core Classes, Reclaiming Core Classes—the five central courses that contain the fundamentals of Reclaiming tradition magic, ritual, witchcraft, ethos, and community. They are Elements of Magic, Iron Pentacle, Pearl Pentacle, Rites of Passage, and the fifth core class, usually referred to as the Community class. The first and original four core classes emerged in the early 1980s in the San Francisco Bay Area and are always co-taught by at least two teachers. The core classes of Reclaiming are integral to understanding the finer details of the tradition, and many Reclaimers return again and again to these classes with renewed curiosity or interest in the continued depths within the work. Core classes are mostly co-taught in person over six weeks or as a three-day or weekend intensive. They are also taught during WitchCamps over four to six days. Sometimes they are offered long-distance utilizing various forms of technology.

Core Worth—the inherent and intrinsic value of each being in the cosmos. This is not given to us, and it cannot be taken away. We are each a fundamentally sovereign being; our worthiness is inviolable. This concept is fundamental to the Reclaiming tradition.

Correspondences—refers to the Western Occult tradition of organizing seemingly disparate information into tables of associations and connections. It is a system of categorizing magical information via the planets or the elements, seasons, directions, etc. Some occultists and witches will refer to tables of correspondences in order to fashion a magical working. For example, using this information, one might take a red candle, inscribe the symbol of the planet Mars into it, fill the carving with iron filings, and on the day of Tuesday (ruled by Mars) during one of the planetary hours of Mars undergo a working for strength, defense, or protection.

Coven—a group of witches who are committed to working magic together, often taking oaths or binding themselves to each other in the name of something larger, such as a tradition or a goddess.

Devoke—at the culmination of a Reclaiming ritual or working, we will usually formally thank and farewell the various spirits, deities, allies, and even elements that we invoked in the beginning. It effectively undoes the invocation and respectfully clears the circle before we release it. Not all Reclaiming witches devoke the elements and deities; some simply thank and honor the elements formally at the end.

Dianic Witchcraft—a female-only magical tradition attributed to the work of Z. Budapest. Related to Wicca, but where only the Goddess is worshipped.

Dropped and Open Attention—a technique originating from aikido practice and adapted within Reclaiming. We gather all of our attention and awareness into one place in the body, and once it is gathered up and concentrated there—for example, in the head—on our next out-breath we drop that attention down to a feeling place within the body, and when it stops, it opens like a flower or like a book. In dropped and open attention, we are more finely attuned and sensitive to underlying and informing forces and patterns.

Energy—a sometimes vague term that refers to the quality or signature of nearly anything. For example, "the energy in this house makes me feel uncomfortable" or "this tree's energy seems content." It is a short-hand way of referring to the essence, nature, or constitution of something. We often talk about raising energy at the conclusion of a ritual to charge our magic.

Evoke—a ritual magic term that traditionally refers to a conjuration of a spirit into visible or perceivable presence. Ceremonial magicians might evoke demons or angels into specially created triangles while they themselves remain in a protective circle. In Reclaiming we usually use the term to refer to the conjuration of a spirit or deity into our own circle or into our lives. See *Invoke*.

Faery or Feri—see *Anderson Faery or Feri*.

The Goddess—a term used in Reclaiming witchcraft to refer to the cycles and processes of birth, growth, death, decay, and regeneration. She is all and nothing. We say the Goddess rather than God or the God because the latter is embedded in patriarchal male-centered assumptions and politics. For many, to re-center the Goddess is to praise and bring balance or focus back to the feminine, but also to restore justice to all those classes of people, beings, states, and emotions that have been maligned and marginalized because they are relegated as female or feminine.

Greenbloods—a poetic and heartfelt way of referring to our friends in nature possessing chlorophyll. Some others might call them the plant people, drawing upon animistic sensibilities regarding all beings as persons or people.

Immanence—the the embeddedness of divinity in and as all things we may encounter. Immanence refers to the divine as embodied.

Invoke—a ritual magic term which traditionally refers to the calling in of a spirit or deity into the vessel of the magic worker. This is how we might begin aspecting or trance possession. In Reclaiming, we use the term to encompass all manner of verbal and nonverbal methods of inviting the spirits to take notice and attend our rites. See *Evoke*.

Invoking Pentagram—in Wicca and the Hermetic Order of the Golden Dawn, pentagrams are drawn in the air with magical tools, such as a knife or wand, to open a portal for a spirit to enter into a ritual space, or perhaps to charge an object or seal a spell. As you are looking at it, an invoking pentagram is drawn from the top down to the bottom left-hand point, up to the top right, across to the top left, back down to the bottom right and up to the originating point. In Reclaiming, we usually encircle the five points of the pentagram and then plunge our tool or hands through the center of the pentagram to activate it.

Kabbalah—also spelled Qabalah (referencing the system utilized by Western Hermetic magicians) and Cabala (referencing a Christian stream), this is the transmission and teachings of certain Jewish mystic streams, especially as formulated in the Middle Ages onward.

Mighty Dead—powerful and self-aware witches, magic-makers, priestesses, healers, artists, and activists who have left this world and retain memory, vitality, and even personality from their lives. Some Reclaimers say the Mighty Dead no longer need to reincarnate in this world and choose—from the Otherworld—to guide, inspire, and assist the living. In the Reclaiming tradition we honor many Mighty Dead. These include: Cora Anderson, Victor Anderson, Raven Moonshadow, Doreen Valiente, and Judy Foster, who are considered five significant Mighty Dead to the tradition. See also *Beloved Dead*.

Mysterious Ones—referring to any and all beings. We might use this term, which was coined by Reclaiming witch Donald Reece-Engstrom, to widen our understanding of kinship to encompass all spirits, beings, qualities, synchronicity, and powers we encounter in the worlds.

Neo-Paganism—an umbrella term used by practitioners, adherents, and academics to describe the recent and current movement of nature-based magico-religious traditions often linked to the revival or reconstruction of pre-Christian European and Middle Eastern folk cultures, customs, and spiritualities. This is largely a North American, Australian, and European phenomenon, though there are vital neo-Pagan communities elsewhere, including South Africa, Brazil, and even India. See *Pagan*.

Nonviolence—denoting the ideologies and philosophies, popularized by Mahatma Gandhi (1869–1948), regarding actions, thoughts, and speech that bring no harm to ourselves and others. There are various angles by which nonviolence can be approached and expressed, including that of Marshall Rosenberg's Nonviolent Communication (NVC).

Pagan—this term has been used to cast negative judgment on non-Christian or non-Abrahamic traditions and practices. It derives from the Latin *paganus,* referring either to someone living in a rural region and therefore outside of the city of Rome, or to a civilian in contrast to a soldier. Modern people who identify with the term *Pagan* are usually describing their religious and spiritual sentiments and identity. A Pagan is generally someone attempting to ground into their locale, become attuned to the natural and seasonal rhythms and cycles, and who connects with spirits in the land and divinities who may be encountered in nature and the body. See *Neo-Paganism.*

Priestess—used in Reclaiming to refer to people of all genders to describe facilitation, leadership, and tending to a space, ritual, or anything necessary or desirable for the community. We often use the word as a verb, as in "I will help to priestess this ritual." We are taking on responsibility toward something for the sake of a greater collective, whether that be a human community or a wider web.

Principles of Unity—a manifesto that was co-written by the original Reclaiming Collective in 1997, after which the collective dissolved. It was written to highlight that Reclaiming had become a distinct tradition of witchcraft that thrived beyond the San Francisco Bay Area of the United States. It has become the one document that unites us as Reclaiming witches; it is sometimes said that all we must do to identify as Reclaiming is agree to these principles and practice Reclaiming-style magic. It has been amended once, in 2012, to change language around gender and the nature of divinity as related to gender. The Principles of Unity is on page xix.

Sabbat—Since the advent of Wicca publicly in the 1950s and the subsequent neo-Pagan movement, this term has come to refer to the eight seasonal festivals commonly called the Wheel of the Year. Sabbat originates as a term applied to secretive meetings of witches during the historical period of the European witch trials in the sixteenth to eighteenth centuries. See *Wheel of the Year*.

Sacred Space—a term used in Reclaiming to describe the setting aside of space and time to dedicate to ritual or magical work. Not everyone in Reclaiming uses this term as some might experience every place and space as sacred. Some of us will say "affirm sacred space" or "create ritual space or working space" instead.

Shamanic—an academic term drawn from an indigenous Siberian tribe's word referring to a person who knows or enters and wields ecstatic states with spirit helpers in order to heal the sick or the possessed (by malevolent spirits including illness), to retrieve lost soul fragments, and who speaks with the spirits on behalf of a group of people. Practices and people like this exist in nearly every culture on this planet. Modern Western practitioners sometimes refer to their practices and rituals as shamanistic, referring to this legacy and centralizing the concept of ecstasy and spirit helpers.

Tradition—In modern Pagan and witchcraft communities, the term *tradition* refers to a particular style, approach, historical initiatory lineage, or specific group of practitioners that are identifiable to each other—and others—by unique traits. Sometimes these traits include secret or private names of certain deities or spirits, or memorised and verified lineage that goes back to a founder or propounder of the tradition; for example, all Gardnerian witches can trace their lineage back to Gerald Gardner, and all Feri witches can trace theirs to Victor Anderson. In general, a Pagan or witchcraft tradition requires some formal commitment, instruction, or even dedication or initiation rite in order for one to fully participate within it. Reclaiming is distinct in that one need only identify as Reclaiming and agree to the Principles of Unity.

Trans*—refers to a more inclusive and broader understanding of trans and gender experiences and identities. The asterisk signals non-binary, genderless, transsexual, and two- and three-spirit individuals.

Wand—a tool, usually wooden, harvested from a tree or from the ground, that is used for ritual and magical purposes. The wand can be wielded to cast the circle and to conjure spirits. Sometimes we might also use it to stir brews and potions or to scratch symbols in the ground. In Reclaiming, it is often associated with fire, burgeoning vitality, and the power to will. Wands can also be made from glass, crystal, or a combination of things.

Western Mystery Tradition—refers to a collection of mystic, philosophic, and occult traditions arising from, but not limited to, Classical (Greek and Roman), Celtic, British, Irish, Egyptian, Nordic, and Semitic cultures. Clear examples include Kabbalah, Gnosticism, alchemy, the Grail Mysteries, and the Hermetic Order of the Golden Dawn.

Wicca—a magical religion founded in the 1940s and '50s by Gerald Gardner (1884–1964), a British civil servant. It was impacted greatly by Doreen Valiente, who was initiated as one of its first high priestesses. The word *Wicca* is, in a stricter sense, more often used for lineages of initiates and traditions deriving from Gerald Gardner, Alex Sanders, and the early high priestesses such as Maxine Sanders, Patricia Crowther, and Eleanor Bone. It is a form of modern witchcraft revering a goddess of the moon and witchcraft and a horned god of death and resurrection.

Wiccans usually work with gender or sexual polarity in magic, and only a woman may initiate a man and vice versa. Each ritual or magical working is conducted in a ritually cast and consecrated circle in which guardians are called from the four directions. Wicca practices three rites or degrees of initiation.

The first degree makes one a priest or priestess and witch, the second degree makes one a high priest or high priestess, and the third degree is a consummation of Wiccan mysteries and a celebration of the previous initiations. The third degree in some lineages also endows special privileges and responsibilities; for instance, the ability to hive off from the parent coven, establish one's own coven, and begin to train and initiate others in that tradition.

Wicca is primarily an initiatory mystery tradition, though many people today might identify as Wiccan without having participated in a lineaged coven. At times the term is even used by Reclaiming teachers or elders. Traditions that fall under the traditional banner of Wicca include Gardnerian, Alexandrian, and Central Valley Wicca.

Wheel of the Year—a neo-Pagan term referring to an eight-spoked wheel symbol and concept that embodies the eight seasonal festivals, or sabbats, of modern-day witches, druids, and religious Pagans. The eight festivals comprise two sets of seasonal rituals merged together: the equinoxes and the solstices and the Celtic fire festivals that are often called by their Irish names by various spellings: Samhain, Imbolc, Beltaine, Lughnasadh. All of these festivals were a part of pre-Christian cultures in European countries and linked to the agricultural and pastural cycles. Largely the symbolism, cultural pretext and inspiration for these festivals in the modern-day derives from Celtic and Germanic folklore and mythology. The eight festivals are commonly marked by Reclaiming witches and communities. In Reclaiming, Imbolc is more often referred to as Brigid, and Lughnasadh as Lammas. See *Sabbat*.

Witch—a term reclaimed from a complex history of Pagan (pre-Christian) tradition, Christian heresy, shamanistic ecstasy, folklore, and persecution. The word *witch* can mean myriad things for each person. Usually the word *witch* is used in Reclaiming to re-center the Goddess and animistic folk cultures and magical traditions of Europe and the Middle East. We might say that it refers to a bender or weaver of fate, or a wise or skilled person with insight into the magical arts and the ways of spirits.

RESOURCES AND RECOMMENDED READING

Reclaiming on-line: http://www.reclaiming.org/

Reclaiming WitchCamps: http://www.witchcamp.org/

Reclaiming and Related

Coyle, T. Thorn. *Evolutionary Witchcraft*. Penguin, 2005.

Meredith, Jane. *Rituals of Celebration*. Llewellyn, 2013.

Meredith, Jane, and Gede Parma. *Magic of the Iron Pentacle: Reclaiming Sex, Pride, Self, Power & Passion*. Llewellyn, 2016.

Nightmare, M. Macha, and Starhawk. *The Pagan Book of Living and Dying*. HarperOne, 1997.

Salomonsen, Jone. *Enchanted Feminism: Ritual, Gender and Divinity Among the Reclaiming Witches of San Francisco*. Routledge, 2002.

Stanfield, Gerri Ravyn. *Revolution of the Spirit: Awaken the Healer*. 2016.

Starhawk. *Dreaming the Dark: Magic, Sex, and Politics*. Beacon Press, 1988.

———. *The Empowerment Manual: A Guide for Collaborative Groups*. New Society Publishers, 2012.

————. *The Fifth Sacred Thing*. Bantam Press, 1994.

————. *The Spiral Dance: A Rebirth of the Ancient Religion of the Great Goddess*. HarperCollins, 1979, 1989, 1999.

————. *Truth or Dare*. HarperOne, 1989.

————. *Webs of Power: Notes from the Global Uprising*. New Society Publishers, 2002.

Starhawk, Dianne Baker, and Anne Hill. *Circle Round: Raising Children in Goddess Traditions*. Bantam, 2000.

Starhawk and Hilary Valentine. *The Twelve Wild Swans*. HarperOne, 2001.

Earth

Griffin, Susan. *Woman and Nature: The Roaring Inside Her*. Reissue Edition. Counterpoint, 2016.

Macy, Joanna, and Molly Brown. *Coming Back to Life: The Updated Guide to the Work That Reconnects*. New Society Publishers, 2014.

Meredith, Jane. *Circle of Eight: Creating Magic for Your Place on Earth*. Llewellyn, 2015.

Mollison, Bill, and David Holmgren. *Permaculture One: A Perennial Agriculture for Human Settlements*. Transworld, 1978.

Seed, John, Joanna Macy, Pat Fleming, and Arne Naess. *Thinking Like a Mountain: Towards a Council of All Beings*. New Catalyst Books, 1988.

Starhawk. *The Earth Path*. Harper One, 2005.

Wohlleben, Peter. *The Hidden Life of Trees*. Greystone Books, 2016.

Air

Adler, Margot. *Drawing Down the Moon: Witches, Druids, Goddess-Worshippers and Other Pagans in America*. Revised Edition. Penguin Books, 2006.

Gilligan, Carol. *In a Different Voice: Psychological Theory and Women's Development*. Reprint Edition. Harvard University Press, 2016.

Linklater, Kristin. *Freeing the Natural Voice: Imagery and Art in the Practice of Voice and Language*. Revised and Expanded. Nick Hern Books, 2006.

Oliveros, Pauline. *Deep Listening: A Composer's Sound Practice*. iUniverse, Inc., 2005.

Rosenberg, Marshall. *Living Nonviolent Communication*. Sounds True, 2012.

Fire

Bonheim, Jalaja. *The Hunger for Ecstasy: Fulfilling the Soul's Need for Passion and Intimacy*. Daybreak, 2001.

Briggs, Beatrice. *Introduction to Consensus*. International Institute for Facilitation and Change, 2013.

Carrellas, Barbara, and Annie Sprinkle. *Urban Tantra: Sacred Sex for the Twenty-First Century*. Celestial Arts, 2011.

Christian, Diana Leafe. *Creating a Life Together: Practical Tools to Grow Ecovillages and Intentional Communities*. New Society Publishers, 2003.

Frater, U. D. *Secrets of Western Sex Magic: Magical Energy and Gnostic Trance*. Llewellyn Worldwide, 2001.

Harrow, Judith. *Wicca Covens: How to Start and Organize Your Own*. Citadel, 2000.

Wade, Jenny. *Transcendent Sex: When Lovemaking Opens the Veil*. Simon and Schuster, 2004.

Water

Bass, Ellen, and Laura Davis. *The Courage to Heal: A Guide for Women Survivors of Child Sexual Abuse.* 20th Anniversary Edition. William Morrow Paperbacks, 2008.

Emoto, Masaru. *The Message from Water: The Message from Water Is Telling Us to Take a Look at Ourselves.* Hado Press. 2000.

Ingerman, Sandra. *Medicine for the Earth: How to Transform Personal and Environmental Toxins.* Three Rivers Press, 2001.

Katie, Byron. *Loving What Is: Four Questions That Can Change Your Life.* Harmony, 2003.

Richo, David. *When the Past Is Present: Healing the Emotional Wounds that Sabotage Our Relationships.* Shambhala, 2008.

Slonczewski, Joan. *A Door into Ocean.* Arbor House, 1986.

Taylor, Jeremy. *The Wisdom of Your Dreams: Using Dreams to Tap into Your Unconscious and Transform Your Life.* TarcherPerigee, 2009.

Spirit

Anderson, Victor. *Etheric Anatomy: The Three Selves and Astral Travel*. Acorn Guild Press, 2004.

Arrien, Angeles. *The Tarot Handbook: Practical Applications of Ancient Visual Symbols*. Jeremy P. Tarcher/Putnam Edition, 1997.

Coyle, T. Thorn. *Kissing the Limitless: Deep Magic and the Great Work of Transforming Yourself and the World*. Weiser Books, 2009.

Dominguez Jr., Ivo. *Casting Sacred Space: The Core of All Magickal Work*. Weiser Books, 2012.

———. *Spirit Speak: Knowing and Understanding Spirit Guides, Ancestors, Ghost, Angels, and the Divine*. New Page Books, 2008.

Parma, Gede. *Ecstatic Witchcraft: Magick, Philosophy & Trance in the Shamanic Craft*. Llewellyn, 2012.

CONTRIBUTORS

Abel R. Gomez—USA

Abel is a queer witch, writer, performer, and activist ever in love with the unfolding grace of the Star Goddess. He was first introduced to Reclaiming through the San Francisco Brigid Ritual in 2006. Since then his involvement has included studying, organizing events, priestessing, and teaching with the Bay Area Reclaiming Community. Also initiated in Hindu Shakta Tantra, his practice is rooted in devotion, gratitude, song, and ancestor veneration. Abel is currently engaged in doctoral studies in upstate New York, researching the intersection of ethnic identities, ceremony, and sacred sites within contemporary indigenous communities. He is teaching and practicing with Reclaiming the Radiant Wild, a Syracuse Reclaiming Circle, and deepening his personal Craft through ongoing practice in the Feri tradition.

Catherine Gronlund—USA

My magical practice is rooted in the earth and ecstatic life-force energy. Each day you will find me connecting with the earth. At home in Seattle it might be the sight of a weed breaking through a crack in the sidewalk or a breath of salt air against my skin. My garden is dedicated to the bees, with plants selected to feed them throughout the year. Wild places along the ocean, in the mountains, and deep in the forest are my second home and the place where it is easiest for me to recharge. I discovered Reclaiming at an Imbolc ritual in 2000 after the Battle in Seattle WTO Protest. I fell in love with the community, our commitment to activism, and the healing power of our magic.

Chuck—USA

Chuck, aka Claire Bohman, first began practicing magic as a child with a small Pagan community in Virginia. She's been involved with Reclaiming since she landed on the West Coast over twelve years ago. She began teaching with Reclaiming in 2011. Chuck is a clinical energetic herbalist as well as a hospital chaplain. She trains people from many spiritual traditions in interfaith spiritual care as well as facilitates herbal and spiritual workshops in unceded Ohlone Territory, aka the California Bay Area. She is currently working in collaboration on developing curriculum for interfaith spiritual care providers on working with trans and gender-variant people. Keep current with her writing and herbal practice through her website: herbalchaplain.com.

Copper Persephone—USA

I have been a practicing witch—doing ritual, performance, and community organizing/activist/social justice work with people who live in poverty—for over twenty years. I walk a spiritual path devoted to erotic and ecstatic communion with spirit in all of its faces and forms, and I am called to help others experience immanence through many roads, including western queer tantric practice and shamanic journey work. I teach workshops internationally in leadership, personal growth, sacred sexuality, and mask making. First teaching Reclaiming classes in 2001, and then at WitchCamps starting in 2003, I am devoted to service and organizing work. Dedicated to Freya and initiated into Reclaiming, the Honey Bee clan and the Bear clan as well as Queer Spirit, those roots and conversations inform my daily life. After living in the San Francisco Bay Area for many years, I moved to Minneapolis in 2016 and am deepening my roots in fertile land fed by the Mississippi River.

Dawn Isidora—USA

International teacher, grounded mystic, mother, and spiritual mentor, Dawn Isidora took her first Reclaiming Elements of Magic class with Rose May Dance in 1983 and fell in love with the tradition. After many years of study, she became a teacher in her own right, offering the Reclaiming core classes as well as her own body of work and training a next generation of spiritual teachers. An initiate of both Reclaiming and Feri traditions, Dawn is also a certified mediator and hypnotherapist who devotes much of her professional life to support individuals in seeking their unique spiritual path. She makes her home with her family on the flank of an extinct volcano in Portland, Oregon. For more information or to contact Dawn Isidora, go to DawnIsidora .com.

Fiona Mariposa—Australia

Fiona Mariposa draws great spiritual sustenance from nature's poetry, and she works as a teacher to share her love of the natural world with people of all ages. Fiona's spiritual practice has been influenced by Reclaiming tradition Paganism for the past twenty years, and she has been working as a teacher, priestess, and events organizer within the Reclaiming community for many years.

Fiona has a deep interest in earth-based practices, including deep ecology and permaculture. She counts many plants, animals, and fungi as her teachers and allies. Fiona is a mother, witch, activist, beekeeper, and passionate gardener and seed-sower. She currently lives in Melbourne, Australia, with her two daughters and her canine, apian, and avian kin.

Fiona can be contacted via e-mail at: fimariposa@yahoo.com.au.

Flame—USA

I was born in the San Francisco Bay Area and have lived here all my life. I moved to San Francisco and became a punk rocker involved in the early days of the San Francisco punk rock scene and had a band named Animal Things. I found no use for religion, capitalism, or heteronormative life. It was then that I discovered the Worship of the Goddess. I started going to public rituals at Reclaiming San Francisco. I took Elements, Iron, Pearl, and Rites of Passage classes and for many years taught them. I was involved in the Pagan Cluster in direct political actions. I served my community on the SF Ritual Planning Cell and the Wheel. I was initiated and taught at WitchCamps. I am a coach for those affected by drug/alcohol addiction/use at Rediscovery Coach. Contact me at dominique.leslie@gmail.com.

Fortuna Sawahata—Netherlands

Fortuna Sawahata is a witch, mystic, and cartomancer with a degree in fine arts. Born in LA, educated in Seattle, and a resident of the Netherlands since 2003, she has taught at Reclaiming WitchCamps in the UK and continental Europe, as well as weekend workshops in Reclaiming core courses. Fortuna holds white and blue cords from Morningstar Mystery School and is an initiate in the Anderson Feri tradition. Her lifetime love of writing has translated into a Native English marketing and communications company, Sawahata Communications; in 2016 she launched Soul Deep Magick (souldeepmagick .com), "real magic for real people," to bring the joy, beauty, and power of tarot, ritual, guided trance, and effective magical workings to the world.

Gede Parma—Australia

I am a dancer, a queer non-binary mischief-maker, an initiate of the Craft, a dirty Pagan, an animist, polytheist, mixed-race child of Ros and John. I am made of the fecund soil of living volcano, of the verdant green of Eire, the chalk of England, the mountains of Scotland, the Brisbane River of Meanjin, and the Cloud Catcher. I am the author of several books on contemporary Paganism, ecstatic witchcraft, and ritual and magic. I co-authored *Magic of the Iron Pentacle* with my beloved friend Jane Meredith. I am a midwife of CloudCatcher Witch-Camp and the Wildwood tradition of Witchcraft. I learned about breath, prayer, ancestors, and the spirits in the forest from my father in Bali, where I was born. I learned about patience, determination, action, justice, and loyalty from my mother. I live on Wurundjeri Country in Melbourne. My website is www.gedeparma.com.

Gerri Ravyn Stanfield—USA

Gerri Ravyn Stanfield is the author of *Revolution of the Spirit: Awaken the Healer*, a guide to liberating the healing superpowers within us. She has been published in *Nailed Magazine, Voice Catcher, Rebelle Society, Elephant Journal, Wake Up World,* and *Tattooed Buddha.* She practices acupuncture in Portland, Oregon, and works with Acupuncturists Without Borders to build world-healing exchange programs. She designs trainings for emerging leaders and healers in the US, Canada, Europe, Asia, and Australia.

Ravyn is a cultural alchemist, writing to transform the heartbreak of our times and reveal the gold in what seems worthless. She creates modern ritual and theatre art, combining music, poetry, and performance to make contemporary offerings of the human imagination. She uses her background in trauma recovery, neurobiology, psychology, writing, and performance to coax more of the extraordinary into the world through the cracks in Western civilization.

Gwydion Logan—USA

Gwydion is a queer man, priestess, witch, teacher, and urban farmer living in San Francisco. He first came to the Craft through the Anderson Feri tradition and found his home in the Reclaiming tradition and community in San Francisco a few years later, in 1988. Having taken classes and worked on the *Reclaiming Newsletter,* he eventually became a Reclaiming Collective member, local and WitchCamp teacher, founding member of the Reclaiming Wheel, and participant in many of San Francisco Bay Area Reclaiming's cells. Gwydion is a devoted science geek who thrives when standing at the intersection of science, magic, and mystery.

Heidi Marian—USA

Heidi is a wild-hearted green witch, social scientist, Reclaiming initiate, and community priestess. Her Craft training is rooted in Anderson Feri and Reclaiming traditions. Born and raised in San Francisco, she makes her home in the South of Market neighborhood, where weeds crack through concrete. Some of the main tools and allies she works with include hearth tending, stone and plant medicine, nonviolent communication, facilitation, and laughter. Her heart's passion lies in the merging of the right and left hand paths of magic, in doing the deep down rooted work of turning the tides, and of living a life of commitment in a complex and perilous world.

Irisanya Moon—USA

Irisanya Moon is a witch, priestess, international teacher, often-vegan, invocateur, ritualist, drummer, writer, moon devotee, Sagittarius, and Reclaiming initiate. She has been a witch since 1998 and moved to California in 2005. A fateful connection with a Reclaiming organizer led her to attend her first California WitchCamp in 2008, take the core classes, organize rituals for North Bay Reclaiming, and teach classes around the San Francisco Bay Area.

Irisanya has been fortunate to teach at WitchCamps in California, British Columbia, Canada, Texas, Australia, and the UK. She is committed to facilitating community growth and connection through ritual creation, storytelling, moon magick, drumming, and embracing beauty in all of its forms. She's devoted to Aphrodite, Hecate, Iris, and the Norns. You'll often find her writing poetry, crafting songs, and looking for a snack. For more details, you can visit www.irisanya.com.

Jane Meredith—Australia

Jane Meredith is an author and ritualist passionately involved in Reclaiming. Her books include *Journey to the Dark Goddess, Circle of Eight: Creating Magic for Your Place on Earth, Aspecting the Goddess,* and *Magic of the Iron Pentacle,* co-authored with Gede Parma. Jane teaches in person and distance courses, including Reclaiming core classes. She lives in the Blue Mountains outside Sydney, Australia, and travels a lot. She adores WitchCamps and is devoted to CloudCatcher WitchCamp, of which she is one of the founders. Some of her favorite things are rivers, trees, white cockatoos, dark chocolate, magic, and ritual. She is excited by co-created ecstatic ritual, great writing, and wild places. Jane's website is www.janemeredith.com.

Jennifer Byers—USA

Jennifer Byers stumbled upon Reclaiming witchcraft in Chicago, Illinois, in 2003. She has since been learning and teaching within Reclaiming across the United States and Canada. In 2013 she moved north to Minnesota, where she is learning to love winter more...and mosquitos less. She is a queer witch-poet who thrives on art and music, with more than twenty-five years of training and experience in professional theatre and performance.

Jennifer works deeply with the ancestors and descendants, focusing her magic/activism on love and justice. She seeks to grow in accountability and awareness, and desires to nurture our capacity to look honestly at the intersections of capitalism, oppression, climate change, and our collective power for right action.

Jennifer has also trained with T. Thorn Coyle and Diana's Grove Mystery School. She often tends toward creativity, embodiment, sensuality, mindfulness, and humor. She strongly values daily practice, self-awareness, integrity, and the potency of kindness.

Kellie Wilding—Australia

Kellie stumbled upon the fact that Reclaiming still existed as a real live tradition in the UK in 2002. She has since attended many camps and events, been involved in organizing and teaching, and has not stumbled out of love with Reclaiming since.

Lisa Lind—Australia

Lisa has been practicing Reclaiming-style magic for twenty years. She has taught Reclaiming-style magic in three countries and has also served her community as a WitchCamp organizer. She grew up with the trolls and gnomes her mother introduced her to, as well as the gods of her blood and bones. Later on she formed deep connections with wild gods from a variety of places. Lisa works with her dead in almost all the magic she does.

Lisa finds her spirituality and scientific training inseparable and is experimental in her magic. Her activism takes the form of rewriting gender policy and creating avenues for indigenous health initiatives and cultural education. She relishes embodied magic, gritty transformational work, and a good old-fashioned belly laugh. Much of her work focuses on recognizing our human divinity.

Pandora O'Mallory—USA

Pandora O'Mallory has worked in the Reclaiming branch of the Feri tradition since 1981. Under the name Anne Brannen, she has been a professor of medieval literature and currently teaches witchcraft classes and does spiritual counseling. She can be reached at www .annebrannen.com.

Paul Eaves—USA

I live in Minneapolis, Minnesota, near the Mississippi River. I have been a Reclaiming Witch for over thirty years and have organized and taught Reclaiming magic in my home community and at WitchCamps in North America and Australia. I am currently retired, which means that I get to pretty much live my heart's desire every day. My passions include my thirty-year romance with my marvelous wife, my two moms, labyrinths, gardening, habitat restoration, social/environmental justice, and working/playing with children. Magic is an integral part of my day-to-day life. I experience magic as an important practice in fostering personal, community, and planetary change.

Phoenix LeFae—USA

Phoenix LeFae is equal parts blue-eyed wanderer and passionate devotee of the Goddess. She is a restless seeker of knowledge, always yearning to learn more, dig deeper, and dive into mystery. Phoenix suffers from the whims of her divine muse (or perhaps muses) and in that suffering experiences a joy that manifests in writing, ritual, teaching, and devotion. Her first Reclaiming ritual was Winter Solstice 1995, and she's been hooked ever since. An initiate in Reclaiming, the Avalon Druid Order, and Gardnerian Wicca, Phoenix has had the pleasure of teaching and leading ritual globally. She is a hoodoo practitioner, a professional witch, a published author, and the owner of the Goddess shop Milk & Honey: www.milk-and-honey.com.

Preston Coyote Vargas—USA

Preston Coyote Vargas has been practicing magic and facilitating group rituals for twenty years. He has been counseling self-identified queer men through recovery for ten years. His ancestors are ever present in his journey. His ritual practice is a blend of Reclaiming witchcraft, shamanic inspiration, Ifa Orisha spirituality, ancestral medicine training, hoodoo, sorcery, and Fey magic. It is interwoven with the knowledge he developed in his postgraduate degrees in philosophy, cosmology, and consciousness, as well as transformative studies. The gifts he offers from his training in indigenous ancestral healing traditions are tempered with healing justice, his awareness of privileged power dynamics, and his commitments to anti-oppression. He believes that the actions we make can stretch backward in time to heal the wounds of all our relations and stretch forward in time to manifest the best possible worlds for our future descendants. His website is www .PrestonVargas.com.

Rae Eden—USA

Nature and dance are my healers. I can be found dancing on the street corner and wandering through the forest. I am a mother, grandmother, and auntie. I came to Reclaiming by way of eclectic witchcraft, mindfulness, Unitarianism, Judaism, recovery, and social justice/ community organizing. I am a member of the Upper Mississippi River Reclaiming community and teachers group in Minnesota. I work in the environmental health field and am in training to be a dance movement therapist. These elements influence my teaching style, where I incorporate movement-based exercises to embody the teachings. I am also a choreographer for Global Water Dances, and I dance with fire in an annual ritual honoring Brighid.

Raven Edgewalker—Britain

Raven Edgewalker is a British witch, teacher, artist, and writer who dwells in the magical landscape of Somerset. She is a Reclaiming and Anderson Feri initiate and has worked within the Reclaiming tradition for around twenty years. She has an ongoing, passionate love affair with the natural world. She sees her work in the world as that of building connections with self, with each other, within community, and with deity and the elements. Raven has been lucky enough to teach Reclaiming WitchCamps and workshops across the world, both face to face and in the last few years as a founder and member of the teaching faculty of World Tree Lyceum, an online Pagan Mystery School. Raven owns the popular Pagan business Greenwomancrafts and makes her living crafting beautiful Pagan tools and jewelry. She is currently writing a book on experiential Ogham and co-authoring a book on techniques of spellcrafting. Visit Raven online at www.worldtree lyceum.org and www.greenwomancrafts.etsy.com.

Riyana Rose Sang—USA

Riyana Rose Sang is a Bay Area Reclaiming Teacher and Certified Western Herbalist, counselor, and all-around witchy woman. She has taught and worked with clients in the SF Bay Area and internationally for over fifteen years. She thinks of herself as a mystical witch and adores experiential, ecstatic, direct experience of the divine and guiding others to get there too, through the tools she teaches and the rituals she helps create. She is devoted to connecting with nature and cultivating relationship with the green ones, animals, and the fey. By utilizing ritual technologies such as aspecting, trance, and meditation, she moves out of the mind and into ecstatic communion with the earth and the divine. When not writing, reading, or playing with witches in the woods, she can be found in Alameda, California, where she lives with her partner, her baby girl Brighid, and two very furry cats. You can connect with her at www.RiyanaRose.com.

Rose May Dance—USA

Rose May Dance, aka Gweneth Dietrich, is one of the Mothers of Reclaiming and has been in the collective since around 1980. She is a teacher and the trainer of many teachers and initiates. Rose specializes in trance magic and is well known for healing work. She is an earth-based political activist and has retired from a career in the AIDS field into a clinical practice of hypnotherapy. She would be nowhere without her sense of humor.

Ruby Berry—Canada

Ruby Berry has been involved in Reclaiming and British Columbia WitchCamp for a long time. She is a witch, activist, ecofeminist, and lover of the wild earth.

Seraphina Capranos—Canada

Seraphina Capranos is a green witch and priestess living on an island off the coast of Western Canada. She teaches herbal medicine and magic in North America. Her website is www.seraphinacapranos.com.

SusanneRae—Australia

SusanneRae teaches mindfulness meditation and yoga courses, and facilitates events and groups at the Meditation Space in Campbelltown, New South Wales. An active member of the Greater Sydney Reclaiming group, she regularly teaches and co-creates festival celebrations in her home community that is in Dharawal Country, Campbelltown, South Western Sydney. SusanneRae's spiritual practice is deeply rooted in her understanding, love, and connection with the earth and her cycles. She feels most at home in deserts, forests, rivers, and other wild places, including her garden. As a mother, grandmother, artist, activist, gardener, traveler, one-time midwife, academic, bureaucrat, and high school art teacher, her pragmatic magic is woven inseparably through and around her everyday life. Her friendships, connections with children, art-making, teaching, activism, knitting, gardening, healing, building labyrinths, and trips to the supermarket all offer opportunities to explore the mysteries and priestess for the earth. Her website is www.themeditationspace.com.au.

Suzanne Sterling—USA

Suzanne Sterling is a musician, yogi, and activist who has been performing and teaching transformational workshops for over twenty years. She is founder of Voice of Change, inspiring others to find their unique voice as a tool for conscious evolution. Suzanne has been featured at hundreds of international festivals and conference centers including Omega, Esalen, Wanderlust, Kripalu, and Earthdance, where she led the world's largest spiral dance.

Since 2007 she has been training leaders in activism and social justice through her co-founded organization Off The Mat, Into the World. As director of OTM's Seva Challenge, she has spent time in the US, India, Cambodia, Haiti, Ecuador, and Africa, working in community resilience.

For twenty-five years she has worked with the International Reclaiming community, creating ritual and training teachers. She created the ongoing Priestess Apprenticeship in Sacred Leadership with Ravyn Stanfield. She has released five solo albums and numerous DVD soundtracks. Her website is www.suzannesterling.com.

Tarin Towers—USA

Tarin Towers is a poet, author, editor, and journalist who teaches and studies in the Reclaiming tradition in San Francisco. She was drawn to Reclaiming for its commitment to social justice, its creativity, and its humor. Tarin's personal practice of witchcraft includes singing, drumming, tarot, altar building, and trance. She's also a ritual planning geek and is one of the founding organizers of Redwood Magic Family Camp and the Mysteries of Samhain WitchCamp. Tarin loves co-creating Elements of Magic classes and has done so many times, both in the Bay Area and at California WitchCamp. Her articles about witchcraft have appeared in such varied publications as *Broadly*, *The Establishment*, and *Atlas Obscura*. Her website is tarintowers.com; for Twitter/Insta/Tumblr/Facebook, @tarintowers.

Thibaut Laure—USA

I am witch, magical geek, world bridger, playful trickster, and shapeshifter. Born and raised in Paris, France, I moved to California nineteen years ago and fell in love with San Francisco, its magic, and its people. I encountered the Craft and the Goddess seventeen years ago, first through Wicca and Shakta Tantra before finding my home in Reclaiming ten years ago, drawn to the community focus on service, openness, and inclusivity.

As a scientist, I find magic and science to be two sides of the same coin and enjoy bringing the science of magic and the magic of science into my workings.

I am dedicated to Hekate, Kali, and Brigitte. I connect deeply with the magic of the Goddess and love working with mystery, shadow work, and rituals to create spaces for healing and transformation.

Willow Firefly Kelly—USA

Activist, witch, queer, shadow-stalker, lover of the fae and the wyrd, I am a music-making, mischief-conspiring priestess of transformation and have been teaching magic in the Reclaiming tradition of witchcraft internationally since the mid-90s. I am a skeptic and a mystic, seeking a glimmer of understanding into this ocean of ineffable wonder that I inadequately call spirit. I experience and priestess transformation through the exploration and integration of shadows, sprinkling my work generously with the ecstatic vibrations of music, energy, play, movement, theatre, devotion, and sound. I thrive on collaborative community building, art, and ecstatic magic. I teach and facilitate classes, intensives, restoratives, rituals, rites of passage, and workshops that hold the common threads of authenticity, responsibility, and transformation. My training in the Reclaiming tradition of Witchcraft, Dances of Universal Peace, the Mevlevi Order of America, and other mystical traditions informs my practices and teaching styles. My website is www.willowkelly.com.

Zay Eleanor Watersong—USA

Zay Eleanor Watersong is an organizer and teacher within the Reclaiming tradition, as well as an environmental and indigenous rights activist, entrepreneur, fire dancer, drummer, and priestess of the Lady of the Lake. She lives in an anarchist permaculturalist urban collective in Syracuse, New York. Over the years she has been involved with the Ithaca Reclaiming Collective, the Pagan Cluster, Bay Area Reclaiming, and Reclaiming Teachers in Training and Service (a Northeast teaching collective), and she is thrilled to be part of growing the Reclaiming the Radiant Wild community in Syracuse. While Vermont WitchCamp is her home camp, Free Cascadia Camp will always be her first. She teaches Elements of Magic, Iron Pentacle, and magical activism classes, as weekend intensives and at camps. Follow her at https://medium.com/@ZayEleanor/.

To Write to the Authors

If you wish to contact the authors or would like more information about this book, please write to the authors in care of Llewellyn Worldwide Ltd. and we will forward your request. Both the authors and the publisher appreciate hearing from you and learning of your enjoyment of this book and how it has helped you. Llewellyn Worldwide Ltd. cannot guarantee that every letter written to the authors can be answered, but all will be forwarded. Please write to:

Jane Meredith & Gede Parma
℅ Llewellyn Worldwide
2143 Wooddale Drive
Woodbury, MN 55125-2989

Please enclose a self-addressed stamped envelope for reply or $1.00 to cover costs. If outside the USA, enclose an international postal reply coupon.

Many of Llewellyn's authors have websites with additional information and resources. For more information, please visit our website at

WWW.LLEWELLYN.COM